D1196604

BUGSY SIEGEL

Bugsy Siegel

The Dark Side of the
American Dream

◆┼◆┼◆

MICHAEL SHNAYERSON

Yale

UNIVERSITY
PRESS
New Haven and London

For Gayfryd

Don't worry, don't worry. Look at the Astors
and Vanderbilts, all those big society people.
They were the worst thieves—and now look
at them. It's just a matter of time.

—Meyer Lansky

CONTENTS

CONTENTS

Of THE NEARLY fifty biographies that so far have constituted the Jewish Lives series, all are of admirable figures. There are no bootleggers among them, no racketeers, gamblers, or murderers. Until now.

Benjamin "Bugsy" Siegel has the dubious distinction of representing all four categories. Through the 1920s, 1930s, and most of the 1940s, he and his longtime partner in crime Meyer Lansky engaged in innumerable acts of violence. By his own account, Siegel himself killed roughly a dozen men; according to one gangster, he oversaw the contract killings of far more. Yet his brute force and reckless ambition were not just focused on crime. As World War II came to an end, Siegel saw the potential for a huge, elegant casino resort in the sands of Las Vegas, a mecca for homecoming GIs and high rollers alike. Everything was converging: cars making the drive from Los Angeles in shorter time, and with air-conditioning; planes making direct flights from thousands of miles away; a war-weary generation eager for fun, the naughtier the better. And no one knew better how to profit from the booze that coursed through casinos like blood.

In a town of cowboy-style casinos with wagon wheels on the walls and sawdust on the floors, Siegel dared to imagine a palace more suitable to Monaco than Nevada. The Flamingo, he called it, and he imported live pink flamingoes to tone up the place. The flamingoes died, and so, not long after, did Benjamin Siegel, murdered at age forty-one in the spring of 1947. Yet a legacy remains, not only in the cornucopia of other Vegas casinos that followed, but also in the impact of gambling and entertainment on American cultural and economic life. For better or worse, the story of the Flamingo, and the criminals who built it, is a Jewish-American story, starting with a Jew who wielded influence, unlike any of the subjects covered so far in Jewish Lives, at the barrel end of a gun.

Siegel's story is compelling on its own. But it laces through a larger one, a generational story of eastern European Jewish immigrants in the early to mid-twentieth century who found the doors of their new world closed and so, as gangsters, pursued their own dark version of the American dream. In so doing, they created a murderously effective business model—gangster capitalism, as one expert on the period defines it—that made them as powerful as the Italian mafia with which they allied, over all the channels of organized crime that seeped through and affected American society.

New York's Lower East Side was, of course, where this story began: the Jewish capital of America at the turn of the century. The immigrants we associate with it were entertainers: George and Ira Gershwin, Irving Berlin, Eddie Cantor, George Burns, Yip Harburg, Zero Mostel, and so many more. Vaudeville and the Yiddish theater welcomed them, and they went on to be stars. Most immigrant families in this rough new milieu were forced to find other escapes from abject poverty. Jacob Riis, a crusading journalist of the period, captured a sense of the odds they were up against. "The story of inhuman packing of human swarms, of bitter poverty, of landlord greed, of sweatshop slavery, of darkness and squalor and misery, which these tenements have to tell, is equaled, I suppose, nowhere else in the civilized world."[1]

Ben Siegel was born into this environment in 1906. Like many of his peers, he left school in the seventh or eighth grade. Weeks before his violent death, he would tell his two daughters, by then teenagers, that he had had no choice: his parents needed him to help support the family.

Children could work in a factory, as Ben's father did, but the work was backbreaking, and dangerous, even deadly. On March 25, 1911, at the Triangle Shirtwaist factory, fire killed 146 mostly young Jewish women, trapped behind locked doors when the flames began to spread. Ben was five years old at the time, old enough to remember the horrifying news. The streets of the Lower East Side offered easier and more lucrative ways to make a living. A boy just had to be tough enough to take the risks.

Nice Jewish boys were studious, obedient, and incapable of raising their fists. "Tough Jews," as popular historian Rich Cohen calls the proto-gangsters in his elegiac book by that title, were scrappy, daring, and all but defined by how well they fought. And for that, they had teachers of their own.

Youth gangs had proliferated since the early days of the immigrant story in the 1880s. They guarded their turf, repelled rivals, and instilled gang loyalty, an exhilarating bond. They also engaged in petty crime and pushed away their parents' Jewish customs, language, and religion. "There was scarcely a Jewish home on the East Side that was free from the friction between parents and children," noted Morris Raphael Cohen, author of *Law and Order* (1933) and *A Dreamer's Journey* (1949). "This explosive tension made it possible for the same family to produce saints and sinners, philosophers and gunmen."[2]

Siegel and Lansky established their own gang and became friends for life. Lansky was short, homely, and cautious. Siegel was nearly five-foot-ten and dashingly handsome, with deep blue eyes, a garrulous grin, and a strong profile. He had a terrifying temper that made his face glow, and a lust for violence that alarmed even his new friend Meyer.

To those who witnessed his fits of rage, Siegel seemed possibly mad, and so earned the nickname he loathed. Being perfectly equipped to fight on a moment's notice may rather have been utterly sane. "If you're in the world he grew up in, and you are characterized by muscle, then you have to play your part," suggests writer and mob historian Nick Pileggi. "There were three jobs: muscle, brains, or the well-connected guy to politicians." Siegel was suited to the first: "Large, tough, and unbelievably headstrong."[3] Albert Fried in *The Rise and Fall of the Jewish Gangster in America* gives Siegel more credit than that. "Both men were exceedingly smart and exceedingly ruthless," Fried notes. "Their qualities of mind and character, not the superficialities of style and manner, accounted for the astonishing success of their joint enterprise."[4]

Soon Siegel and Lansky were consorting with an older group of gangsters. These were Jews who had graduated from petty crime to more lucrative undertakings, like racketeering. That the merchants they squeezed were fellow Jews bothered them not at all, nor that their victims spoke Yiddish as they did. The Lower East Side had winners and losers; which you were was up to you.

Some years ago, Malcolm Gladwell in the *New Yorker* wrote one of his signature pieces on why immigrants turned to crime, and what happened after they did. His source was *The Crooked Ladder*, by sociologist James O'Kane. "The Jewish gangsters of the early twentieth century couldn't hope for the rewards of hard work; they couldn't conform when no one would let them try," Gladwell related. "Yet they revered America and all it stood for." Barred from most professions by antisemitism, they climbed, instead, the crooked ladder of social mobility. "Crime was the means by which a group of immigrants could transcend their humble origins," Gladwell wrote, channeling O'Kane. "Criminal activity, under those circumstances, was not rebellion. It wasn't a rejection of legitimate society. It was an attempt to join in."[5]

A brand-new way up the crooked ladder came a century ago at midnight on January 17, 1920, with the start of Prohibition.

Within weeks, Siegel and Lansky were making midnight booze runs for Arnold "The Brain" Rothstein, grand panjandrum of gambling and fixer extraordinaire. There were no social barriers to this new criminal life of bootlegging, no minimum age. Siegel was fourteen, Lansky not quite twenty. It was a golden opportunity, a great, collective, inconceivable dream come true.

Fortunes were made overnight, but there were costs, as rivals ambushed one another's booze-filled trucks on late-night country roads. Most of the shoot-outs occurred along ethnic lines. By the late twenties, the gangsters began trying to end the mayhem. The turning point came in 1931, when Lansky and Siegel, along with Lucky Luciano, brought Irish, Italian, and Jewish bootleggers together to establish order in their underworld. The Syndicate, as it became known, would be American in the truest sense: an amalgam of immigrants making their way in the New World. A *business* in which money, not murder and revenge, would be the modus operandi. The gangsters were gangster capitalists now, engaged in the business of making a profit for all.

With the end of Prohibition in 1933, the Syndicate, flush with bootlegged millions, slid into gambling: legal and illegal, East Coast and West. Lansky moved to Miami and focused on building a gold coast of gambling joints. Siegel went to Los Angeles to muscle in on the local lords of vice. Soon he was prospering in the lurid L.A. of *Chinatown*. He owned pieces of nightclubs and restaurants, dog and horse tracks, an offshore gambling ship. There was a whole other fortune to be made by the race wire: illegal off-track horse betting by telegraph. Siegel was working on that, too.

Drawn to the ultimate trappings of wealth, Siegel built a mansion in Holmby Hills, north of Sunset Boulevard. With his movie star good looks and seemingly limitless bankroll, he entertained Jimmy Stewart, Clark Gable, Cary Grant, Charles Boyer, Fred Astaire, Marlene Dietrich, and more. The stars were dazzled, as only gangsters could dazzle them. They studied his mannerisms and thrilled to his stories. He was a gangster capitalist *and* a gangster celebrity: Gatsby with a penchant to kill.

Siegel hated almost everything about the state that spanned California's eastern border, starting with its desert heat. But by the mid-1930s he came to see the promise of Nevada as his next big act. It had legalized gambling in 1931—the only state to do so—and thousands of workers on the new Hoover Dam had flocked to Las Vegas on Friday nights, eager to blow their paychecks on games of chance. Up in Reno, gambling was held by a handful of Christian families—no Jews welcome—but Las Vegas was wide open, and just five hours by car from L.A., close enough to draw a swanky crowd. "Siegel shared his idea with Lansky, and Lansky liked it," relates Stephen Birmingham in *The Rest of Us*.[6] "There was no reason why they couldn't have the southern part of the state to themselves."

Siegel wanted more than a few modest, moneymaking joints. He sensed the potential for a "carpet casino" more suited to Europe than the desert sands of Nevada. Others tried. But as Fried says, Siegel was the one with vision. "None of them, not even Lansky, had his audacity, his sense of the grandiose, his courage (or foolhardiness) to attempt the really big move. None had his genius."[7] And so was built the Flamingo, after its first visionary, an L.A. entrepreneur named Billy Wilkerson, took in Siegel and Lansky as investors, only to be pushed out.

Siegel had hoped the Flamingo would let him go legit, the hope of every Jewish-American gangster. He told his backers not to worry that costs had soared, from $1 million to $6 million. He saw the fortunes about to be made. *He* knew what to do; they were lucky to have him. His backers weren't used to being talked to that way. For some months after the Flamingo's disastrous opening in December 1946, Siegel's friendship with Lansky kept him safe—until it didn't.

Despite Siegel's murder on the night of June 20, 1947, or perhaps because of it, the Flamingo took flight at last, redolent with gangster mystique. Along with twenty-four-hour gambling, it offered famous entertainers, a trend other casinos embraced. Families could stay the night in its richly appointed rooms, then play golf or ride horses by day. This was the business model: a grand destination that would grow, in time, to be the new Las Vegas and affect gambling world round. Ultimately, its ill-gotten gains would be fully absorbed by a casino industry in which the underworld and big business merged. Siegel had all but driven the Flamingo into bankruptcy. Yet his death gave it new life, luring crowds with its ambiance of anything goes: casino noir.

Jewish gangsters built nearly all of the Vegas casinos that followed, but without Siegel's swagger and pomp. And then, one by one, they disappeared. Settled as they now were in American society, a new generation of Jews did all they could to put their gangster days behind them. They enrolled their children in private schools and Ivy League colleges, pushing them to become lawyers and doctors. They lived in wealthy suburbs, often antisemitic ones: the push, as before, was to assimilate. "Most people have never heard of Jewish gangsters," suggests Cohen in *Tough Jews*. "They do not believe they ever existed."[8]

Gone with those larger-than-life characters is a particularly vivid chapter of early-twentieth-century history in which crime and keen ambition pulled a generation up from poverty to glamour, riches, and power. The names of those upstarts echo dimly today, though Bugsy's seems one of the most enduring, his story carried farthest from its time to the present. It resonates because Siegel was both beautiful *and* violent, a scintillating mix that goes through us in jolts of excitement, sensuality, and fear.

This short biography is meant to keep Bugsy's memory and importance alive, as a testament without judgment that a century ago, a small band of immigrant Jews did what they had to do to succeed in a harsh new world, assuring that their offspring would get to traverse the bright side of the American dream.

1

The Lure of the Streets

THE STREETS WERE what struck any immigrant first—the teeming, poverty-steeped streets of New York's Lower East Side. Max Siegel and Jennie Riechenthal, future parents of one of America's most murderous gangsters, experienced that visceral onslaught on July 1, 1900, when they disembarked from the SS *Etruria*, along with the ship's eight hundred other immigrants in steerage.[1] Their time on the ocean from Liverpool, England, had been so horribly uncomfortable that they never discussed the passage with their family—not a word.[2]

Max was twenty, his future wife nineteen. They came from Galicia, a poor region in the Austro-Hungarian empire, from which a steady, westward migration of desperate Jews was flowing.[3] Later, family members would suggest both Max and Jennie came from the same town, not in Galicia but in Ukraine.[4] Ukraine was a crown territory between Galicia and Russia, so both versions may have denoted the same place.

For that matter, so could Russia, the country Max Siegel identified as his homeland on the *Etruria*'s manifest. Many Ukrainians in the late nineteenth century identified themselves as "Little Russians," rejecting Galicia and embracing the czarist empire. Max may have been making a political statement of solidarity, even as he recognized that America was his only hope for a new and better life. He may also have been induced to leave Galicia by recent shows of bigotry: in 1898, a priest's antisemitic rants had led to massive damage inflicted on Jewish property, and mobs had gathered.[5] On the *Etruria*'s manifest, Max noted that his father had paid for his passage, and that he was joining a relative on Division Street, which may or may not have been true. Basically, Max and Jennie were on their own. According to the *Etruria*'s manifest, Max had $15.

Together if not yet married, Max and Jennie joined a next great wave of Jewish immigrants to America, less intent on religious reform than on escape from persecution and a chance for their children to rise. In the decade between 1900 and 1910, nearly one million immigrants a year came to America. The vast majority were from eastern Europe, and most of those were Jews.[6] They made their way from the docks to the Lower East Side with their bundles of meager belongings, hoping for new lives in this American shtetl of more than one million people, four thousand residents per block, more tightly crammed than the population of Bombay, India.[7]

Years later in a police interrogation, Siegel would say he was born in Brooklyn, "right around the bridge."[8] There was a case to be made for Brooklyn as the family's first borough. Rents were even cheaper than the Lower East Side. The Williamsburg Bridge opened in 1903, making Brooklyn more accessible, especially for Orthodox Jews, who could walk on the Sabbath to and from their synagogues. Back in Galicia, Max had been a skilled tailor. In New York he got work as a presser in a pants factory, and felt lucky to have it. His salary was about $650, one census report noted, the equivalent of $17,000 today: abject poverty.[9]

Wherever the Siegels lived in those first few years, their new home was easy to describe: a three-room apartment up a narrow, dark stairway with no running water or indoor plumbing, the only light provided by kerosene lamps. Many if not most of the apartments were family-run sweatshops, where piecework from the nearby factories would be finished into garments, by the dozens a day, the family members gathered at their sewing machines by the light of their street-front windows. For the Siegels, as for so many others, Yiddish was the only language spoken at home. Neither parent had any formal schooling. Their marriage in 1903 was a triumph of hope for Max at twenty-three, Jennie at twenty-two.[10] Though perhaps Jennie Siegel hedged her bets in a sense: decades later, on her application for social security, she would identify herself as Jennie Riechenthal, with Max Siegel her spouse.

A first child, Esther, was born in 1905. Benjamin was born the next year. By then, the Siegels were clearly living on the Lower East Side: Ben's New York state birth certificate put them at 88 Cannon Street. The Siegels' secondborn was Nick, named Berish, or Little Bear, a tribute to Max Siegel, whose Hebrew name was Dov Ber—Bear in English—though the Little Bear would soon go by Ben, or Bennie. The state certificate noted his birthdate as March 4, 1906, but the U.S. census reports of 1910, 1920, and others would all list his birth date as February 28. According to the 1910 census, two more daughters, Bessie and Ethel, were born soon after Ben. The fifth and last sibling, Morris or Maurice—the good son—would be born in 1916.

In the humble hierarchy of Lower East Side streets, Cannon was among the humblest, a short, dreary side street that ran north-south, just up from the East River, dead-ending at the Williamsburg Bridge. Tenements of five and six stories lined much of either side. Life was hard, but after much legal jousting, tenement landlords had been forced to provide running water—cold water, but water just the same—and indoor plumbing, to a degree. Four families on each floor now shared two toilets: ten or more people per toilet. Gaslight was also installed, alleviating the gloom.

Conditions were grim, but family ties were tight. All day, a tenement mother tended the kitchen coal stove, making meals and doing the laundry; once a week she bathed her children, also in the kitchen, in a wooden barrel, the water heated by the coal stove. Four or more family members slept in the bedroom, with more in the parlor if need be. The Siegels took in two boarders to help pay the rent. The 1910 census duly noted that the Siegels' apartment count included Rose Stolla, age eighteen, and Lillie Persel, seventeen. They, too, slept in the bedroom, often on eight-hour shifts. The floor's two communal toilets, adjacent to each other, were situated down the hall.

This was the classic tenement. "In winter, fumes from coal stoves, gas from lamps, and vapors from boilers plagued residents," observes Laurence Bergreen in *As Thousands Cheer: The Life of Irving Berlin*, "and in the summer, the smell of decomposing garbage and human and animal waste were inescapable." So squalid were these slums, so desperately poor its residents, that some immigrants eventually went back to their old country.[11] And yet in this shtetl were all the touchstones of Jewish culture: synagogues, Orthodox services, kosher food from peddlers' carts, and the soothing prevalence of Yiddish.

For Ben Siegel, one indelible memory of childhood was the ceaseless, metallic thrum of trolley and subway traffic on the Williamsburg Bridge. The streetcars creaked slowly up each rising side, suspended high over the river, then paused before gathering speed down the other side. Ben would have played with his pals within the bridge's shadows and bars of light, and walked along the East River, watching the barges float by.

Cruising the nearest streets as a boy, Ben took in curious

signs. He had no idea why women with too much makeup flounced up and down the commercial streets, but he sensed the crowd's disapproval of them. In fact, most of the Lower East Side's prostitutes were Jewish, catering to immigrants whose wives remained an ocean away: a vast and lonely clientele. He saw boys no older than he picking pockets, rolling drunks, and getting in fights. Socially prominent Jews—Schiffs, Loebs, Mayers—blamed overcrowding, and said it led to disease, vice, and crime. One young and typical delinquent was future entertainer Eddie Cantor, who recounted "wandering the streets all night with older children, singing popular songs, making noise and getting into trouble." Before long the future comedian, singer, and actor was stealing food from pushcarts and helping stage burglaries, since he was the "skinniest and most agile of the younger boys . . . employed to crawl through narrow bars and fanlights to open doors and secret passages for the marauders." At sixteen, he tried his luck as a performer at Miner's Bowery Theatre. That got him into vaudeville, and out of a future in crime.[12]

Long before Ben became Bugsy, he somehow acquired a middle name he loathed. Hymen was a common boy's name bestowed upon the children of first-generation Jewish immigrants. It was a simplified version of "L'Chaim," the Jewish toast to life.[13] But for the Americanized boys who bore it, Hymen was an embarrassment. It sounded Jewish, not American, and of course it had another connotation. The taunts were as obvious as they were inevitable, and in Ben's case may have inspired his first street fights. No one was going to call *him* a virgin.

Like all Lower East Side boys, Ben played outside as much as he could. The paved streets were perfect for marbles and rolling hoops. There was stickball, stoopball, and a similar version of street baseball called "one o' cat," in which a batter gave a homemade wooden "ball" enough of a tap to put it in play. "The wood would rise a few feet off the ground from such a tap."[14]

Jennie Riechenthal Siegel must have chosen Cannon Street in part because it had a large new lovely school: PS 10, later renamed PS 110. It was a five-story, white-stone building surprisingly ornate for a public school, with neo-Gothic towers. It served the middle grades; next door was an old Baptist church, given new use as the primary school. Both buildings stand today, both still there as PS 110, on Cannon's southeast side. The tenements of Cannon's north side, where the Siegels lived, have long since been replaced by a red-bricked housing project.

Ben attended PS 110 until the seventh or eighth grade. Possibly he recalled the day in about 1915 that classes were cut short by gunfire. Monk Eastman, a Lower East Side gangster at the peak of his prowess who lived just down Cannon Street, had decided to use the school's high, wide-paned windows as target practice. "Bullets rained through the schoolrooms, and the children were in panic," recalled Miss Adeline E. Simpson, the principal, in a later publication honoring the school. "Without stopping to think that he might transfer his attentions to me, I ran out and remonstrated with him, telling him that his own children were being endangered. He looked at me a moment, pistol in hand, and then said, 'yer all right. Yer a good sport for not calling the cops.' And he did as I asked him."[15] If Ben was indeed in school that day—and at eight or nine years old he probably would have been—Monk Eastman's fusillade must have seemed like a trumpet blast from a world he longed to join.

The Siegels were Orthodox Jews, so they naturally joined the Bialystoker, an Orthodox synagogue two blocks away. Its name honored the northeastern Polish city of Bialystok, from which most of its congregation had come. It too still stands, at 7–11 Bialystoker Place, a late-Federal building in fieldstone. Originally a Methodist Episcopal church, it was purchased in 1905 by its new congregation. Today it stakes claim as the oldest synagogue in use in New York City. Inside are scores of memorial plaques. One is for Max Siegel, died April 17, 1947. Directly below it is a plaque for Benjamin Siegel, his fiery death coming two months later, on June 20. Here in this once bustling neighborhood—with its school, its synagogue, its peddler-filled sidewalks, and the Williamsburg Bridge above—are the echoes of a painful relationship between poor Max Siegel and his ambitious son, marked by Max's disapproval of the life Ben chose to lead and, on Ben's side, by resentment that his parents failed to appreciate all he did for them. A story shared among today's congregation is that the contract hit on Ben "Bugsy" Siegel was delayed that spring of 1947 to let the son mourn his father after all those difficult years.

By the age of twelve, Siegel was essentially spending his days as he pleased—but what he pleased to do, more than play games, was embark on petty crime.

Ben learned to hit up pushcart peddlers for protection; those who declined to pay a weekly fee might find their push-carts torched. He learned that the drivers of horse-drawn carriages could be threatened as well: without protection, their horses might be poisoned. Arson and poisoning were crimes of choice for street urchins: "property crimes" easy to do without guns.[16]

For a boy Ben's age, the gangs were irresistible. "It was the exceptional, almost abnormal boy who did not join the gang," recalled one veteran gang member. "The gang was romance, adventure, [and] had the zest of banditry, the thrill of camp life, and the lure of hero worship."[17] Lincoln Steffens, the famous muckraker, saw those children up close. "We would pass a synagogue where a score or more of boys were sitting hatless in their old clothes, smoking cigarettes on the steps outside, and their fathers, all dressed in black, with their high hats, uncut beards and temple curls, were going into the synagogue, tearing their hair and rending their garments. . . . Their sons were rebels against the law of Moses; they were lost souls, lost to God, the family, and to Israel of old."[18]

What separated Siegel from his fellow urchins was an utter absence of fear. He loved the adrenaline rush of breaking rules and taking risks. Siegel became known as a *chaye*—a beast. He scared even his mother. "I never sent Maurice to talk sense into Benjamin," Jennie was quoted as saying years later, "because I was afraid for my younger son, my baby. Benjamin's temper, I knew. He would have probably beaten him up. So I sent the girls after him. But it did no good. Benjamin wouldn't listen. He told the girls that he was a man and that he wanted to lead his own life."[19] Some years later, Ben would pay for Maurice to go to college and medical school, but that would remain a family secret, to Ben's enduring hurt. Maurice, as a niece observed, felt shame for taking the money, and may not have forgotten the pummeling he took from his older brother when both were young.

In the early years of the twentieth century, a whole generation of immigrant boys took to the streets. "Unsupervised, the boys of the Lower East Side spent much of their time in front of the pool rooms and salons which dotted the neighborhood," notes Lower East Side historian Jenna Joselit, "hoping to be called upon to perform an errand for one of the regulars." Underworld characters became their role models, taking the place of sad-sack fathers. "The underworld characters were so fascinating because on top of everything else they exemplified the cynical truth behind the American dream," notes Albert Fried in *The Rise and Fall of the Jewish Gangster in America*. It was "the incontrovertible fact that vice and crime were escape routes to freedom and that all the preaching at home and in school and in the press were so many lies and deceptions. Success taught its own lessons."[20]

Later, Siegel recounted his first actual crime, robbing a loan company. "I had to run like hell for about ten blocks, car-

rying two bags full of small change, before the guy chasing us
ran out of breath and quit. It might have been better if they'd
caught me because after that I was game for anything."[21] Already, the lineaments of a violent character were emerging. Ben
was gleefully daring, impulsive, always ready for a fight. At the
same time, he was willing to learn.

Siegel's lifelong friendship with Meyer Lansky began with
another close call. At sixteen, Lansky stumbled upon a street
fight and saw that a gun had slipped from one of the fighters'
hands. A boy, not quite a teenager, was reaching for it as a police posse rounded the corner. *"Drop the gun,"* Lansky ordered
him. The boy looked up, saw the police, and took Lansky's advice. When the two were safely away, the young Ben Siegel
asked, "Why didn't you let me kill that bastard?"

"If you'd been caught with the gun you'd be in deep trouble," Lansky told him. "Only a *schlimazel* would shoot with the
cops in sight. Use your head."[22]

Lansky was born in Grodno, Russia. His was the classic
immigrant's story, with a father who came to America first and
saved enough to bring over his family. When Meyer reached
Ellis Island at age ten, the authorities changed his surname from
Suchowljansky to Lansky.

Meyer was an excellent student, picking up English on his
own, reading avidly, and discovering a love for mathematics.
But he was beguiled by gambling, beginning with street games
of chance that he mastered by learning how the dealer and shill
worked together to cheat a hapless mark. Like Ben, too, he was
a scrappy fighter, despite his Lilliputian height of about five-
foot-four. Sensing a kindred spirit that day he met him—and a
boy, at five-foot-ten, big enough to protect him—Meyer asked
Ben to join him in a gang he was forming, a gang for self-defense.

The threats came from either side of the Lower East Side's
Jewish enclave: Irish on one side, Italians on the other. Con-
stantly exposed to antisemitism, young Jews felt lucky to hand

over their nickels with only a light beating from one or another of the roving gangs. Back in Grodno, Meyer had seen Jewish families terrorized by Russians, but he would always remember a night at his grandfather's house when a fiery activist had addressed the local farmers. "Jews," he shouted. "Why do you just stand around like stupid sheep and let them come and kill you, steal your money, kill your sons and rape your daughters? Aren't you ashamed? You must stand up and fight."[23]

To Meyer, Ben resembled that activist. "He was young but very brave," Lansky later said of Siegel to a troika of Israeli biographers. "He liked guns. His big problem was that he was always ready to rush in first and shoot. No one reacted faster than Benny."[24] In the Russian pogroms, no one had been able to fight. In America, the young Jewish gang members could stand up to any threat.

Robert Rockaway, in an article in *American Jewish History*, recounts how the call would go out in Newark, New Jersey, when Irish thugs swept in. The streets would resound with "Ruff der Langer": Call the Tall One! In a flash, future New Jersey crime boss Abner "Longy" Zwillman, nicknamed for his height, would martial his Happy Ramblers to drive out the intruders. "As a result," notes Rockaway, "Longy acquired a reputation for assisting Jews that stayed with him his whole life."[25]

Siegel won some of that acclaim, too, and it resonated. When Ben's daughter Millicent Siegel died in 2017 at eighty-six and Las Vegas residents objected to having a daughter of Bugsy Siegel buried in their cemetery, Rabbi Mendy Harlig, a Chabad-Lubavitcher, pushed back. "You don't know what he and his friends did for the Jewish people on the Lower East Side," he told his congregation. "The Italians and the Irish were horrible to the Jews." Ben Siegel had protected those people.[26] Millicent Siegel was buried in Harlig's Chabad of Henderson after all, and because she died with almost no money, Harlig's Chabad paid for the burial.

Sometimes in these ethnic battles, a standoff between rival gangs led to mutual respect. An Italian gang led by one Salvatore Luciana cornered Meyer Lansky and demanded the usual tribute. "Go fuck yourself," Lansky spat out. Lansky was shorter than Luciana and completely outmanned. Luciana was amazed by the teenager's courage. "We both had a kind of instant understanding," Luciana later explained. "It was something that never left us." Luciana would come to be known as Charles "Lucky Luciano," and he, Lansky, and Siegel, among others, would form the multiethnic group known as the Syndicate.[27]

Along with stealing and small-time racketeering—forcing vendors to pay up or else—Siegel and Lansky held mundane day jobs. By the late 1910s, Ben was working for a trucking company, while Meyer was at a tool-and-die shop, fabricating parts for cars. They had money, but they were small fries, still living at home, destined to be caught for one crime or another and thrown into jail. Or worse, to sink into workaday lives like their fathers, both, as it happened, named Max. Siegel and Lansky dreaded the thought. "I'd have done anything not to be poor," Rockaway recalls Lansky saying decades later.[28]

Meyer's chance, and Ben's, came on January 17, 1920, with the start of Prohibition. With it came their graduation from urchins to *farbrekhers*—Yiddish for criminals—and almost unimaginable wealth.

"The transformative power of Prohibition cannot be overstated," says mafia historian and screenwriter Nick Pileggi. "These guys went from being stickup men and thugs and tough guys who didn't want to work for a living like their fathers into seeing a whole new way to make money." A way not only to get rich but to rub shoulders with bankers, lawyers, even the president. "Harding had his own bootlegger," Pileggi notes. "Frank Costello was invited to FDR's inaugural."[29]

At the start, there were choices to be made. Should aspiring bootleggers import booze from beyond the U.S. border? Set up distilleries and make their own? Or hijack other boot-leggers' hauls? Siegel and Lansky needed a mentor. They found one in Arnold "The Brain" Rothstein, the first gangster to jump into bootlegging on an international scale.

It was all the most amazing serendipity. Lansky met Roth-stein at a bar mitzvah in Brooklyn, and the older man—all of thirty-two—was impressed enough to invite the eighteen-year-old to dinner at the new Park Central Hotel, a few blocks south of Central Park, where he lived. They talked for hours, Roth-stein eventually laying out his plan to bring liquor by ship from England.[30] Not the cheap stuff. From his years of running high-class gambling joints in Manhattan, Rothstein knew his customer. Wealthy social imbibers wanted the best, and Roth-stein would get it for them. The beauty of trafficking booze from England, or Canada for that matter, was that it was legal until it crossed the U.S. border. What Rothstein needed was a network of operatives who could get it from there to warehouses and speakeasies. Specifically, he needed dozens of drivers, mus-clemen, ships' crewmen, warehouse owners, middlemen, and gun-wielding guards. Rothstein liked what he saw in Meyer Lan-sky, and said so. It was the most thrilling moment of Lansky's life to date. He told Rothstein he would happily be a driver, getting shipments from ports to warehouses. He had another driver Rothstein could trust too, he said: Benjamin Siegel.

Ben and Meyer soon learned as much about fashion from Rothstein as they did about organized crime. "Stylish dress emerged as the foremost symbol of Jewish transformation in the American city," notes historian Andrew R. Heinze in one Bugsy biography. Rothstein was the style setter. "He taught me how to not wear loud things, how to have good taste," Lucky Luciano later said. "If Arnold had lived longer, he could have made me pretty elegant; he was the best etiquette teacher a guy could have—real smooth." A smart wardrobe spelled business success, and no one grasped the connection better than Rothstein. "He understood business instinctively," Lansky recalled of Rothstein, "and I'm sure if he had been a legitimate financier he would have been just as rich as he became with his gambling and the other rackets he ran."[31] Siegel, at fourteen one of the youngest of Rothstein's recruits, saw the older man as the father he wished he'd had: brash, debonair, a man of the world, with all the money he wanted.

Unlike most Jewish gangsters, Rothstein had grown up on the Upper West Side. His own father was a wealthy businessman, chairman of the board of New York's Beth Israel Hospital, a senior member of his Orthodox Jewish community. Arnold could have been a great success in his father's world. But he loved gambling and the excitement it brought him. Rothstein hobnobbed with New York mayor Jimmy Walker and the rest of New York's elite. He was more than a gambler: he was a fixer, a financier, helping politicians and police chiefs, union bosses and Broadway producers. He was said to have fixed the 1919 World Series, but that may have been a useful legend. The bootlegging was for real.

A test run from England was a dark nocturnal drama crowned by great success: a booze-laden ship anchoring off Montauk, Long Island, motorboats shuttling on a moonless night from ship to shore, trucks carrying the liquor to warehouses in Queens. Soon Siegel and Lansky began renting trucks for bootleggers. The garage they used may have facilitated another new business. "Auto theft was their entrée to the big time," says mafia historian Thomas Reppetto. "Siegel stole them, and Lansky fixed them up for resale."[32] The market for English liquor in America was constant and bottomless, and brought with it other profitable vices: gambling, for one; prostitution, for another.

Along with Siegel and Lansky, "The Brain" hired Salvatore Luciana and his fellow Italians Frank Costello, Vito Genovese, Albert Anastasia, and Giuseppe "Joe Adonis" Doto. Grudgingly, the Italians worked hand in hand with the Jews, among them "Waxey" Gordon, "Dutch Schultz" (born Arthur Flegenheimer), Abner "Longy" Zwillman, Louis "Lepke" Buchalter, and Jacob "Gurrah" Shapiro. All except Rothstein had come up from the streets of the Lower East Side or the old country. All were on their way to national notoriety. Their credo was simple. "No one gives it to you," Costello reportedly said. "You have to take it."[33]

A year later, after eleven successful voyages, Rothstein was out. A ship's captain had snitched, and to Rothstein, the consummate gambler, the odds no longer looked good. His junior partners, including Siegel and Lansky, rushed to fill the gap. The Jews among them viewed Prohibition as rather silly: aside from sipping sacramental wine on holy days, most Jews, even criminals, had little taste for alcohol. But they saw the fortunes waiting to be made, and as fellow Jews, they trusted one another, up to a point. "To me, the whole thing was a matter of organizin' a business," Lucky Luciano later declared.[34]

Lansky and Siegel handled all aspects of the business, from setting up illicit stills in Canada and bringing in booze by boat across the Great Lakes to offshore runs along the Atlantic coast. They even ran a couple of Lower East Side speakeasies, one on Broome Street and one on Lewis, as one gangster, John Barrett, later recalled.[35] What they didn't do was claim a particular turf, as the tall and dapper Longy Zwillman did in parts of New Jersey, and Dutch Schultz did with the Bronx. They were freelance bootleggers, importing high-quality liquor from Canadian distillers like Samuel Bronfman and selling wherever they could.[36] They were also enforcers, hiring out as guards for other bootleggers' truck runs. That was when they became known, and feared, as the Bugs and Meyer mob.

Booze-filled trucks were subject to ambush, and no one was better than Ben Siegel at retaliating. One night, as one of Frank Costello's drivers later related, Siegel, working for Costello on that run, saw a tree trunk across a country road, ahead of the truck he was guarding. Siegel told the driver to jam on the brakes, and raced into the forest to circle around the attackers he felt sure were there. Sweeping the woods with tommy-gun fire, he drew fire in return, from three directions. He fired a flare gun that illuminated the scene, along with an attacker running right at him. Siegel killed the man with a burst of fire, then kept shooting. When a backup team of Costello's men arrived at the scene, they found a teenager "standing guard over four frightened men and a full truck of liquor, untouched."[37]

At some point, such crazy courage earned Siegel his nickname. It was a name he hated and bridled at whenever he heard it. Soon, in the world of organized crime, it became known that a good way to get killed was to greet Ben Siegel as "Bugsy."

The name, of course, had a darker connotation: that Siegel really was crazy as a bedbug, so quick to flare, so willing to kill. The FBI, in one of its later memos about Siegel during its surveillance of him, casually called him "insane along certain lines."[38] Journalists after his death called him a sociopath, someone capable of violent acts without conscience. Certainly he could kill without any apparent remorse. But no one ever heard of Siegel taking to a psychiatrist's couch, and the symptoms, from murderousness to megalomania, were just that: symptoms, and secondhand ones at that.

Some aspects of Siegel's character seemed incongruous with "sociopath" or "psychopath," even used loosely. Siegel had many close friendships that he maintained for life. He adored his daughters and felt, until the end, a certain loyalty to his wife, at least as the mother of his children. Loyalty was his most admirable trait. He remained loyal to Lansky, Luciano, and the rest of the Syndicate's higher-ups, until Siegel's last few nerve-wracking months, when he *may* have skimmed from the till and stolen from his partners, as he struggled to keep the Flamingo afloat. At that point, with the very real prospect that his partners might kill him, he grew more physically abusive and may, in some sense, have lost his mind. But that was all later.

By chance, a psychologist did offer a seat-of-the-pants analysis of another gangster, Frank Costello, which had some bearing on Siegel. The shrink, who came to know Costello through the gangster's lawyer, ventured a few conclusions. "An enormously fascinating man," he declared. "Egocentric, but with insecurities in several directions. He is absolutely sure of his own ability, and his own intelligence. And he has a thirst for power that's extraordinary. But let's look at his background. . . . He saw his father reduced to working with a pickax for slave wages." Siegel's father had endured equally grueling and degrading work. Both gangsters had grown up in New York slums— East Harlem in Costello's case—and moved, as soon as they could, to fancy neighborhoods of high social status. Neither man would ever forget the horrors of his childhood. The shrink who befriended Costello felt the gangster would do anything— anything—to keep from slipping back into poverty. So, it was fair to say, would Ben Siegel.[39]

By the mid-1920s, bootlegging had made Siegel a rich man who indulged in daily trips to the track. A very young rich man of barely twenty-one. For these outings, he wore checked sport jackets of houndstooth plaid, high-waisted pants with pegged cuffs, and custom-made alligator shoes. At night, he went out garbed in well-cut suits, with the colorful ties and monogrammed shirts of a dandy, fending off the winter chill with a hard-shelled derby hat and a velvet collared, full-length cashmere coat.[40] He was a long way from his days as an urchin on the Lower East Side.

And yet, as Meyer Lansky observed, Siegel didn't cling to money, fearful that his next haul might be his last. He spent extravagantly, as if money didn't matter at all. Getting it was a game, spending it just an excuse to play the game again. Perhaps he took some satisfaction in flaunting his newfound wealth to his father, who was still working as an operator in a pants factory.[41] To make money, you had to be ready to lose it. Max Siegel would never understand that simple truth. He let his fear keep him chained to that pants machine, making his pittance with no chance of earning more, the minutes of his life ticking away one by one, trapped by a world he'd thought would make him free. Real freedom meant knowing you could always earn more, as much as you liked, if only you knew how to do it.

On his evening rounds, Siegel loved making an entrance at one of the city's top speakeasies: the West Side's Club Durant, the 21 Club on West 52nd Street, and Chumley's in the Village, where the literary crowd gathered. More for business than anything else, Siegel and Lansky also hung out at the Back of Ratner's, a garage-cum-speakeasy behind Ratner's delicatessen by the Williamsburg Bridge. There the gangsters would rent cars and trucks to other bootleggers. Florabel Muir, a society columnist who worked both coasts, often ran into Siegel on her rounds. She invariably found him "arrayed in the habiliments of an easy money guy," and was struck by his cold blue eyes.[42] Two decades later, Muir would be the first journalist to reach Ben Siegel's murder scene and would note, being the dispassionate reporter she was, that one of those cold blue eyes had been propelled by a bullet into the living room's far wall.

Before Prohibition, no Jewish gangster would have been welcomed by the company in those nightspots. Lawyers, financiers, judges, and debutantes—all would have barred the interlopers from their nightclubs. Now they had no choice but to check their antisemitism at the door and socialize with them. The Jews, after all, had the money, the muscle, and the booze.

Bootleggers were glamorous, with the alluring hint of a dark side. Not by chance did F. Scott Fitzgerald make Jay Gatsby a bootlegger. Nor, by chance, did he have Gatsby meet up at a speakeasy with Meyer Wolfsheim, himself a bootlegger. Wolfsheim was based on Arnold "The Brain" Rothstein, to judge by Gatsby's aside to Nick Carraway that Wolfsheim fixed the 1919 World Series. But he could just as easily have been Ben Siegel.

Siegel enjoyed the women he met on his rounds, and went from one to the next, often with introductions made by his good friend Mark Hellinger, the Broadway newspaper columnist who affected tinted glasses, black suits, black shirts, and white ties. Hellinger was on his way to fame as a theatrical and Hollywood producer. He prided himself on using true-to-life crime stories provided by Lucky Luciano, Dutch Schultz, and Bugsy Siegel, and they loved recounting them over drinks at Sardi's. "Broadway was the gangsters' ideal cultural milieu," notes Albert Fried. "Its very existence served as their vindication."[43]

Still in his early twenties, Siegel now had the patina of class, and prided himself on it. "Class, that's the only thing that counts in life," he said. "Class. Without class and style a man's a bum, he might as well be dead."[44] Along with class, he had the brute force, so it was said, to claim a dollar a case of liquor—a dollar for *every* case of liquor—that came in to the New York docks. That was a lot of power, and a lot of cash. But he was about to reach for more.

2

---◆◄◆►◆---

Marriage and Murder

BEN'S FIRST BRUSH with the law came in January 1926, when a woman filed rape charges against him in Brooklyn. Doc Stacher, Meyer Lansky's right-hand man, explained years later what seemed, for Siegel, a most untypical crime.[1]

Siegel was barely twenty when he ran into a woman at a bar who reminded him, bitterly, that they had met before. Back when Siegel was fourteen, she had accused him of making an Irish youth disappear. Siegel had then pushed his way into her apartment and roughed her up. Apparently he had tried to rape her, only to fumble in the clutch. On seeing him again, the woman mocked his manhood. A furious Siegel followed her out of the bar and raped her in a nearby hallway. Or so said Doc Stacher. The woman, doubtless under pressure, soon withdrew the charges. No further charges of rape or any such crime ever darkened his docket.

Siegel's next charge seemed more in keeping for a now-notorious enforcer. He was arrested for carrying a concealed weapon in Philadelphia.[2] The mug shot taken on that date— April 12, 1928—offers the first known image of Ben Siegel, a snap-brim hat pulled low on his forehead over an icy, baleful stare. The police photographer must have decided the hat had to go: his profile shot has Siegel bareheaded, with a handsome profile, aquiline nose and strong chin. He seems more relaxed in profile, even bemused. Together, the front and profile shots seem to reveal two sides of the man: the murderous and the urbane. Siegel chose to skip his $1,000 bail and become a wanted man in Philadelphia, a harmless enough risk since New York showed no interest in extraditing him.

Early that November 1928, Arnold Rothstein was found shot and near death in his suite at the Park Central Hotel. Gambling had made his fortune but sealed his fate: always a gambler himself, he had become an addict, making ever wilder bets and appearing distracted, even mentally ill. Possibly he had gone into international drug trafficking and become a major dealer, but if so, this was a startling sideline for his Jewish colleagues, who so far had generally avoided drugs. Almost certainly, Rothstein owed his death to an unpaid debt, though he refused to say who had shot him, and why.[3] There was a lesson in that for Ben Siegel, not to let his own gambles get the better of him, but it was one he would fail to heed again and again, to Meyer Lansky's chagrin.

By the late twenties, Siegel and Lansky were said to be bringing more booze into the United States than any other bootleggers in the land.[4] Rumors, never substantiated, had them overseeing their share of narcotics trafficking, too.[5] There was, of course, no Dun & Bradstreet to gauge their business success.

For both men, marriage seemed an appropriate next step. In 1927, Siegel and Lansky began double-dating two Lower East Side girls. Ben went with Esther Krakauer, also known as Esta

and Estelle, whose family were onetime neighbors of the Siegels on Cannon Street. Her father, like Ben's, was a tailor. "Not
a looker," recalls Wendy Rosen, one of Esta's granddaughters—
and Ben's. "A very tall, lanky woman with Lucille Ball red hair."
Also, says Wendy, "a very unusual nose, prominent, with a flat
bridge, like an eagle's nose. And very tall and bony." Esther did
have beautiful blue eyes, Rosen says. More important, she was
crazy about her dashing beau. According to her granddaughter,
she always would be.[6]

Meyer chose Anna Citron, also dark-haired, also a longtime family friend, but from a considerably higher social sta-
tion than either the Lanskys or Siegels.[7] Anna's father had started
as a produce wholesaler and risen to command his own chain of
fruit markets. He wore pinstriped suits and lived on a New Jersey estate near Longy Zwillman in South Orange, an appropriate town for a produce king.[8]

The girls didn't mind that their boyfriends were bootleggers, though when asked, they were careful to say that Siegel
and Lansky ran an auto garage. They liked swanning as a four-
some into a speakeasy and drawing all eyes. But both were proper
young women, ready to start families. According to Wendy
Rosen, neither knew how deadly their fiancés were.[9]

Siegel married first. The ceremony was held on January 27,
1929, at 332 Rogers Avenue, a brownstone in then-bourgeois
Crown Heights, Brooklyn. Ben listed his occupation as "salesman" and his address as 546 Gates Avenue in Brooklyn's Bedford-
Stuyvesant, also a good neighborhood at the time. Esther, at
seventeen, was underage, and so a consent certificate was needed.
It was signed by Esther's father; her mother was noted as de-
ceased. The most striking fact in the marriage certificate was
that a rabbi officiated. His name, in flowing script, is illegible on
the form; the address on Rogers Avenue may have been his own.

Meyer Lansky married Anna Citron less than four months
later, on May 9. Again, a rabbi officiated: Rabbi Isaac Leib Ep-

stein. Lansky listed his residential address as 6 Columbia Street on the Lower East Side, and his business as "auto rental," rather amusing if he was, indeed, still selling stolen cars. Anna's father's name was Moses, her mother was Selma; both parents were Jewish and had been born in Russia. The two grooms served as each other's best men.[10]

The presence of rabbis at both services was telling. Lansky and Siegel might have no ties with local synagogues. Yet they had chosen to enter Jewish marriages and identify themselves as Jews. If they had given any thought to marrying without a rabbi, they had acted otherwise, doing what they most strongly felt: to honor the faith of their fathers and, unlikely as it might seem, to recognize that the same bonds that held them together as gangsters held them together as Jews. These included the presence, if not the practice, of religion; Yiddish as the communal language if no longer the dominant one; and the resonance of Jewish values, shunted aside if business required, but always there in the fabric of their lives. Most emphatically, they embraced the shared destiny of the Jewish people, unfurling here in America with opportunity, one future day, for all.

The ever-practical Lansky arranged for his honeymoon to take place during an Atlantic City conclave of top-tier gangsters in mid-May, 1929, a meeting he himself planned and headed up. Dozens of attendees gathered, from Lucky Luciano and Frank "The Prime Minister" Costello to Vito Genovese, Joe Adonis, Longy Zwillman, and, to be sure, Ben Siegel. During the meetings, Lansky's and Siegel's brides lounged by the pool with other gangsters' wives and girlfriends. When business was done, the gangsters joined them or took pensive strolls along the beach, their shoes and socks in hand, their trousers rolled up. The gathering was a first formal attempt to plan for the inevitable end of Prohibition. How would the gangsters sustain the cash flow that bootlegging had brought? Ending the bloodshed among rival gangsters was the other urgent order of business, following the Valentine's Day massacre of the preceding February in Chicago, where Al Capone had orchestrated the murder of seven rival gangsters. Capone was at the conference, too, his temper even less in check than Siegel's.[11] Atlantic City was where the notion of a national Syndicate was first aired, with strict rules for all, but more blood would have to be shed before the gangsters agreed on who should lead them, and how the pie of vice should be divided, vice by vice and market by market.

Charming and collegial as this interlude seemed, Siegel and Lansky had come very close to killing a man just months before—using him, as they later put it, for target practice. Racketeering was becoming as big a business as bootlegging, and as gangsters who had started by threatening to torch peddlers' pushcarts, Siegel and Lansky brought the same concept to the garment industry: pay for protection, or else. The most feared racketeers were Louis "Lepke" Buchalter and Jacob "Gurrah" Shapiro, friends of Lansky and Siegel from the early days of Prohibition, when all had worked for Rothstein. Lepke and Gurrah ruled the garment industry and often hired Siegel and Lansky as enforcers. The gangsters got paid by garment company owners to break up union strikes, then hired out to the unions for acts of revenge, breaking owners' legs or burning their factories.

Despite their tactics, Lepke and Gurrah were almost rabbinical in manner. "Lepke avoided all flamboyance and displays of bravado," notes Albert Fried. "He was reserved in speech, manner and dress, and while he occasionally gambled, drank and womanized, he was rarely seen in the popular haunts. And Gurrah lived quietly with his family in the predominantly Jewish Flatbush section of Brooklyn."[12]

The near-homicide was the result of a routine job involving pricey furs from a Bronx wholesaler, a job that took a bad turn when Lansky and Siegel realized they were several furs short.

Under questioning, a low-ranking hood named John Barrett admitted he had taken the furs. He felt that Siegel and Lansky's share of the take on jobs like these was unfairly high.

That night, Lansky and Siegel took Barrett on a ride out of town. With them was Red Levine, an Orthodox Jewish contract killer who tried not to kill on the Sabbath—but if the job had to be done, kissed his mezuzah, said his prayers draped in a tallit, and wore a skullcap under his hat as he headed out.

"Even the most violent of the gangsters saw themselves as good Jews, people of the Book," suggests Rich Cohen in *Tough Jews*. "They went to temple on High Holy Days, thought of God when things went bad, had their sons circumcised and bar mitzvahed. Being a Jew was not something they were thinking of all the time, but they were aware of themselves as Jews, as players in a larger story—the Temple, the Exodus. How did they square their criminal life with the life of the Bible? Well, like most people, they made a distinction: This is the life of the soul; this is the life of the body. Next year in Jerusalem. But this is how I live in the Diaspora."[13]

Barrett felt sure he was about to be killed. With nothing to lose, he jumped out of the moving car in a rural area. The gangsters screeched to a stop and piled out to open fire on Barrett's zigzagging figure. Barrett was "a hell of a runner," another gangster recalled with awe, but he did get hit four times.[14] Somehow he managed to flag down a taxi and get to the Lower East Side's Gouverneur Hospital.

Over breakfast the next morning at Ratner's, the Delancey Street deli where Siegel and Lansky often met with pals for long, schmoozy breakfasts, Lansky announced to a new arrival, "You really missed the party!" He meant the shooting-target practice that Barrett had provided. Over their bagels and coffee, the boys decided to finish off Barrett by sending a poisoned chicken to his hospital room: the hospital was barely a block away. Barrett, no fool, winged the chicken out the window.[15]

All this was highly amusing to Siegel, who despite his penchant for violence retained a childlike sense of mischief. From atop buildings in Brooklyn, he would drop water balloons onto policemen below. "When one dripping cop stormed into Siegel's hotel looking for the villain," reports Dean Jennings, Siegel's first biographer and in some ways his best, fellow Rothstein bootlegger Albert Anastasia snarled, " 'For Christ's sake, Ben, why in hell you keep pulling this kid stuff?' "

" 'Because I get a kick out of it,' " Siegel replied.[16]

Soon Siegel was dropping those water balloons from a suite at the Waldorf Astoria, having moved his family from Brooklyn to the city's largest first-class hotel when his first daughter, Millicent, was born January 14, 1931. Instead of Ratner's, he started his day at the Waldorf's Norse Grill, or in one of his fellow gangsters' suites. Frank Costello, a longtime racketeering pal, had a suite at the Waldorf, too. So did Siegel's and Lansky's close friend Salvatore Lucania, who had earned his nickname "Lucky" in 1929 after being taken for a ride by rival gangsters, beaten, cut, and left for dead at the side of a road. Some good Samaritan had taken Lucania to a hospital, and he had survived. He emerged from the ordeal with a deep, long, menacing knife scar down one side of his face—and a new name.[17]

The Waldorf's plush grandeur appealed to the gangsters, and the security was good. Lansky was a frequent breakfast guest. "We sort of met there mornings," Lansky recalled. "I spoke often about gambling to Frank, Charlie and Ben."[18]

For Siegel and Lansky, the American dream had come true, even if their version of it required bootlegging, racketeering, and the occasional contract killing. And how young they were! Lansky was twenty-nine years old in 1931, Siegel just twenty-five. Now, however, they found themselves caught in the crossfire of two mafia clans.

Mussolini, of all people, had managed in 1926 to banish Joseph "The Boss" Masseria from Italy and Salvatore Maranzano from Sicily, along with each man's murderous army. In the New York turf war that followed, as many as fifty underlings died. Masseria recruited Lucky Luciano as an enforcer. Luciano, in turn, hired Lansky and Siegel.[19]

With the gang war still red-hot in early 1931, Luciano got word from one of Masseria's top lieutenants, Joe Adonis, that Luciano was no longer in favor: too big for his britches, Masseria had decided. He wanted Luciano killed. He wanted Lansky and Siegel killed, too. He didn't much like working with Jews.[20]

Quietly, Luciano switched his allegiance to Maranzano and suggested to his new boss that he lure Masseria into a trap. Luciano asked Masseria to lunch on April 15, 1931, at a Coney Island restaurant, and the two talked for some time. Legend has it that Masseria, a huge man, wolfed down a massive plate of spaghetti, but as Bugsy biographer Larry Gragg notes, Masseria's stomach, when pumped the next day, showed little or no food consumed.[21] True to legend, though, Luciano did excuse himself to go to the bathroom, and a large sedan did appear outside the restaurant, with gun-toting gangsters piling out to blow Masseria to smithereens.

Whether Siegel was among them is a matter of dispute. Gragg finds no firm evidence he was. Mafia historian Robert Rockaway puts Siegel in the car along with Albert Anastasia, Vito Genovese, and Joe Adonis. Meyer Lansky's trio of Israeli biographers goes so far as to suggest Siegel led the vengeful posse. Job done, they report, "the four gunmen ran for their car. Their driver stalled out the vehicle twice. Bugsy Siegel punched him and shoved him aside, then took the wheel himself and calmly drove off at high speed." This version is also credited by Thomas Reppetto in his *American Mafia*. The hapless driver, he suggests, was one Ciro Terranova, the Artichoke King.[22]

With Masseria dead, Maranzano convened a meeting of all the top gangsters and formally recognized their families and bosses. Luciano was one of them, in recognition of his role in eliminating Masseria. Maranzano made just one mistake: he put himself above all others, as boss of bosses.

Siegel, Lansky, and Luciano heard the grumbling. They also knew that Maranzano had drawn up a kill list, and that Luciano was on it. For that matter, Lansky and Siegel were on it, too. Together the three came up with a plan to be carried out at the heavily guarded midtown offices that Maranzano had just taken for himself at 230 Park Avenue.

The plan was that a handful of putative Internal Revenue Service agents would knock on Maranzano's front office door, there to check for evidence of tax evasion. None of the agents would be Italian: that might raise the suspicions of Maranzano's bodyguards. They would, instead, be Jewish contract killers, mostly brought in from distant states.

The plan came off without a hitch. On September 10, 1931, the uniformed faux agents flashed their badges and showed their inspection documents. Once inside the front office, they drew their guns and lined the bodyguards against a wall, warning them to stay silent. Then they burst into Maranzano's private office. The Jewish killer Red Levine, the one who tried not to kill on the Sabbath, stabbed Maranzano six times. (It was a Thursday.) Others riddled his bleeding body with bullets. The killers then fled down the back stairs to a waiting car. Some versions put Siegel at the wheel of the getaway car; true or not, he could take gleeful credit, with Lansky and Luciano, for the plan.[23]

With that, Lucky Luciano became the unchallenged ruler of gangland, flanked by Siegel and Lansky. Wisely, he claimed no such title. There would still be five families, as Maranzano had decreed, but they would be free to do whatever business they pleased. "There's no such thing as good money or bad money," he reportedly said. "There's just money."[24] Luciano reiterated the credo first aired in Atlantic City. Italians, Irish, and Jews would work together, both to minimize bloodshed and to maximize profits; all hits would have to be sanctioned by the family heads of what would now be known officially as the Syndicate. Along with Luciano, Lansky, and Siegel, the Syndicate's top members included Frank Costello and Giuseppe "Joe Adonis" Doto. They would be the ones sitting in judgment, meting out shootings as needed.

To hash out how racketeering would be handled in this new day, nine nattily dressed gangsters convened on November 12, 1931, at New York's Franconia Hotel on West 72nd Street. Among them were Lepke Buchalter and Gurrah Shapiro, terrors of the garment industry. There, too, was Ben Siegel. A tipoff to the police led to a roust, as gangsters put it: all nine men were brought in for fingerprints and mug shots. The cops lined them up for a group shot as well. It was quite a picture: all nine men dapper-hatted, with snappy ties protruding from their elegant overcoats. That was the picture that made the newspapers the next day: the public's first image of Ben Siegel.[25]

Siegel was furious. The cops had no charges to slap on any of the gangsters. They were just rousting for the sport of it. Siegel argued that his arrest was a breach of his privacy. So was publication of that group photograph. Since he had no previous record in New York, he prevailed. He had his fingerprints and mug shots returned to him, and got the police to snip him out of the group photograph. Ben Siegel was determined to be a gangster *and* a member in good standing of Café Society.[26]

Despite Luciano's stern new edict that no killings should occur without permission, gangsters had a way of taking matters into their own hands. Waxey Gordon had nursed a grievance against Siegel and Lansky for years, ever since "Bug and Meyer" had hijacked one of his booze trucks. To Waxey's greater indignation, Lansky and his brother Jake then provided evidence of tax evasion on Gordon's part to United States Attorney Thomas E. Dewey. Waxey had made himself an obvious target: in 1930, he had earned roughly $1.5 million and paid taxes of exactly $10.76.[27] Now Waxey was indicted, and would soon be serving a ten-year jail term, in large part thanks to the Lanskys. He was livid, and intent on revenge.

One day in the fall of 1932, Siegel got a call from one of Waxey Gordon's lieutenants, Charles "Chink" Sherman, asking for a meeting at Broadway and 34th Street. Sherman had left the Waxey Gordon mob, he said, and wanted to throw in his lot with Siegel and Lansky. Whatever Sherman said, it was enough for Siegel to head uptown from the headquarters he and Lansky kept on Grand Street on the Lower East Side with one or two bodyguards in a bulletproof sedan. As they reached 34th Street, another car drew up alongside, and its passengers raked Siegel's car with machine-gun fire. One of Siegel's men was shot in the rear; the rest were unhurt.

Back on Grand Street, a seething Siegel convened a war meeting. That was when the second attack came. One of Gordon's henchmen had lowered a bomb down the room's chimney, and he managed to detonate it. He just hadn't realized that the chimney made a ninety-degree turn, and then another, above the fireplace. The bomb, as a result, went off in the chimney, not in the fireplace. Still, Siegel was hit in the head by a flying piece of brick and rushed to a nearby hospital.[28]

Siegel felt sure that a Gordon mobster named Tony Fabrazzo had planted the bomb. There was bad blood between him and Siegel, since Siegel had had something to do with killing one or both of Fabrazzo's brothers, one of them reportedly in a phone booth. On the high-speed drive to the hospital, Siegel's mobsters swore they caught a glimpse of Fabrazzo in a chase car, angling for an open shot.

In his private hospital room, Siegel came up with a plan. On his second or third night of recuperation, he donned a suit, plumped up pillows under the covers to resemble his sleeping form, and sneaked out of the hospital. Whisked into his bullet-pocked armored car, Siegel rode out to Fort Hamilton, Brooklyn. His pals parked up the street from the house of Tony Fabrazzo's father, where the last of his three sons was staying, and rang the doorbell. The father opened the door to what he thought were three police detectives, dutifully flashing their badges. Called down by his father, Tony Fabrazzo came to the doorway and was promptly shot with three bullets in the head. Siegel and his pals fled back to the hospital, where Siegel crawled into his private-room bed, thrilled with his perfect alibi.

The year that Prohibition ended—1933—Siegel moved his family from the Waldorf Astoria to a five-bedroom, Tudor-style house in Scarsdale, New York, at 46 Bretton Road. His second daughter, Barbara, had just been born, and Siegel wanted what everyone who moved to Scarsdale wanted: an upscale Westchester County suburb with good public schools. For a homeowner who worried that he might get shot, the house was perfectly situated at the intersection of three streets—three escape routes, that is. For a boy from the Lower East Side, Scarsdale was country: on a U.S. census report, Siegel would say that he and his family lived on a farm.[29]

Still, Scarsdale was an odd choice for a Jew at that time. As a social history of the town makes clear, Jews were not welcome. "Realtors, normally eager for clients, tried to discourage Jewish couples from buying property in Scarsdale," writes Carol A. O'Connor. "If dissuasion failed, the realtors had an agreement whereby they refused to show Jews the houses in certain areas." Ultimately, wealthy Jews managed to buy homes in the most affluent neighborhoods: money prevailed, as it often did in real estate. One notable resident at the time Ben bought his house was Sidney Weinberg, of the investment firm Goldman, Sachs. Another was entertainer Al Jolson, quite possibly the Broadway acquaintance who inspired Siegel to move to

Scarsdale in the first place. But as O'Connor writes, social acceptance rarely followed. "The small number of Jews who moved into the village discovered that non-Jews refused to associate with them socially. Although they could join the local civic organizations, they were not admitted to the Scarsdale Golf Club."[30] Siegel could hardly have been unaware of the antisemitism. He may have felt he could tough it out in Scarsdale, and charm his way into his neighbors' social circles. Anyone who declined to receive him, after all, might find himself taking a ride in the back of a Packard, down a long dark country road.

This sylvan suburban scene was marred by the news that a new and progressive New York mayor, Fiorella La Guardia, had embarked on an all-out campaign to rid the city of organized crime. His sidekick was Thomas E. Dewey, the mayor's specially appointed prosecutor, who had just won his first case—against Waxey Gordon, thanks to the Lansky brothers.[31] Now Dewey was vowing to break the rackets, starting with Lepke Buchalter and Gurrah Shapiro. The Bug and Meyer mob could hardly be far down Dewey's list. Perhaps it was time for Siegel to make himself scarce.

Siegel had another incentive to lie low. His alibi for the killing of Tony Fabrazzo was looking less than perfect; the authorities were asking around. Lansky had a suggestion. The Syndicate had awarded Lansky and Siegel the rights to any and all gambling operations outside of New York. Cuba was promising; so were the Bahamas. And so was Las Vegas. But clearly the hottest opportunities lay in and around Los Angeles, now that Prohibition was ending and booze would no longer be the Syndicate's top source of income. Lansky wanted Siegel to explore how the Syndicate might muscle in on L.A. gambling operations, make book at the Santa Anita track, squeeze racketeering proceeds from the movie industry—and maybe bring in narcotics, including heroin, from south of the border. Handsome and suave, with a still-clean record in the eyes of the law but a fearsome reputation in the underworld, Ben Siegel was the perfect advance man, sure to command the respect of shady gangsters in that sunny clime. As for Siegel, he loved the prospect of fun amid stars and starlets while his wife stayed back in Scarsdale, watching over their daughters. Hollywood! It was, in retrospect, a perfect marriage of the man and the moment, a move Ben Siegel was born to make.

3

Sportsman in Paradise

ON HIS FIRST TRIP to L.A., in 1933, Ben Siegel stayed at the towering Ambassador Hotel, famous for its Cocoanut Grove nightclub.[1] His first call was almost certainly to George Raft: fellow gangster, Broadway dancer, old friend, and rising movie star. Raft was Bugsy's entrée to Hollywood.

Raft had grown up in a cold-water flat in Hell's Kitchen and, like Siegel, had become a scrappy fighter with a volatile temper, adroit enough with a knife to be called The Snake. His gang boss, Owney Madden, had a yen for entertainment: he started the Cotton Club, where jazz greats from Cab Calloway to Duke Ellington, Benny Goodman, and Louis Armstrong performed. It was Madden who first noticed Raft's gift for dancing and encouraged him to work the midtown dancehalls, where lonely women paid to be whirled around the floor. Later, Fred Astaire described Raft as "the neatest, fastest Charleston dancer ever. . . . He practically floored me with his footwork."[2]

With the dawn of talkies in the late twenties, Madden began pushing Raft to give Hollywood a try. One day in 1930, the two of them set out for the Golden State together in Madden's car. Their timing was perfect: the era of the hard-boiled gangster movie had just begun. Hollywood's screenwriters, however, had no idea how gangsters actually talked. Raft was their answer: a Hollywood-handsome bona fide gangster. His breakthrough was the 1932 *Scarface*, based on the life of Al Capone. It was an instant classic, making George Raft a star. No one who ever saw him do his coin-flip trick in the movie ever forgot it.

On that first trip, Siegel spent hours at a time with Raft at the Santa Anita horse track, ruminating on how the Syndicate might muscle in on the so-called horse race wire. Gentlemen went to the track and placed their bets at pari-mutuel machines. But a whole world of off-track operators had figured out how to send race results by telegraph wire, circumventing the tracks altogether. The beauty of it was that transmitting results by wire was entirely legal. Only the bookies paying to receive those results in so-called horse parlors were committing a crime, and all they had to do was pay off the police to make everyone happy. Siegel was set on cutting the Syndicate into the race wire, whatever it took. He seemed, at the track, something of a wastrel. But he had ambitions. "Damned few people knew what made him tick," Raft said later of Siegel. "But I did. He came out here because he wanted to be somebody."[3]

In his youth, one of Bugsy's few legal pleasures had been the nickelodeons, where he sat mesmerized by early silent film stars like Theda Bara and Rudolph Valentino. He yearned to meet the stars and studio heads whom Raft was gadding around with, but he knew he had to prove himself first. He had made a million dollars over the previous few years, he told Raft, only to lose a lot of it in the stock market. "If I had kept that million, I'd have been out of the rackets right then," Siegel said. "But I took a big licking, and I couldn't go legit."[4] Bugsy would have to make big money again—and build a big house to go with it—to start socializing with stars. And since the only kind of money he knew was easy money, he knew who that put him up against.

Sicilian-born Ignazio Dragna, known as Jack, had become the Al Capone of California bootlegging and headed up his own L.A. crime family, only warily affiliated with the Syndicate. Dragna had made his previous boss disappear, and would have enjoyed nothing more than to do the same with Siegel, but Lucky Luciano intervened. Siegel had the Syndicate's blessing, Luciano told him, and Dragna would have to cooperate, as long as Siegel didn't interfere with Dragna's own schemes. Siegel began horning in on the racetracks, demanding cuts of the pari-mutuel pool. Nightclubs and private casinos were other obvious targets. There, in addition to dealing with Dragna, Siegel had to take on . . . the Octopus.

Casino owner Guy McAfee was a former head of the Los Angeles Police Department vice squad. They called him the Octopus because his tentacles reached into gambling, bootleg liquor, bookmaking, and prostitution, among other vices, with the city's top politicians and police in his pocket. One of his prize holdings was the Clover Club, on L.A.'s Sunset Strip, a top-tier speakeasy enjoying the last days of Prohibition, thanks to its backroom casino, where one-way mirrors warned of impending raids so that the gaming tables could be flipped. The Clover was haute Hollywood, and Siegel wanted in. McAfee had a trigger-happy manager, Eddie Nealis, who found himself disinclined to accept Siegel's kind offer. Nealis, in turn, had a tough enforcer on his payroll, one Jimmy Fox. Siegel had Fox shot, not quite fatally, and then went after Nealis, who somehow sensed a waiting assassin outside his home and fled to Mexico City, never to be seen on the Strip again. Part of the Clover's nightly spoils were now funneled to Siegel by his surly new business partner, Guy McAfee.[5]

The following year—1934—Siegel rented a house on Arden Drive in Beverly Hills. America was flat broke, except for Hollywood, whose stars and studio heads had money to burn. With Prohibition's end, L.A. was filled with former speakeasies now serving as bars and gambling joints. The horse tracks were packed, and the telegraph wires were burning with off-track race wire results. Meanwhile, the ex-bootleggers still had their trucks and garages, useful for drug trafficking.

Siegel's family stayed on the East Coast in Scarsdale, which made Siegel a man about town for weeks at a time. He did his share of womanizing, and fell hard for a blonde French actress named Ketti Gallian, who had come to L.A. with a screen contract from Twentieth Century–Fox. According to Raft, Siegel spent $50,000 trying to help Gallian lose her accent. The effort was in vain. Her 1934 American debut, *Marie Galante*, was a bomb, and a second film did no better. Gallian went back to France, her contract bought out and her romance with Siegel dashed.[6]

Siegel may have felt some guilt about keeping Esther and the girls in Scarsdale through these dalliances. Probably to placate her, Ben had his sister Ethel live at the Scarsdale house to help Esther with the girls. Also, according to a U.S. census covering 1935, the Scarsdale house contained a live-in maid, a cook, and John the butler.[7] All three in staff were listed as Negroes. Their presence provided not just household help, but social status in class-sensitive Scarsdale.

To anyone back in Scarsdale who asked, Siegel purported to be a sales broker with his own office.[8] In L.A., he called himself a sportsman. It was a title that suggested wealth and social prominence: an owner of racehorses, or a big-game hunter. For Siegel, it was a euphemism for gambling, with a little extortion and the occasional killing thrown in. But he was reinventing himself in the town of reinvention, a most American enterprise.

The horse tracks—Santa Anita for one, Agua Caliente for

another—were Siegel's great passion and profit rolled into one. He made bets of his own virtually every day. While he sometimes lost, he more often won, thanks to the inside word he seemed to get on which horse was about to go lame, or which was doped up and likely to win. Later, a close friend would say that betting was Siegel's main occupation by the mid-thirties and that he earned hundreds of thousands of dollars a year doing it. From all proceeds, the Syndicate took its skim: 25 percent, according to the FBI.[9] As the Syndicate began building casinos in Florida—Lansky's turf—Siegel shared in those profits as well.

Some of Siegel's earnings at this time went to education—his younger brother Maurice's education, that is. Maurice became an internist with a private practice in Beverly Hills. One account suggests he was, for a time, a studio doctor at Columbia Pictures.[10] According to Wendy Rosen, Ben's granddaughter, Maurice came to occupy a seat on the board of Cedars-Sinai Hospital. Years later, Maurice asked Wendy whether she knew about her late grandfather. It was the one mention of his brother he ever made to her. Ben had paid for his education, Maurice admitted, but that was all Maurice wanted to say on the subject. "If Ben came up in conversation, my aunt Lil, Maurice's wife, would shuffle around the house," Wendy said. "It was like he didn't exist."[11] It was a classic scenario in gangsterland: a life of crime justified—ennobled, even—if the money could buy a family member's escape into legitimacy. Lansky would do the same thing by sending his son Paul to West Point.

By 1935, Siegel was ready for a move up. He rented the large Beverly Hills home of Metropolitan Opera singer Lawrence Tibbett at 326 South McCarty Drive. The way the story unfolds in Barry Levinson's Oscar-nominated 1991 film *Bugsy*, the house isn't for rent. Siegel, played by Warren Beatty, just likes it as he drives by it, tells George Raft to pull over, strides in, and flashes such a big roll of bills that Tibbett is persuaded to leave on the spot. None of the more credible biographies mentions the scene, but the house on McCarty was the one to which Siegel brought his family to live.[12] Unfortunately, Siegel found himself forced to make trips to New York even as he settled his family in L.A. The Syndicate had a problem for which Siegel's help was needed.

Like Siegel and Lansky, Arthur "Dutch Schultz" Flegenheimer had gotten his start with bootleg whisky runs for Rothstein. He was a German Jew, not Dutch, but he liked his nom de crime because, as he put it, "it was short enough to fit in the headlines. If I'd kept the name Flegenheimer, nobody would have heard of me."[13]

As the beer baron of the Bronx and the numbers boss of Harlem, Schultz was well known, so much so that he made an irresistible target for newly named Manhattan Special Prosecutor Thomas Dewey, who indicted him, as he had Waxey Gordon, for tax evasion.[14] Schultz's first trial ended in a deadlocked jury; for the second, his lawyers succeeded in moving the venue an hour's drive north of New York to the sleepy town of Monroe, where Schultz charmed the locals and beat the rap. He came back to Manhattan bent on revenge. Dewey must die, he told his fellow gangsters. They were stunned. Did he have any idea how much heat that would bring on them? "Alright," Schultz growled, "I'll kill him myself in the next 48 hours."

With that, Schultz signed his own death warrant. The gangsters resolved to dispatch him before Schultz got Dewey. And so they did, sending three of their best contract men to murder "Dutch" and his guards on October 23, 1935.[15] Finding them was easy: the entourage dined every night at the Palace Chop House in Newark, New Jersey.

Dutch fled to the bathroom as the shooting broke out, so one of the killers, Charlie "The Bug" Workman, went back to finish him off. When Workman emerged, to a scene of mayhem and cowering diners, he found his fellow killers gone, along with the getaway car. Workman couldn't believe it. He ended up walking across to Manhattan, appalled by their treachery.[16] One of Bugsy's early biographers, George Carpozi, claims Siegel was one of the gangsters Workman could blame for abandoning him.

"A little reported facet of this rub-out was Bugsy Siegel's role in Schultz' actual killing," Carpozi explains. "After Lucky Luciano had dispatched [the killers] to New Jersey, he called in Bugsy. 'Benny, you take a couple of boys and go out there to Newark. Don't get mixed up in this deal unless [they] mess it up.'

"Thus Bugsy, accompanied by Harry Teitelbaum and Harry 'Big Greenie' Greenberg, waited in their parked car a short distance from the restaurant as a second line of defense," writes Carpozi. Once they saw the first car of killers tear away, they drove off at a law-abiding speed and melted into the night.[17]

It's a good story, but as with so many of Siegel's early exploits—driving the getaway car from Joe Masseria's murder in Coney Island, planning the killing of Salvatore Maranzano by "IRS agents," and sneaking out of his hospital bed to put a bullet in Tony Fabrazzo's head—it's a story none can confirm. Gangsters rarely tell their own tales, at least not the true ones, and those who speak for them tend to embellish, until over time the story becomes a legend, even a myth. Did Bugsy Siegel really kill a dozen men himself, as he apparently told his contractor in Las Vegas? Or did he kill thirty, as the FBI suggested in an interoffice memo?

The truth of those early tales would never be parsed. Meanwhile, Ben Siegel was on his way to becoming a public figure. Increasingly his moves would be set down in type by a diligent and delighted press. There wasn't anything Siegel could do about that but grin and hope his luck prevailed.

One of the first stars Siegel met in Hollywood was Jean Harlow, the platinum blonde bombshell who had become

MGM's leading lady in her early twenties. He met her through Longy Zwillman, the New Jersey gangster nicknamed for his commanding height, who knew Harlow's mobbed-up step-father, one Mario Bello. Zwillman was enamored of Harlow and procured her a two-picture deal at Columbia Pictures by giving studio head Harry Cohn a sweetheart loan for $500,000.[18] Unfortunately, Harlow failed to reciprocate his feelings. Still, Harlow began coming as Zwillman's date to dinners at the Siegel house. Siegel's older daughter Millicent, then about five years old and on her first summer vacation in L.A., was speechless when introduced to Harlow. Soon enough, the actress agreed to become Millicent's godmother. Not officially, since the role had no formal place in Jewish families—just informally. One of Harlow's biographers, Irving Shulman, suggests that Harlow resented her stepfather and his crowd, including Zwillman, and tried to keep her distance, agreeing to be Millicent's "godmother" only as a sop to an innocent girl. But Harlow enjoyed the diversions. She put on an apron and cooked; she gave Millicent baths.[19]

There was a seamier side to this cozy scene. Siegel was soon set on sleeping with Harlow. She had had a fling with actor Jimmy Stewart, and Siegel saw that as his way in. "Jean's a good friend of yours," he said to Stewart. "How about you tell her to go out with me." To which Stewart apparently responded, "You go to hell." Stewart told his future wife, Gloria, that he had been terrified Siegel would pull out a gun and plug him on the spot. But Stewart's height seemed to keep Siegel from doing anything rash.[20]

It was, for the Siegels, a dazzling but short-lived friendship. Only twenty-six, Harlow died of a cerebral edema and uremia on June 7, 1937. The Siegels were among the hundreds who attended her funeral; according to Gloria, they were observed weeping copiously.[21]

The Tibbett house was suitable for modest entertaining,

but it lay in the Beverly Hills Flats, below the demarcation line of Sunset Boulevard. Above Sunset was where the hills rose and the homes grew grand, with sweeping views of the valley. Siegel was set on building a house that would draw in Hollywood royalty. He bought a 1.7-acre plot on 250 Delfern Drive, above Sunset Boulevard in the Beverly Crest neighborhood of Holmby Hills. In 1937, he started building his 10,000-square-foot dream house.

That house and grounds would cost $180,000, at a time when the average cost of a home in America was just under $3,000. It would be a white-bricked, two-story structure with imposing gates and a wide, curving driveway that announced grandeur within. The front door would open into a two-story classic hall with sweeping staircase, a sixty-foot-long living room containing a piano no one could play, and a bar with a slot machine at either end. There would be an oak-paneled library, gourmet kitchen, and capacious dining room with a table to accommodate thirty guests before adding extension leaves. Siegel was enthralled. More than Lansky, he needed the trappings of wealth to prove he had come as far as he had, the Lower East Side street kid literally on top of the world he'd dreamed of entering a decade ago. This was the American dream, all right, and Siegel was proof that anyone with guts, good taste, and a gun could grab it, assuming he kept striking fear into those who might otherwise make his dream their own.

The house had twenty-three rooms in all, including six bedrooms. The master bathrooms and dressing rooms were especially striking. Ben's was done entirely in red marble, while Esther's had a mirrored ceiling and walls. There would be six "vanity rooms" for female guests, equipped "with crystal bottles containing exotic perfumes and comb-and-brush sets trimmed with turquoise, amethyst, silver and gold."[22]

Out back, a long lap pool was being installed, along with a pool house, fountains, and formal rose gardens. Already Siegel swam almost every day to stay fit, either at the local YMCA or in George Raft's pool in Coldwater Canyon. Soon he would use the lap pool on Delfern, along with a sprawling workout room, steam, and sauna. He was obsessed, too, with calisthenics, acquiring, after several years of daily workouts, the body of a gymnast. The whole property would be surrounded by a high wrought-iron fence and state-of-the-art security system. Some seventy-five years later, in February 2013, the house and grounds would be sold for $17.5 million to hedge fund director Jon Brooks and his wife Shanna. By December of that year, everything on the site would be gone but for the tennis court, which would soon be removed as well. Construction of a new house was under way in early 2019.[23]

The bills kept coming, but Siegel could afford them: almost every day, he bet up to $5,000 on horse races, baseball games, and prize fights, and almost never lost.[24] As the house went up, Siegel badgered the contractor every step of the way. Often he went back again after dark, with George Raft in tow, the two of them lighting wooden matches so that they could inspect the progress.

One night, with the house far along, Siegel brought Raft to the master bedroom. As Raft later explained, the wall beside the bed had a sliding panel controlled by a concealed button: a trapdoor, like a dumbwaiter. "Who needs it?" Raft teased.

"I do," Siegel retorted. "I got two others in the house. Maybe some day I gotta get out of here in a hurry." In the library, a set of fake bookcases slid open to reveal cabinets and a safe in which he kept his jewelry, papers, and two guns: a Smith & Wesson .38 caliber revolver and a .38 automatic.[25]

Cheering on the project was a wealthy woman whom Esther Siegel must have resented, for Siegel soon became her man about town.

Dorothy di Frasso, born Dorothy Taylor, had inherited $10 million from her father's $50 million New York leather goods company. She had had one failed marriage—to famed English aviator Claude Grahame-White—and one unhappy, ongoing one, to a destitute but titled Italian much older than she. Count Carlo Dentice di Frasso lived in a sprawling villa on the outskirts of Rome and spent his wife's money. Dorothy, in exchange, became the Countess Dentice di Frasso, often apart from her husband for weeks at a time in Beverly Hills, entertaining at her own mansion on North Bedford Drive. According to society columnist Elsa Maxwell, the countess set up a boxing ring at her first major party and staged three bloody bouts. Maxwell said of di Frasso that she had a "racy wit, did the most outrageous things."[26]

Di Frasso had just ended an affair with Gary Cooper when she looked over from her box at the Santa Anita track and saw a handsome stranger marvelously dressed.[27] She decided, moments after meeting Ben Siegel, that he was a perfect successor to the screen idol. At di Frasso's next dinner party, Hollywood journalist Florabel Muir was shocked to see Siegel and di Frasso heading up the receiving line together. "She gave spectacular parties," reported Louella Parsons, another well-known society chronicler. "She wore magnificent jewels." At one party, Parsons related, di Frasso put Dictaphones under the chairs and divans, "and the upshot was that guests heard their supposedly best friends commenting caustically on their clothes, boy friends, and peccadilloes, all of which was highly amusing to the hostess, but spread social havoc among the hapless victims."[28]

Di Frasso was, by one report, known for "her black hair, blue eyes and seductive figure."[29] In her youth she had been quite beautiful, but two decades of cigarettes and cocktails had taken their toll. Now in her late forties, she was somewhat heavier, and quite the older woman to Siegel, who had just turned thirty. Di Frasso may have charmed Siegel into bed, but the two probably settled into a friendship that served them both. Di Frasso got a handsome walker in Siegel, who gave off a tantalizing aroma of danger. Siegel got entrée into Hollywood's best homes, including Pickfair, Mary Pickford and Douglas Fairbanks's mansion.

Between George Raft and Dorothy di Frasso, Siegel came to know most of Hollywood's swells. "Practically everyone had met Bugsy through Dorothy," Louella Parsons wrote in 1944. Or as screenwriter Charles Bennett noted, "Bugsy was so smooth, so charming, he was accepted in Beverly Hills society."[30]

Gambling was Bugsy's most lucrative line, but as the house on Delfern Drive approached completion, he made serious efforts to build a Hollywood racket. A couple of Chicago-based gangsters, Willie Bioff and Johnny Roselli, had shown that Hollywood could be fleeced as easily as the garment industry. They paid a call to the Chicago-based Balaban and Katz Theater Corporation, or B&K, whose founders had made their fortunes not by making films but by building the ornate theaters in which those films were shown, including the first to be air-conditioned. The mobsters demanded that all of B&K's theaters have two projectionists at all times, not one. The projectionists' union would strike if the owners failed to comply. The shake-up created jobs, but all the union projectionists, new and old, had to pay hefty union dues, a sizable fraction of which went to the gangsters as a "war fund" in case of a strike.

Bioff and Roselli were spotted in Hollywood, riding fancy cars and squiring classy women. They had bigger ambitions now. They took over the ten thousand–strong stagehands union and threatened the studio heads with a strike if payoffs weren't forthcoming. Each of the big studios wrote a check for $50,000, while the smaller ones paid $25,000 each.[31]

Siegel was furious at not being cut in to that action, but the Syndicate was firm. It was getting its share of Bioff and Roselli's operation; it had no need for Siegel to intervene. Siegel responded by starting his own racket, in league with the Syndicate, of course. He zeroed in on the stage extras union. Extras were humble workaday actors, but no film production could do without them, any more than it could without stagehands. Where would a street scene be without its bystanders? Or a crowd scene without its crowd? After winning the union's blessing to speak for it, Siegel began making social visits to the studio heads, asking them for sums to assure that those extras would show up for work. Sidney Kent, then president of the board of directors of Twentieth Century–Fox, told FBI agents that Siegel came in more than once to muscle him, and the studio did hand over a loan or two: paperwork to that effect was later found in Siegel's home vault. But the amounts were modest, and no strike was called.[32]

If the touch was light, there was a reason. Siegel wanted something else from these studio heads. He wanted to be an actor. He even had footage of himself acting, if the studio heads cared to look.

The footage came courtesy of George Raft. On set, while Raft was making a film with Marlene Dietrich, Siegel sat rapt in the shadows. When the director called "Break!" he opened a briefcase to reveal his own 16-millimeter camera. He then turned to actor Mack Gray, another gangster-turned-star. "Okay, Killer," Siegel told Gray, using the nickname Carole Lombard had come up with for him. "I'm going to do this bit and you shoot it for me."[33]

To Raft's astonishment, and Gray's, Siegel reenacted Raft's part in the scene he'd just witnessed. He had not only memorized the lines, Raft later recalled, but used Raft's gestures.[34] Siegel was pretty good, Raft had to admit, but if the footage went any further than Siegel's home projector, Raft never heard about it. As much as Siegel wanted to be on the silver screen, he was far too hot-tempered to prostrate himself before some studio head.[35] An audition might have ended in bloodshed.

If Siegel couldn't be an actor, he could at least look and act like one. He was not just a fitness fanatic but a health nut, weighing just 160 pounds with a frame a tad under five-foot-ten. He neither smoked nor drank, aside from a celebratory cigar or an occasional snifter of brandy. He did like candy, however, and usually had some with him. Candy was a throwback to his youth, one of the only pleasures he could afford in those desperate years. For the 1930 U.S. census, he had called himself a candy salesman. He carried candy with him like a charm.

Almost daily, Siegel went to Drucker's, one of Hollywood's top barbershops, usually for the works: a haircut, shave, manicure, shoulder massage, and shoe shine. Drucker had started at the Waldorf Astoria in New York, and come west with his well-known clients. Siegel was one of them, but when the gangster went back east, which he often did, other barbershops stood ready to serve. One was Benny Newman's in Newark, New Jersey, where Siegel often went to meet with Longy Zwillman. Siegel was observed there, on at least one hot summer day, sitting jaybird naked in a barber's chair. When Newman was done administering to him, Siegel stood in front of a long mirror, admiring his coif and buffed body. Only then did he put on his clothes.[36]

Shaved and trimmed in L.A., Siegel would sail out on his rounds in one of his $200 Louis Roth suits. He would be wearing one of his $25 silk monogrammed shirts, and a flashy tie, and handmade, pointed shoes. Every day, he chose his wardrobe from the lighted glass cabinet in his dressing room, where his clothes were hung like museum pieces.[37]

No less important was Siegel's nighttime regimen. He started by rubbing cream over his face to keep his skin smooth. Then he fitted himself with an elastic chinstrap to keep his jowls from sagging, and slipped between the covers with a copy of *Reader's Digest*. He especially liked the section "It Pays to Increase Your Word Power," and practiced the new words he saw. When he felt himself dozing off, he turned out the bedside light and covered his eyes with a sleep shade. Raft would say later that Siegel obsessed over his thinning hair, and feared he might one day lose it all.[38]

All this was vanity, but not *just* vanity. Siegel sensed the power he radiated with his picture-perfect physique, his vulpine good looks, and his visible grooming. No one he met with on his rounds wanted to see even the hint of a scowl cross those features.

How many people Siegel actually killed in his L.A. "sportsman" days is, of course, unknown. As yet, his record in California remained clean, his name unsullied. An October night in 1937, however, brought the brutal demise of a gangster with whom Siegel had just had harsh words. Siegel stood to be implicated in the murder.

George "Les" Bruneman had started as a West Coast bootlegger, then moved, after Prohibition, into gambling and bookmaking. Siegel was a partner in Bruneman's Redondo Beach gambling joint, and the two men worked with fellow gangsters Jack Dragna and Johnny Roselli. But Bruneman apparently got greedy. He started encroaching on his partners' gambling turf and skimming the proceeds. And when Siegel decreed that all independent operators like Bruneman kick back 10 percent of their profits to the Syndicate, Bruneman declined. Bruneman was even said to be muscling in on the screen extras racket, Siegel's own latest caper.

The end for Bruneman came in two acts. One July night, the bald and bespectacled criminal was promenading outside his Redondo Beach Surf Club with one of his "hostesses" when he took three bullets in the back. Bruneman survived, and in fine gangland style, declined to name his assailants. He was still recovering on October 25, when he went with his nurse for a late-night dinner at the Roost Café, one of L.A.'s most notorious gangland hangouts. Two men burst in with automatic rifles and fired more than a dozen shots, killing Bruneman and wounding his nurse. A waiter was also killed when he ran outside to get the license number of the getaway car.[39]

Given Siegel's close ties with Dragna, and the anger both felt at Bruneman's infringements on their turf, the chances seemed high that Siegel at least knew about the hit in advance.[40] Still, he kept his name out of the papers, and a low-level bank robber, Peter Pianezzi, was charged with the crime. For the next several decades, Pianezzi would deny any role in the Bruneman killing. In 1981, he was exonerated by Governor Edmund G. Brown Jr., who found the case for his innocence compelling. Whether Siegel had been one of the shooters or just advised from afar, he appears to have doomed a low-level hood to a near-lifetime behind bars for a murder he hadn't committed. Soon another gangland killing would hit the tabloids, one in which Siegel played a direct and all but indisputable part, changing the course of his life.

4

The Masterminds of Murder Inc.

BACK EAST, Thomas Dewey had moved on from Dutch Schultz to a new target: Lucky Luciano. This was a matter of no small concern to Siegel, Lansky, and the rest of the Syndicate.

Compared to Dutch Schultz, Luciano seemed a model citizen, and Dewey struggled to pin major crimes on him. As a fallback, in July 1936, he indicted Luciano on a dubious charge of engaging in forced prostitution.[1]

Luciano had never consorted with prostitutes, he protested, much less acted as their pimp. Dewey knew this. He knew that Luciano's underlings were the ones who had managed prostitutes and set up a network of brothels. But Dewey argued in court that Luciano was liable for all activities under his management, including prostitution. When Luciano took the stand, the prosecutor made a fool of him, getting him to mutter malapropisms in his broken English. What had he been doing when stopped with two shotguns among other street guns? "Shooting birds," Luciano replied. What kind of birds? "Peasants," Luciano said, and watched the courtroom erupt in laughter.[2] To the Syndicate's indignation, Luciano was found guilty on 558 counts, and sentenced to thirty to fifty years. For Siegel and Lansky, the verdict was like a death in the family.

Dewey's next targets were two more of Siegel's and Lansky's closest associates. Both Lepke Buchalter and Gurrah Shapiro had come a long way since their bootlegging days with Rothstein, but of the two, Lepke had come farther. The quiet king of racketeering in the New York garment industry, he was said to take in the current-day equivalent of $18 million a year from rackets in industries ranging from leather goods to shoes to millinery and handbags, from trucking to rabbit furs. He and Shapiro oversaw a small army of 250 men, ready to break up a union protest or sweep through a garment factory, breaking arms and legs. As he grew rich from the rackets, Lepke made contributions to his mother's synagogue, attended High Holy Day services, and helped support his brother, a rabbi.[3]

In the fall of 1936, Dewey charged Lepke and Gurrah with racketeering in the rabbit fur industry. The racketeers knew their sentence for that crime would be relatively light—two years or so—but they feared Dewey wouldn't stop there. They knew how many men they had killed, and how many garment businesses they had torched. What they feared, above all, was their own men: gangsters who might betray them, giving Dewey the goods for a trial that would put them in the electric chair.

To the astonishment of all, Gurrah jumped bail and vanished. Overnight, he became one of America's most-wanted men, tracked by an army of detectives led by the relentless Dewey, with a $25,000 reward for his capture. He surrendered after less than a year, lonely and depressed, and spent the rest of his life in prison. By then, Lepke had skipped bail, too.

From the moment he vanished in 1937, Lepke became the object of the largest international manhunt in the FBI's history.

He may have moved from one hideaway to the next, as the agency theorized, but he may have stayed right in Brooklyn: one account had two of the Syndicate's most trusted killers, Albert "The Mad Hatter" Anastasia and Abe "Kid Twist" Reles, guarding Lepke in Brooklyn for the whole two years he was pursued, from an apartment above the Oriental Palace dancehall in Coney Island to various apartments nearby.[4] Word of his whereabouts must have traveled to lower echelons of the Syndicate, yet none ratted for the sizable reward.

Lepke had an odd way of thanking his hoodlums for their discretion. Unable even to venture outside, he became deeply paranoid, brooding over which of his henchmen he could trust. Eventually he embarked on an audacious campaign to kill anyone who might incriminate him for murder. For that, he recruited the newly formed Murder Inc., essentially Ben Siegel and Meyer Lansky. This was the Syndicate's enforcement arm, the former Bug and Meyer mob, renamed and amped up. In their new guise, Siegel and Lansky took kill orders directly from Lepke, Frank Costello, "Joe Adonis" Doto, and the imprisoned Lucky Luciano. Most of the kills were done by a far-flung cadre of murderers on retainer. By the late 1930s, Murder Inc. would be said to have killed close to one thousand men. Even if the low estimate of four hundred was closer to the mark, that was still a shocking and unprecedented run.[5]

The execution plans were usually elaborate, involving an out-of-state killer unknown to the victim. One minute the victim was alive, the next he was dead. "If you can believe it," a detective later said, "Bugsy preferred to do the job himself. He wasn't content just to give the orders and collect the fees. He enjoyed doing the blasting personally. It gave him a sense of power. He got his kicks out of seeing his victims suffering, groaning and dying."[6] Was the perpetrator of these atrocities a sociopath? A megalomaniac? Or just a sportsman of sadism? Surrounded as he was by gun-toting antagonists, Siegel may simply have felt that the terror these stories generated was an insurance policy to keep the next target from eliminating him first.

In *Tough Jews*, Rich Cohen describes what made Murder Inc. so effective—and terrifying. "A stranger arrives, kills, is gone. The local cops are left with nothing . . ." By the mid-1930s, Cohen adds, "the contract killer had become a national character like the frontiersman or logger, who embodies aspects of the American personality. To some he was kind of an existential cowboy, riding the line between being and not, the mysterious stranger of Mark Twain who carries death in his pocket."[7]

For the two years Lepke was on the lam, Murder Inc. became more than a killing machine of second- or third-tier gangsters. It became a business, countrywide. If the pay was good enough, Murder Inc. would kill pretty much anyone, and not just on the streets of New York or L.A. Siegel himself featured in one of the most chilling stories, in which a millionaire businessman was allegedly dispatched to a watery grave in northern Minnesota.[8]

Herbert H. Bigelow had founded a company in the 1920s that printed playing cards and pinup calendars. He had done well, but on principle declined to pay federal income tax and landed a three-year term in Leavenworth prison. In an adjacent cell languished one Charlie Ward, a rough character who volunteered to protect Bigelow from other prisoners.

After serving eight months, Bigelow was pardoned by President Calvin Coolidge. When Charlie Ward was released, Bigelow not only hired him as his corporate heir apparent: he bequeathed him $1 million of his $3 million fortune.

Bigelow was in one of three large canoes on Minnesota's Basswood Lake in 1934 when conditions turned rough and his canoe overturned, drowning him and a companion. Investigators noticed perforations in the canoe that appeared to be bullet holes, shot from a rifle on shore. But there was nothing more to go by—except two letters that would turn up in Ben Siegel's vault when detectives searched his mansion in August 1940. The letters were sent by Ward's lawyer, referencing a payment of $100,000 due to Ben Siegel.

Ward had a fascinating explanation when tracked down by the press. He said he and Siegel had met when Ward was visiting Hollywood. So charmed was Ward by Siegel that the Minnesotan had lent him $100,000 for "a dog track or something." But as the letters made clear, Ward hadn't lent Siegel anything. Ward *owed* Siegel $100,000 for some service rendered.[9] Given the $1 million inheritance hanging in the balance for Ward, the service seemed all too clear.

Just how many channels of cash seeped in to Siegel's business network by the late thirties was impossible to know. "Bugsy is said to control almost everything for the mob on the west coast," an informant later told the FBI. "But he doesn't get directly involved because he wants to stay in good standing in California. Siegel is the only Jew who has built a record of high accord among his colleagues."[10]

"He is attempting to enjoy a good reputation there," another FBI informant noted. "He prides himself on the fact that he has never been convicted of a criminal offense of a major nature."

According to the FBI, Siegel was said to have a 25 percent interest in a gambling setup at Redondo Beach, the one co-owned by the ill-fated Les Bruneman, whose greed at not sharing gambling proceeds had contributed to his untimely death. Siegel owned 5 percent of the Agua Caliente racetrack, 5 percent of the dog track in Tijuana, and a piece of the Culver City dog racing track. He was said to oversee one of the biggest numbers game in southern California. From his bootlegging days, he was said to get a kickback—still—from all sales of certain brands

of Scotch. Along with his share of the Clover Club, he was re-
puted to own part of the Beverly Wilshire hotel, and a nightclub called the Chi Chi. By now, too, suggests Lansky biographer Robert Lacey, Siegel was "running floating crap games in
the private homes of the famous movie moguls, ferocious bettors to a man."[11]

The biggest business by far was the race wire. Siegel would
have liked to start his own wire, but he and his fellow southern
California vice lords, Jack Dragna and Guy McAfee, were up
against the kingpin of the business. Moses Moe Annenberg was
a Prussian-born, Chicago-based, up-from-the-bootstraps newspaper publisher who early on had become William Randolph
Hearst's general in the bloody newspaper circulation wars of
the day. Annenberg had bought a modest publication called the
Daily Racing Form, which supplied customers with key facts for
the day's races. Then came the ingenious move: hitching the
Racing Form with the telegraph wire to relay the results. By
the mid-1930s, Annenberg's Nationwide News wire service was
used by most of the fifteen thousand bookie joints in 223 cities
across America.[12] Annenberg himself was one of the country's
richest and most powerful men, closely allied with the Chicago
mob. Siegel and his cronies would have to content themselves
with betting on Annenberg's wire until the millionaire somehow tripped up.

The opening of Siegel's home on Delfern Drive in 1938
brought Siegel's glamorous life to a new level. He and Esther
began giving grand parties. In came the stars, intrigued by the
mansion and its mysterious host. Cary Grant was among them,
as were Clark Gable and Gary Cooper. George Raft was a
regular, of course. So was Jimmy Durante. And so was Frank
Sinatra, who knew more of Siegel's story through his own mob
friends than most other guests. Comic actor Phil Silvers's wife,
Jo-Carroll Dennison, said her husband and his pals were en-

thralled. "They would brag about Bugsy, what he'd done and how many people he'd killed. Sometimes they'd argue about whether Bugsy preferred to shoot his victims or simply chop them up with axes." Dennison never forgot "the awe Frank had in his voice when he talked about him. He wanted to emulate Bugsy."[13]

"He was one of the most fabulous characters ever to take part in the social activities of the city where fabulous characters gather like bees on clusters of sweet grapes," wrote columnist Florabel Muir. "He was the storybook gangster to the romantic, emotional, almost childlike adults who populate the movie colony. He bowled them over with his suave manner, his immaculate hand-tailored shirts, his two-hundred-dollar suits, his twenty-five dollar ties. For women, especially, he had a strange fascination. Perhaps it was the imagined menace that shadowed his handsome face or the quick boyish grin he flashed for those he liked. Some of them who would never have dared date him enjoyed a delicious tingle along their spines at the thought of doing so."[14]

The holdout was Jimmy Stewart. Appalled by Siegel's burgeoning notoriety, the earnest actor tried to talk his fellow stars out of seeing Siegel at all. Cary Grant replied, rather winningly, "Look, Jim, the guy's best pal is George Raft, and George says if Benny wants you to be his friend, you *be* his friend." That was a bit disingenuous, Stewart's wife, Gloria, felt. Stars liked even bigger stars; for them, she said, "the only people who could be remotely more glamorous were royalty and big-time gangsters."[15]

Stewart did more than lecture his friends in private. He came right up to Siegel in public and denounced him to his face. The gangster's famous temper flared, and George Raft feared the worst. "Let me talk to Benny," he told Stewart. "Try and calm him down."

"If Siegel wants to try his luck with me," Stewart seethed, "let him take his best shot."

"If he takes his best shot," Raft said, "it'll be the last shot you hear."

Gloria Stewart had her own theory for why Stewart didn't take a bullet from Siegel. "I think it's just possible that it was Jim's belligerence that kept him safe."[16]

Socializing and snooping weren't the only reasons Siegel's Hollywood stars came to dine. Siegel ran his own floating craps game at the house on Delfern Drive. He was a gracious host, quick with a quip and a laugh. One by one, though, the stars noticed something disconcerting about him. He asked them all for loans. Individually, the loans weren't that large: a thousand dollars here and there, pocket money for a Hollywood star. But they added up. Later, a record book found in one of Siegel's secret compartments at the Delfern Drive house would tote hundreds of thousands of dollars in loans from the Hollywood set to their elegant host.[17]

The loans were never repaid. Siegel was so charming that his friends felt it somehow beneath them to ask for their money back, and Siegel always had some promising investment he was about to make with their cash: a new nightclub in which he might get them a piece, a new horse about to win at the track. But then, too, there were those stories from back east, of Siegel as a bootlegger, handy with a gun. No doubt the stories were exaggerations, and yet . . .

As another way to gamble, Siegel took an interest in the SS *Rex*, a casino ship rigged up by a gangster named Tony Cornero, who had made a first fortune robbing bootleggers. Cornero took the *Rex* three miles off Santa Monica, just beyond the reach of the law, and shuttled guests back and forth in high-speed water taxis twenty-four hours a day. Soon a dozen other gambling ships were anchored offshore, a veritable navy for the nabobs of southern California.

Whether Siegel invested his own money in the *Rex* is unclear. He did ask George Raft to lend him $20,000, a wad of cash that would buy the two of them a share of the boat's profits, he said. Raft said he was between films and didn't have the money. "So get it," Siegel told him. The next day, Raft drove 140 miles to a summer resort southeast of Hollywood where producer Myron Selznick was staying. With an arched brow, Selznick wrote him a check against future fees for a film Raft owed him.[18]

In its first six months, the SS *Rex* sat profitably at anchor off the coast, earning $236,940, of which a chunk went to Siegel.[19] This may have been the most lucrative period of Siegel's career. Along with his various nightclub investments, the gambling dens and dog tracks, Siegel may have been taking in as much as $500,000 a year, ten times the amount he claimed to the IRS.[20] In today's dollars, that would be more like $9 million. But change was in the air—and sea. Earl Warren, the newly elected, reform-minded California attorney general, made it his mission to stop the gambling boats. He started by pushing federal authorities to expand the limit of international waters from three miles to twelve. When that failed to drive the *Rex* and its ilk out of business, the future U.S. Supreme Court justice sent authorities to dump $100,000 worth of slot machines and other gambling equipment into the ocean. That was it for the gambling boats—and, for George Raft, most of the $20,000 he'd lent his good friend. Records showed Siegel repaid Raft just $2,000, plus checks for $500 "here and there," as Raft put it. With Siegel, the cost of friendship ran high.[21]

Another offshore adventure at that time showed just how far Siegel would go in pursuit of easy money. Dorothy di Frasso told him of a talk she had had in New York with a man who rolled out a hand-drawn map and told her of a great buried treasure, worth $90 million, on Cocos Island, some miles off the coast of Costa Rica. The hard-boiled Siegel thrilled to the very mention of it.[22]

Days later, a most peculiar entourage left Santa Monica on the *Metha Nelson*, a three-masted schooner. Along with a hired captain and crew, it consisted of Siegel, Dorothy di Frasso, and, among others, the late Jean Harlow's mobbed-up stepfather, Mario Bello, and a young, attractive nurse whom Bello married three days out of port.[23]

Siegel, recalled one of the passengers, showed a flair for leadership, and kept his famous temper in check. He had brought dynamite for blasting, gas-powered rock drills, and spades and shovels for all. Expectations diminished after an obligatory stop in Puntarenas, where the Costa Rican government claimed a third of any treasure that might be found. Siegel was daunted, but not for long. After all, he declared, "We'll still have sixty million left."[24]

Cocos Island, it turned out, was uninhabited for good reason. It was a rock outcropping, tropically hot. With Siegel urging them on, the group spent ten days blowing up promising sites and digging rocky soil before abandoning the dream. Later, Dorothy di Frasso waved off the rumors of romance on the trip with Siegel. "Ben is one of my closest friends," she told one reporter. "But as for romance, it's absurd. He has a wife and I have a husband, and any other interpretation is ridiculous."[25]

Sunburned and blistered, the group headed back north, stopping first in Panama, where Siegel abandoned the passengers and crew, including di Frasso, and flew home on his own. When the ship at last reached Santa Monica, after weathering a typhoon, FBI agents pounced, investigating rumors of drug trafficking and the possibility that Lepke Buchalter, the world's most wanted man, was onboard. The questioning led nowhere, but Siegel's name was linked to the story, and an enterprising editor of the *Los Angeles Examiner* began researching just what kind of sportsman Ben Siegel was. Remarkably, not one Los Angeles reporter had yet published a story that linked Ben Siegel with bootlegging or illegal gambling, let alone contract killing. After getting his image removed from that group shot of 1931 at New York's Franconia Hotel, Siegel had gone seven years without having his past exposed, beyond the mentions in social columns of "sportsman" Ben Siegel. All that was about to change.

Siegel had been gone many weeks on a boat, with a woman not his wife, through the fall of 1938. He returned to a family confused and depressed, but still going through the rituals of upper-class life in one of America's most fabled milieus. He and Esther had joined the Hillcrest Country Club, an exclusively Jewish enclave, and made new friends. Millicent and Barbara had been enrolled in a fashionable girls' school. They took daily lessons at the DuBrock Riding Academy, where one of their riding mates was Elizabeth Taylor. They took piano lessons at home. When a grown-up gave her father a violin, Millicent recalled, she had to learn to play it, too.[26]

Decades later, Millicent told one interviewer that Siegel as a father had been both strict and indulgent. He wanted his daughters to be well mannered, well groomed, and capable of speaking on issues of the day.[27] At dinner they had to discuss the news of the day. Siegel's insistence that his family conform to these social strictures said more about him than it did them. How could he head off on a pirate adventure while leaving them on their own, and still expect them to be happy when he came back home? Perhaps because of his own dichotomous role growing up—the breadwinner and the ne'er do well in one odd package—Siegel saw nothing strange about acting in such contradictory ways as husband and father. He was still the provider, but on his own terms, as he was with his parents and siblings. As soon as he got home, the family fun began, with Siegel at the center of it, splashing the girls in the pool as his wife held the movie camera. Decades later, Millicent would view the fading footage, trying to make sense of the father who laughed and engaged in horseplay, only to vanish again.

Deep down, Siegel may have realized he couldn't have his family and his freedom, any more than he could live as a gangster and gain social acceptance from a public appalled by his crimes. Only here, in his dream house on Delfern Drive, could all the incongruities of his life come together. Only here, within its walls mounted by surveillance cameras, could he feel safe and at ease. He would have been shocked to know that a journalist was in the house, watching his family's every move.

William Bradford Huie was an ambitious reporter who would go on to pioneering civil rights coverage, prying loose the confession of Emmett Till's killers among other coups. At twenty-eight, as a freelancer newly arrived in L.A., he was intrigued to pick up a copy of the *Los Angeles Examiner* on December 16, 1938, and see a feature about the ill-fated voyage of the *Metha Nelson*. Sniffing an even better story in Bugsy Siegel's rise from poverty, he drove over to 250 Delfern Drive and knocked at the service door with an armload of magazines, presenting himself as a subscription salesman. As Huie later recalled in a long report in the *American Mercury*, the cook invited him in and soon related that the lady of the house was in desperate need of a butler: her father was arriving from New York for a Christmas visit, with her in-laws—Max and Jennie Siegel—already in residence. Huie went to the employment agency the Siegels used and presented himself as a fancy butler just in from the South.

Huie interviewed the next morning with Esther, who surprised him. "She wasn't the movie version of the big-shot gangster's wife," he related. "She was a serious, not unattractive blonde in her early thirties. . . . Now she was working hard at making like a rich woman, but I sensed that she was lonely. . . . She was almost pathetically glad to see me. She hired me much too quickly."

Huie assumed that Esther's husband would be in residence, too, but as he later wrote, "Bugsy had double-crossed me."

Huie had assumed the *Metha Nelson* would be docked by now, and that Siegel would be home for Christmas. Apparently he was still making his way. Huie found himself tending the rest of the family: making breakfast for Esther, waxing the floors and cleaning the Venetian blinds, taking Millicent and Barbara for their horse riding lessons, and chauffeuring Esther nightly to a local bar where she drank quite a bit with other young Hollywood wives.

Huie was particularly struck by Siegel's father, Max, a "portly, mustachioed old gentleman who had worked hard peddling suits all his life." Apparently, Siegel's parents had come to live with him at last—or so suggests the 1940 U.S. census, in which Max would note he was no longer working for pay. But life at 250 Delfern was no less lonely for Max than for the others. As Huie put it, "He had great difficulty passing the time. He liked to talk with me, and on afternoons when Mrs. Siegel went shopping he'd come into the pantry and help me polish the silver. But he'd be careful to run and pick up a newspaper at her approach."

With Siegel still gone on Christmas Eve, Huie filled in. "I carved the turkey and served dinner in the rumpus room for twelve; I changed into a Santa Claus suit, parked my reindeer on the roof, bounded back into the rumpus room, and was a solid hit as St. Nick." As the Christmas tree indicated, Siegel appeared to be farther than ever from his Judaic roots. "They were really a forlorn family, living there in that big house that Christmas. . . . Mrs. Siegel was the loneliest of all. Each night, after the others had gone to bed, she'd either go with me or send me after the papers. Then she'd trudge wearily up to her room to read about Bugsy and his voyage on the Metha Nelson."

With Siegel not yet home, Huie made late-night visits to the gangster's study, and managed to pry open his file cabinet, in search of incriminating documents. "It was nervous work," as he put it, because the floor was carpeted and Huie wouldn't hear a family member approaching until it was too late. He came away with what seemed only some of Siegel's papers—but enough. "They clearly indicated his connections and activities; and they contained more than enough evidence for legal action."

On December 30, without warning, Siegel returned. "I went to answer the front doorbell and there he was—the sportsman himself in a two-hundred-dollar tweed suit, snap-brim hat, and plaid tie," Huie wrote. Siegel gave Huie a cool, appraising look and swept in, followed by two beefy bodyguards. He had bagsful of Christmas presents for Millicent and Barbara, but soon repaired to his office, where he began making rapid-fire calls. Lawyers and accountants went in and out; amid their murmuring, Siegel's harsh laughter dominated. The man of the house was home.

That evening, Huie served the family dinner in the ornate living room. He felt Siegel's eyes on him. "I kept telling myself that he wouldn't be as easily deceived as his family. A successful racketeer suspects everyone." But Siegel seemed distracted by his wife and daughters.

That night, when his family had gone to bed, a big meeting convened in Siegel's office. Despite his fear, according to Huie, he went through the kitchen and pantry to listen in through the drawing room. He was about fifty feet from the office door, close enough to see cigar smoke rolling out, but too far to hear what was being said. All he could tell for sure was that Siegel was mad, and that a rough edge had come into his voice. "He had reverted to his old gang argot," Huie wrote.

Determined to hear details, Huie tried a new approach. He went out back from the kitchen, where two large and menacing dogs lurked; fortunately they recognized the butler. The drawing room's windows were cloaked by Venetian blinds, but days before, Huie had stretched two of the lower slats far enough apart to get a narrow view on his knees. The windows were

closed, but Huie could hear much of what was being said, particularly Siegel's voice. Through the slats, he saw the brightly
buffed shoes of the gangsters, and their raffishly patterned socks.
He would be safe unless Bugsy grew suspicious and flicked the
switch on his desk, floodlighting his entire grounds."

Bugsy's visitors, Huie knew, "were his hoods, the muscle,
the force by which a front man like Bugsy 'moves in' on the
gambling at Redondo Beach, or 'cuts himself a piece' of the
foreign book at Caliente, or 'muscles in' on Las Vegas or 'takes
over a territory' for bookmaking or distributing heroin. They
were the collections agents, the intimidators."

When the meeting broke up, Huie recalled creeping to his
bedroom and sneaking a look out the window. There below was
Siegel, talking to the dogs and seeming to sniff the air himself.
He came back inside, and started up the staircase by the garage
that led to the staff quarters. "I was baffled," Huie wrote. "If he
suspected the truth he wouldn't be coming after me this way;
he'd call me and ask me to drive him somewhere. But neither
would he be paying me a friendly visit at 3 A.M."

Huie wrote that he heard the footsteps coming closer. He
flattened himself against the wall by the door, a gun in hand. "If
he opened the door I'd have no choice; I'd have to shoot him."
Huie heard Siegel's steps outside the door. "I heard him switch
on the light in my bathroom; then he went back downstairs and
reentered the house." Apparently, Siegel was just the proud
homeowner, surveying his gracious domain.

Not long after that, Huie found Siegel playing with his
daughters, only to be waved over. " 'They tell me you been taking them to their riding lessons, Robert,' " Siegel said, using
Huie's borrowed name. " 'How they doing?' "

Huie said they were doing just swell. Why, he added politely, didn't Siegel go riding with them one afternoon.

" 'Me? Hell, I can't ride. When I was a kid I didn't ride
nothing but the subway.' "

By January 4, 1939, Huie wrote, he began to feel seriously endangered. He took a moment when Esther was in the kitchen and Siegel was up in his bedroom to tell Esther a plausible story. Huie's mother had had a stroke in Arizona, the journalist improvised. He had to go home right away. Esther was disappointed, but gracious: she made him take a full month's pay of $115 rather than the three weeks he'd earned since his arrival. With that, Huie called a taxi, then dashed over to his bedroom and grabbed his luggage. "I felt certain that while I was with the kids, Mrs. Siegel had told Bugsy. A light might flash on for him."

As Huie made for the waiting taxi, he heard the kitchen door slam, and a voice cry out "Robert!" He felt sure that Bugsy was about to appear from behind the wall, gun in hand. But no: it was Ben's father, Max. "The old man was rushing to tell me goodbye, to express his sympathy, and to offer to lend me money. Had he not called to me I might have killed him."

Huie managed to hurl himself into the taxi before Bugsy appeared. He was safe—just barely. Three days later, after Huie had tipped off the authorities that Siegel had incriminating documents in his home, a raid was enacted at 250 Delfern Drive. Siegel was standing in the doorway to welcome the officers. He flashed them a big grin. "Why didn't you bring Huie along?" No incriminating documents were found.[28]

An abridged version of Huie's adventures in the Siegel household was published in early January 1939 in the *Los Angeles Examiner.* It helped stir buzz all over town about Siegel's bizarre voyage, with accompanying stories about his gangster life back east. The details were enough to prompt Ben and Esther Siegels' expulsion from the Hillcrest Country Club. At school, one of Millicent's classmates, the son of Edward G. Robinson, asked whether Millicent realized her father was a gangster. Millicent was too hurt to be struck by the irony that her classmate's father had become a star by emulating thugs.[29]

Dorothy di Frasso, apparently reconciled with Siegel after

his abandonment of her in Panama, drove up to the hilltop castle of San Simeon to dissuade its owner William Randolph Hearst from running stories on her dear friend in his newspapers. In one version, Hearst heard her out and laughed: this was exactly the kind of story he wanted his papers to run, he said. In another, Hearst declined to open the gates at the bottom of the hill when she announced herself and her reason for coming.[30]

Siegel cared about his public image, but he had bigger concerns. Lepke remained a fugitive from Thomas E. Dewey's tireless pursuit into the summer of 1939, with serious implications for Siegel's longevity. Increasingly paranoid, Lepke kept adding possible traitors to his list, and the hired guns of Murder Inc. kept killing them off. Not happily, though: even his top men were getting sick of the murders. Singlehandedly, Lepke was destroying the Syndicate.

Enough was enough, agreed Siegel, Lansky, and the imprisoned Luciano. Together, they drew up the deal that brought Lepke in from the cold.[31] Essentially they deceived him, persuading him that he would only have to face the racketeering case he'd skipped and serve a maximum sentence of two years. He wouldn't face Dewey and a stack of other charges, including drug smuggling and murder. In just two years he would be a free man, running the rackets again.

All but broken by his long sequester, Lepke agreed to the deal. There was just one issue that troubled him, one loose-lipped traitor who stood ready to tell the whole Syndicate story and who had to be stopped: Harry "Big Greenie" Greenberg. On two recent occasions, contract killers had tracked him down, only to have him squirm away. Lepke wanted no more failures in finding the weasel. He wanted the best, most reliable hit man he knew: Ben Siegel.

The problem was that Siegel was in Italy with Dorothy di Frasso, and wasn't easy to reach.

Di Frasso and Siegel had let a new scheme captivate them. Somehow, di Frasso had been made aware of a new explosive called Atomite that detonated without sound or flash.[32] With her Italian connections, di Frasso had pitched Atomite to Mussolini. The Italian leader was so interested in it that he advanced $40,000 to di Frasso to have the scientists with whom she was dealing scale it up. In the spring of 1939, di Frasso and Siegel sailed over to Rome with a large cache of Atomite in their possession. The trip was also a chance for di Frasso to show Siegel her husband's Roman compound, Villa Madama.

Unfortunately, the Atomite failed to explode and a furious Mussolini demanded his money back. Di Frasso was evicted from her husband's villa by the dictator, who announced that he had important guests to install there. One was Hermann Göring, head of the German Luftwaffe and creator of the Gestapo. A second may have been Paul Joseph Goebbels, Hitler's minister of propaganda. Bugsy biographer Larry Gragg suggests the mention of Goebbels might have been fanciful, but that Göring did seem to arrive while Siegel and di Frasso were there. Gragg found a note to that effect in the personal journal kept by Mussolini's son-in-law, Count Galeazzo Ciano.

"Dentice di Frasso has given us information about an astonishing American invention of a very powerful smokeless, colorless, and flashless gunpowder," Ciano wrote. "Dentice vouches for this claim, but I am skeptical about such inventions." The note was recorded in January 1939, plausibly dated some months before Siegel and di Frasso's late spring trip to Italy. It was Ciano who noted that Göring had arrived in April and stayed at the Villa Madama. But the diary has no mention of Goebbels.[33]

Even with only one top Nazi in shooting range, Siegel still felt his adrenaline pumping. He started casting about for the best vantage point for a clean shot—or two. Hitler had just invaded Czechoslovakia, violating the Treaty of Munich, and Jews in America would have rejoiced if Siegel had managed to kill even one of the Führer's right-hand men.

Dorothy di Frasso put a quick end to the scheme. Did Siegel realize, she exclaimed, what a position the shooting would put them both in? Di Frasso would lose her villa or worse; her husband could be imprisoned. For that matter, they could be imprisoned, too, if not tortured and killed. Reluctantly, Siegel let the idea go. But for the rest of his life he would regret not having taken those shots. Lansky would have done it, he knew. Already, his old friend was doing his part to take on the Nazis.

One of the fondest chapters of Meyer Lansky's life, unfolding even as Siegel and di Frasso tested Atomite, had begun with a call from a New York judge asking Lansky to help counteract the Nazi Bund rallies cropping up in and around New York's Germantown. The judge would pay Lansky for mobilizing his men. He just wanted Lansky's word that no one would be killed. Lansky refused the money, and agreed not to leave anyone dead.

Years later, Lansky recounted his first attack on a Bund rally to his trio of Israeli biographers. "We got there in the evening, and found several hundred people dressed in their brown shirts. . . . The stage was decorated with a swastika and pictures of Hitler. The speakers started ranting. There were only fifteen of us, but we went into action. We attacked them in the hall and threw some of them out of the windows. There were fistfights all over the place. Most of the Nazis panicked and ran out. We chased them and beat them up, and some of them were out of action for months. We wanted to show them that Jews would not always sit back and accept insults."[34]

Rich Cohen says Lansky and Siegel understood, more than most law-abiding Jews, the threat the Nazis represented. "They knew what men are capable of, how far someone like Hitler would go, and they knew it could not be fought with reason or treaties or sanctions. The gangsters, who cared mostly about

getting rich, knew some things were not just about money."
Mafia historian Robert Rockaway wonders whether a need to
atone was also a motive, at least for Lansky. "Perhaps this was
his way of compensating for his other, less heroic life."[35]

Siegel came home with di Frasso, the world's list of hid-
eous Nazis undiminished, to learn that Lepke was looking for
him. He had a pretty good idea of what Lepke wanted, and even
now, for all the trouble the crime boss had stirred, Siegel would
do all he could to help.

5

‎—◆◦◆◦◆—

Going After Big Greenie

DAYS BEFORE HIS surrender, Lepke sat holed up in a little apartment on Foster Avenue in East Flatbush, Brooklyn. That was where Siegel came to pay his respects and take a last job that might keep the terrified murderer from the electric chair.

Harry "Big Greenie" Greenberg had been a Syndicate killer for years, and a friend to all, none more so than Siegel. But Big Greenie had made the very serious mistake of threatening to talk if he wasn't advanced a $5,000 loan. Lepke had sent a pair of killers to Montreal, where Greenberg had gone into hiding, only to have him give them the slip. The killers had picked up his trail in Detroit, yet failed again to nab him. Now Lepke had word that Greenberg was living incognito in Los Angeles.

"Don't worry," Siegel told Lepke. "If he's in L.A., he'll never leave."[1] No more failed hits, Siegel added. He would take on the job himself.

One of those at the meeting was Doc Stacher, Meyer Lansky's right-hand man. Decades later, he would recount the scene to Lansky's Israeli biographers. "We all begged Bugsy to keep out of the shooting," Stacher recalled. "He was too big a man by this time to become personally involved. But Bugsy wouldn't listen. He wouldn't even listen to Lansky the way he used to." Stacher could only protest so much. As he later put it, "Greenberg was a menace to all of us, and if the cops grabbed him he could tell the whole story of our outfit back to the 1920s."[2]

It was Lepke's last kill order. Days later, he came out of hiding to surrender.[3] The handover, on August 24, 1939, was the stuff of great drama. Walter Winchell had won the gangsters' trust with his nightly radio shows and was drafted by the FBI to help bring Lepke in. Following instructions from an anonymous caller, Winchell drove out first to Yonkers. The gangsters just wanted to be sure no G-men were tailing him. Winchell was then instructed to drive to a certain street in Chelsea, on the West Side of Manhattan. Like clockwork, Lepke emerged from a big black Packard and slid into the passenger seat of Winchell's car. Winchell then drove Lepke down another West Side street to the FBI director's idling limousine. His hands shaking, Winchell rolled up beside the car and nodded to the figure in back. "Mr. Hoover, this is Lepke," Winchell said.

"How do you do?" Hoover asked drily.

"Glad to meet you," Lepke said, and climbed into the back seat of Hoover's car, beside the FBI director. "Let's go."[4]

The pledge of one trial, and one trial only, lasted about as long as it took for Lepke to be driven to prison. The Syndicate's bosses had double-crossed him. Lepke would be tried first for racketeering, then for murder, the latter by none other than Thomas E. Dewey. Still, if Siegel could take out Big Greenie, Lepke might avoid the chair, and the Syndicate's other killers might sleep more easily, too, including Ben Siegel.

Harry Greenberg was a rumpled, heavyset immigrant from Poland who had been deported from the United States once already. Nothing if not resourceful, he had jumped ship as Le Havre came into view, and managed to stow his way back to America. For years he had worked for the Syndicate as a loyal contract killer, but he had let his financial straits, and a tendency to gab, get the better of him. Now he was using all his wiles to stay alive, with a pair of killers on his trail.[5]

Big Greenie and his wife, Ida, had rented a modest apartment in Hollywood, close to the Hollywood Freeway, living as Mr. and Mrs. George Schacter. When not working as a part-time chauffeur, Greenberg stayed in the apartment, except at about 11 P.M., when he made a quick run in his yellow Ford convertible to the drugstore at Hollywood and Vine for the next day's newspapers. Somehow Siegel tracked him there, and began planning the hit to the last detail, with a perverse sense of fun.[6]

At Siegel's direction, an East Coast hit man named Albert "Allie Tick Tock" Tannenbaum, one of the killers originally assigned to get Big Greenie, went to the Newark, New Jersey, airport, where Longy Zwillman gave him a package containing two guns, along with $250 in cash for his plane fare to Los Angeles. Why Tannenbaum couldn't have flown to California first and *then* picked up guns there was one of those details he knew not to question, not when Siegel was doing the planning.

A gangly, gregarious fellow, Tannenbaum had come to the business in atypical fashion: his parents bought land in upstate New York and started a family-run summer camp popular among Jewish mobsters. "In much of the old world, Jews were forbidden to own property," Rich Cohen notes, "so for many of them, land became a kind of grail, a dream, something worth fighting for."[7] Gangsters especially loved upstate resorts: they could congregate in peace. By age sixteen, Tannenbaum was on a first-name basis with almost every figure in New York organized crime.

The former camp counselor was met in L.A. by Frank

Carbo, another hit man recruited for the job. They went to meet Siegel at a Hollywood apartment. "We met several times planning the job," Tannenbaum later testified, "spotting 'Big Greenie's' house and making arrangements for a getaway."[8]

The plan was rife with Siegel's signature details. As Greenberg returned from his evening newspaper run, two idling cars would emerge from the shadows. The lead car would be driven by Tannenbaum, with Carbo in the passenger seat. Siegel would be in the following car, his own new 1939 Buick convertible. When Big Greenie walked from his car to his front door, Carbo would run up to him and blast away. Meanwhile, Siegel and Tannenbaum would switch cars, with Siegel now in the lead car, and Tannenbaum following in Siegel's Buick. If any car tried to follow the little motorcade, Tannenbaum would crash into it, giving the killers in the lead car the time they needed to make their getaway.

To any veteran of drive-by shootings, the plan seemed absurd. Why use Siegel's new Buick as the follow-on crash car, running the risk of demolishing it, and having its papers identify it as Siegel's? But this was classic Siegel, an extra wrinkle in the plan. Siegel was willing to sacrifice a new car for the *perception* that he couldn't have been part of the shooting posse because his own car would have been the lead getaway car, not the crash car.

Peculiar as it was, the plan came off without a hitch. "We got set and after a while, 'Big Greenie' drove around the corner," Tannenbaum testified. "Carbo was already out of the car and standing in the dark. He stepped over to 'Big Greenie's' automobile and let 'Greenie' have it five times. Then he got in the car with Siegel and they drove away, with me following."[9]

If Siegel and Lepke thought killing Big Greenie would plug the last Syndicate leak, they were grievously mistaken. Early in the new year of 1940, one of their most trusted men and top enforcers, Abe "Kid Twist" Reles, astonished the crime world by telling the whole decade-long story of Murder Inc., corroborating everything Big Greenie might have said.

What had led Reles to spill? His wife, Rose, who was pregnant, begged her husband to talk in the hope that their child might grow up with two parents.[10] Reles had committed many of these killings himself, and knew his chances of dying in the electric chair were high. He made a deal with Assistant District Attorney Burton Turkus, later a coauthor of the classic 1951 book on the Syndicate, *Murder, Inc.*[11] Reles would recount all the crimes of the Syndicate's contract killers in return for having no charges brought against him. Turkus himself would become the subject of a 1960 movie, *Murder, Inc.*, portrayed by actor Henry Morgan; Reles would be played by Peter Falk.

Reles's confessions filled twenty-five stenographers' notebooks, and either solved outright or gave clues to what he claimed to be one thousand murders during a ten-year period. To the Syndicate's horror, Allie "Tick Tock" Tannenbaum chose to squeal as well. This was not a good development for Lepke, whose charges were soon bumped up from racketeering to murder. For Siegel, still unindicted, it was a potentially life-ending one.

In an unmistakable warning to stool pigeons, a low-level gangster associated with Big Greenie's murder was shot dead August 1, 1940, on New York's Delancey Street. Whitey Krakower, who had provided the stolen lead car used for the rubout, now was said to be gabbing. Curiously, Siegel chose just that week to come to New York. After Krakower was gunned down, Siegel's lawyer provided a receipt for several nights' stay in early August by Ben and Esther Siegel in a Newark hotel, as if a forty-minute drive could serve as an alibi for murder on a Manhattan street.[12] Siegel was never charged with the murder, nor was anyone else.

Shortly after Krakower's shooting, a grand jury in L.A. began deliberating in the matter of Big Greenie's murder. To help the jury in its investigation, the city's district attorney decided to see what a search warrant of Siegel's home might reveal. Early on the morning of August 16, 1940, four carloads of detectives showed up at the front door of 250 Delfern Drive. None would ever forget what they found inside.[13]

A black butler answered the door—this was nearly two years after William Bradford Huie's undercover stint as a butler for the Siegel family—and glowered at the group until a search warrant was presented. The detectives then asked to see Ben Siegel.

"He's not home," the butler said.

The detectives politely replied that they would determine that for themselves. Guns drawn, they went up the sweeping staircase to the master bedroom. The bed was empty, its top sheet and coverlet pushed aside. One of the detectives put his hand on the mattress. "Still warm," he said. Another noted the leather bedroom slippers askew on the plush carpet.

One of the detectives opened the bedroom clothes closet to find hanging suits and pants, but no Ben Siegel. Then, on a low shelf, the detective saw a footprint on linen. Above was a closed trapdoor to the attic. The detective climbed up and saw a hand on one side of the brick chimney. "Hey, Ben," the detective said, "we want to talk to you."

A sheepish Siegel appeared, wrapped in a silk robe, his hair unkempt.

"What are you doing up here?" the detective said.

"I'm going to the barber shop," Siegel said.

The detectives found that hilarious. "That's doing it the hard way," one of them said.

Siegel asked why the detectives had come.

"Big Greenie," one said.

"Big Greenie?" Siegel replied. "Never heard of him."[14]

The detectives gave Siegel just time enough to throw on some clothes, and packed him into one of the four cars. Rather than take him to headquarters, they drove him to the Kipling Hotel on West Third Street and took him up to room 521. There were no Miranda rights to recite: some twenty-five years would pass before they became the law of the land. As a result, Siegel had no lawyer at his side. Nevertheless, he gave little away.

Siegel denied any involvement with Tony Cornero and the SS *Rex*, and he professed complete bewilderment at mention of the race wire. "I don't know nothing about that," he said. "I don't even know how it runs—sidewards, backwards, anything about it."[15]

The detectives rolled their eyes at that. Just weeks before, Moe Annenberg had pleaded guilty to massive tax evasion on his own race wire, Nationwide News Service. In exchange for dropping charges against his son, the IRS had accepted a settlement of $9.5 million from Annenberg.[16] The fallen titan had also agreed to sell Nationwide for a pittance, and to serve three years in Pennsylvania's Lewisburg federal prison. Siegel and his cohorts were actively vying to seize Nationwide for themselves.

As to the killing of Big Greenie, Siegel had no recollection of what he was doing the night of November 22, 1939. He did admit to knowing Frank Carbo, based on their mutual love of boxing and Carbo's management of various boxers.

The detectives drove Siegel to the county jail, where a crowd of news photographers awaited him. That was the only time Siegel lost his composure. He couldn't be photographed yet, he said, not with his hair unbrushed and an open-collar shirt. One of the detectives lent him a comb; another provided him with a tie. "I want a mouthpiece"—a lawyer—Siegel declared.[17]

With Siegel secure in a Los Angeles County jail cell, the detectives returned to 250 Delfern Drive for a closer look. They found a button in the library that slid open a panel, revealing a strong box with a double-barreled shotgun, loaded and ready to go. Within the strong box were personal treasures: gold watches, gold cuff links, a gold cigarette lighter, and more.

There, too, were the guns Siegel had shown George Raft: a .38 caliber revolver and a .38 Colt automatic.

Of more interest to the detectives were account books that had unlisted phone numbers of Hollywood stars and studio heads. There were daily bets recorded, to show that Siegel had been to Santa Anita almost every day. There were also loans noted, from both stars and studio heads, as well as the intriguing correspondence between Siegel and the Minnesota ex-convict who by this time had repaid the $100,000 he owed Siegel.

For a court appearance the next day, Siegel was the best-dressed man in the room, with an impeccably pressed blue pin-striped suit, a snow-white shirt, dark blue tie, and a fedora. To the press he fiercely denied the story of hiding in his attic. "I was just getting up and getting dressed Friday morning when I looked out of the window and saw four cars with a lot of men with guns piling out. I stepped into the linen closet, waiting to hear who they were when they announced themselves to the maid. I hadn't the slightest suspicion they were police officers. They didn't announce themselves but came right on up. Then I stepped out of the linen closet. I was never in the attic, and the mark[s] the detectives say I left on the linen in the closet climbing up [to] the attic were made by the officers themselves."[18]

As for the story that stool pigeons "Kid Twist" Reles and "Allie Tick Tock" Tannenbaum were about to tell a grand jury of Big Greenie's murder, it was, as Siegel put it, ridiculous. "For instance, take Al Tannenbaum. Al Tannenbaum is singing because he was promised immunity. I would like to say right now that he is a liar.

"Tannenbaum says he was driving my car the night Greenberg was killed," Siegel explained. "Wouldn't I be a sucker to allow a thing like that, and to take a chance that Tannenbaum, a well-known no-good, would crash a car registered to me? I am laughing."[19] Ah, that extra wrinkle in the plan!

Asked what he did for a living, the thirty-seven-year-old Siegel declared himself "retired."[20]

Siegel was remanded to the county jail without bail. A day or so later, the grand jury was mesmerized by the appearance of Reles and Tannenbaum, flown out from New York to L.A. under heavy guard. The two testified for hours, relating the Big Greenie story in scintillating detail. They declared that Siegel swung more weight in the mob than Lepke, and that in his bootlegging days, Siegel was, as Tannenbaum put it, the "absolute king" of the liquor business in New York.[21]

By the time the duo flew home, again under close guard, five men were charged with Big Greenie's murder. Along with Ben Siegel, the defendants were the imprisoned Lepke and three others now on the lam: "Champ" Segal, a boxing promoter; Mendy Weiss, one of Lepke's lieutenants; and Frank Carbo, the trigger man. (Reles and Tannenbaum had traded their testimony for their freedom.) Rumors swirled that one or more of the three might soon meet Big Greenie's fate. But in the courtroom, Siegel waved off the thought. "Just let me get to a telephone and I'll have them for you within 24 hours," he told the judge. His offer was declined.[22]

Some days later, Siegel was back in court to make his formal plea. Not guilty, his lawyer declared. The lawyer tried to win his client bail by calling him "a good citizen and family man whose business interests would be incompatible with flight."[23] The judge declined this proposal as well. That meant an immediate return to county jail, where Siegel would remain until his trial.

It took time for the press to discover how different jail was for Siegel than for his fellow inmates. He had stylish, hand-tailored uniforms with notched lapels that were made of a soft, high-quality denim. He had an inmate to iron those uniforms and shine his shoes. He got to sleep on the prison doctor's comfortable bed and to use his private shower. He had takeout food from local restaurants, including caviar and roast pheasant from Ciro's restaurant on the Sunset Strip. Often, he entertained women visitors in the jailer's quarters. Unrestricted phone use was de rigueur.[24]

Siegel even had his freedom, more or less. By mid-November, he would be granted nineteen daily leaves, each from 9 A.M. to 4 P.M., within his forty-nine-day stay. Most of his outings were listed as meetings with his dentist or lawyer. Some may have been with his daughters, to give the impression he was out and about, busy with work, and if so then also to check in with Esther, as well as his parents, who by now were apparently living at the house on Delfern Drive.

Of Siegel's many "leave" days from county prison that fall of 1940, at least a few were rendezvous with Wendy Barrie, the new woman in Siegel's life.

Barrie, the daughter of a distinguished lawyer, had grown up in England. She made her screen debut at twenty, resplendent with red-gold hair and sapphire blue eyes, and soon brought her accent and élan to Hollywood, where she played opposite Spencer Tracy (*It's a Small World*) and Jimmy Stewart (*Speed*). She was at the peak of her career in 1940, with five films that year alone, when she came into Siegel's life, unbothered by the fact that her date was a gangster.

George Raft, ever the self-sacrificing friend, found himself recruited into taking Barrie to the county jail for an extended visit with her new beau. Raft did give her a serious warning on their drive home. "If you go around with Ben Siegel you'll get hurt," Raft said. "And I mean hurt. Suddenly nobody will want you in pictures." Barrie was resolute. "I'll take that chance," she said.[25]

Days later, a prison guard drove Siegel to Lindy's restaurant on Wilshire Boulevard, where he met up with Barrie for a meal after having his handcuffs removed by the thoughtful guard.

Unfortunately, the crusading editor of the *Los Angeles Examiner*, Jim Richardson, had heard rumors of Siegel's day leaves and assigned a reporter to follow the gangster as he was driven about town in a county vehicle. Plastered on the front page of the *Examiner* the next day were pictures of the happy couple.[26]

The city was outraged, especially when further investigation revealed the role that county jail doctor Benjamin Blank had played in the scandal. Blank was the one who had sanctioned all those luxuries. In return, he had accepted multiple checks totaling $32,000. Record of the payments was found in Siegel's strongbox. Oddly enough, Dr. Blank had been one of the luckless treasure hunters aboard the *Metha Nelson*. He was also Maurice Siegel's roommate in medical school. A short proceeding led to his formal ouster as county jail physician. He vowed to fight it, after accusing his fellow jailers of "making life miserable" for Siegel, who was, as he put it, "a personal friend," whom he would "not permit . . . to be so treated.[27]

The negative coverage did nothing to cool Barrie's ardor for Siegel, nor his for her. When Barrie told him about Raft's warning, he was incensed. As soon as Siegel was released that December, he would drive up to Raft's Coldwater Canyon home and charge in with gun drawn, threatening to shoot his friend dead. Raft knew how to calm him down, using a soothing nickname he liked: Baby Blue Eyes. But long after Siegel left, Raft was shaking. He was sure that anyone else in his shoes that night would have been a dead man.[28]

The coziness of L.A.'s county jail could do only so much to ease Siegel's anxiety about his upcoming trial. Another court performance from "Kid Twist" Reles and "Tick Tock" Tannenbaum might leave him facing the death penalty, and L.A.'s long-serving district attorney, Buron Fitts, was eager to see justice done. But Siegel had a get-out-of-jail card to play. With Fitts running for a fourth term as D.A., Siegel managed to make a $30,000 contribution to Fitts's rival, John Dockweiler. That was a fortune for a D.A.'s race in 1940, and one that probably tipped the outcome, yet Dockweiler seemed not to notice it.

Days after his victory, Dockweiler made a show of preparing for the Big Greenie murder trial. That brought an angry letter from Siegel, who had expected his immediate release to be Dockweiler's first order of business. He announced his $30,000 contribution to the press and demanded its return. Dockweiler responded by sending the money back immediately, claiming he had no idea it had come from Siegel.

Nothing Dockweiler did in his first days in office persuaded outgoing D.A. Fitts or Brooklyn D.A. Bill O'Dwyer to risk sending their star witnesses to testify. Consequently, Dockweiler had no case, which appeared to be just what he wanted. The judge had no choice but to adjourn the trial. An investigation by Fitts's outgoing team of attorneys excoriated Dockweiler and found his office mired in corruption.[29]

Before the judge's gavel came down, halting the case, Siegel offered a statement. "I am keenly disappointed in the dismissal of this case," he told the court. "I am absolutely innocent of this offense and have sought nothing but the opportunity to establish my innocence in a fair trial before a Los Angeles court and jury."[30] With that, Siegel reclaimed a pair of gold cuff links from the jail's front office and walked out a free man, home in time for Christmas.

Siegel wasn't quite off the hook yet. In the early summer of 1941, he was charged in New York with harboring a fellow suspect in the Big Greenie murder case: Lepke Buchalter. With an armed escort, he was flown east from L.A. and once again sat in a courtroom, this time just a few seats from Abe "Kid Twist" Reles and Allie "Tick Tock" Tannenbaum, whose threat to Siegel's continuing freedom remained keen.

Reles took the stand to say that Siegel had attended the meeting called by Lepke in August 1939 in which the decision was made to kill Greenberg. The meeting lasted twenty to thirty minutes, Reles recounted. That was when Siegel declared that he would take care of Big Greenie in L.A. over the others' protests. Reles testified that he had known Siegel at that point for ten years.

When Siegel was called to the stand, he testified that he had never met Reles. As for the meeting just before Lepke's surrender, he said that he couldn't have been there because he'd been sailing to Naples with Dorothy Di Frasso on a ship called the *Conti di Savoy*. Upon reaching Italy, he added, he and di Frasso had attended an audience with the pope. They had met the king of Greece, King Victor Emmanuel of Italy, and the duke of Spoleto, who later became the king of Croatia. The court was stunned. Siegel went on to say he had returned from Europe to New York on June 5, 1939, and immediately returned to Los Angeles. Thus he could not have attended the supposed meeting with Lepke in August of that year.

Asked what he did for a living these days, Siegel described himself as a stock and bond operator worth $500,000, but added that he was also in real estate. At that moment, he was trying to sell his mansion on Delfern Drive. "If somebody offered me $75,000 for the place I'd take it and throw in the furnishings," he declared.[31] Siegel probably meant what he said. As Lansky had noted, Siegel didn't seem to care what he did with his money once he got it. The game of getting it—the adrenaline rush—was what exhilarated Siegel, just as it had when he was a ten-year-old boy, tearing off with a bag full of change on his first neighborhood theft, the market owner racing after him until he lost his breath.

If only out of embarrassment, L.A. district attorney John Dockweiler decided by the fall of 1941 that a Big Greenie murder trial must go forward after all. On the East Coast, the Brooklyn D.A. Bill O'Dwyer had gotten what he needed from Reles and Tannenbaum in his New York case against Lepke for murder.

Now he was willing to send the songbirds back to L.A. to testify once more against Siegel, protected by some of his best men.

For once, Siegel seemed to lose his swagger. On September 18, 1941, with a grand jury about to convene, he disappeared. His lawyer said he was vacationing at Lake Tahoe. A grand jury in late September heard riveting testimony from Tannenbaum, but Siegel was a no-show in the courtroom. His absence seemed to hearten Tannenbaum. With gusto, he described Siegel as "what is known in gangster parlance as a cowboy, which is the way the boys have of describing a man who is not satisfied to frame a murder but actually has to be in on the kill in person." Tannenbaum added that in one sense, Siegel was underappreciated. For more than a decade, he said, "Ben Siegel was the supreme gangster in the U.S., the top man, he had been the big boss for the last ten years throughout the country." Six days later, Siegel was still absent. When the judge asked why Siegel's chair was empty, there was only "mocking silence," as one newspaper account had it.[32]

With his life in the balance, vacationing on Lake Tahoe was the last thing Siegel was apt to be doing. Tannenbaum's testimony was devastating, and soon the grand jury would hear worse, if that were possible. Reles was due to address the grand jury in November. Siegel was almost certainly meeting with Syndicate stalwarts to see what could be done about Reles before the start of Siegel's reconvened trial.

For months, Reles had resided at the Half Moon Hotel on Coney Island under around-the-clock armed guard provided by the government. Reles was, according to Rich Cohen, "a jerk, lighting matches and throwing them at the officers, pouring pepper all over his food. The cops had to grit their teeth and bear it, for Reles was implicating one gangster after another in the many murders of *Murder Inc.*"[33] Now he was about to do the same with Siegel.

At about 3 A.M. on the night of November 12, 1941, Captain

Frank Bals had six policemen on the midnight-to-eight shift guarding Reles and three other squealers on the hotel's sixth floor. He brewed himself a cup of coffee and turned to see Reles emerging from his bedroom—623—into the sixth-floor common area. "No thanks," Reles said when asked if he wanted a cup of coffee himself, and retreated into his bedroom, closing the door behind him.

At around 7:45 A.M., a guest on the fifth floor looked out the window to see a gray-clothed body tangled in bed sheets, spread-eagle and very dead on the roof of the hotel's second-floor extension. From Reles's own window dangled a makeshift escape line of sheets knotted together and extended by wire, suggesting to the detectives that Reles had meant to escape, possibly by swinging outward and then swinging back through the window directly below him, which happened to be unoccupied. But that was just one of many theories.[34]

The mystery was never solved, but Meyer Lansky's version was as good as any. "The way I heard it was that Frank Bals stood in the room and supervised the whole thing," Lansky later told his Israeli biographers. "Reles was sleeping and one of the cops gave him a tap with the billy and knocked him out. Then they picked him up and heaved him out." Doc Stacher, the garrulous Lansky man, said he had overheard Frank Costello say, shortly before Reles's death, "It cost us a hundred grand, but 'Kid Twist' Reles is about to join his maker."[35]

Siegel's life was almost certainly saved by Reles's demise. For lack of corroboration on Tannenbaum's testimony, both Siegel and Frank Carbo were freed, and the Big Greenie story came to an end at last in a California courtroom in February, 1942.[36]

Reles's death saved Lepke from one dire fate, but not another. On December 2, 1941, Lepke was found guilty of first-degree murder of another gangster, Joseph Rosen. Two of Lepke's lieutenants, Mendy Weiss and Lou Capone, were found guilty of the same charge. All three were sentenced to die in the electric chair—and did, on March 4, 1944. Weiss's last words were ones of gratitude. "I want to thank Judge [Irving] Lehman. He knows me because I am a Jew. Give my love to my family . . . and everything."

The Big Greenie ruling was Siegel's chance to go legit at last, in a grand, ambitious way. He would buy his way into the burgeoning Las Vegas casino business, and for a brief, shining moment, all of his dreams would come true.

6

The Flamingo

IN 1941, the drive from Los Angeles to Las Vegas on U.S. 91 took nearly six hours. "It was horrendous," recalled John Cahlan, the first newspaper reporter to make Vegas his beat. "It was paved, but lots of ups and downs, and two-lane all the way. If you got behind a truck you might as well forget it. And no air conditioning in the cars of those days." Drivers had to take extra tanks of gasoline; God forbid they should run out in the long stretches between stations. Worst were the sandstorms that rose up from the desert without warning. "It would pit the windshield," Cahlan recalled, "just as if you were being sand-blasted, and it would take the paint right off the car." These storms could get so thick that the sky turned dark and a driver had to pull over until the skies cleared. "It didn't rain like it does now, it just blew instead," Cahlan said.[1]

Vegas had a scattering of small, western-style casinos in early 1941 that catered to the locals. Later, Siegel would be credited as the first to envision the glamour palaces to come. In truth, a hotel owner from Sacramento named Tommy Hull had the jump on him. "He had a flat tire one time he came up here," recalled Cahlan, "and he just counted the automobiles passing by."[2] Enough, Hull sensed, for a larger casino than Las Vegas had yet seen, midway between Salt Lake City and L.A., not just with gaming tables and slot machines but with rooms for the night: *a hotel-casino.*

When Hull's El Rancho Vegas opened in April of that year, the first hotel-casino on lonely Highway 91, it was an overnight success, thanks to its 110 guest rooms. Guests could drink and gamble late into the night, then just toddle upstairs to bed. That November came a downtown competitor, the even grander El Cortez. It had colorfully lit landscaping, replete with a man-made waterfall.

The Flamingo was five years away, not yet a gleam in Ben Siegel's eye. Still, he understood the money to be made in Vegas from the new hotel-casinos. Nevada was still the only state to permit gambling, a deeply comforting thought. And now, along with more gaming tables and slot machines, where gamblers could bet all night, the new El Cortez and El Rancho Vegas could take the race wire. Bettors could bet by wire all day on horse races around the country. All Siegel had to do was take control of the race wire in Vegas, and not let his rivals get there first.

For Siegel, this was the very embodiment of a new, soul-restoring chance. Siegel knew he had botched his chance for legitimacy in southern California. The Hollywood stars who had come to the mansion on Delfern to socialize with its dapper owner came no more, not even to gamble. With Big Greenie's murder and the publicity that followed, Siegel had become persona non grata in Hollywood, accepted only by George Raft and Dorothy di Frasso. When his murder case was dismissed a second and final time, Siegel put his hopes and outsize ambition on the dust-blown, boom-and-bust town of Las Vegas.[3]

Long before gamblers came to try their luck at the slot machines and roulette wheels, Las Vegas had drawn its share of risk-takers. Despite the surrounding desert, pioneers had begun making it a stop on the Old Santa Fe Trail in the 1830s, and frontier explorer John Frémont had led a settlement party there in 1844. They, and the Mormons who followed, were all drawn by the astonishing meadows—a great oasis—that gave Las Vegas its name.

Las Vegas was farmland, alfalfa its chief crop, sheep its main livestock. "They would bring in sheepherders from the Pyrenees," a doctor's wife of the period explained. "Those sheepherders would stay out months on end." The doctor always took his compass on house calls. "Otherwise he would get lost and wander for hours," his wife said, "and we would have to send a search party."[4]

In 1905, all that changed with the arrival of a railroad baron and U.S. senator from Montana, William Andrews Clark, who declared his intention to build a train line from Los Angeles to Salt Lake City. Las Vegas was halfway: perfect for a stopover. Clark's engineers could sink artesian wells and supply water to their trains, and his work crews could build a trackside depot for on-the-spot repairs. Clark, all business, dispensed with the name Las Vegas. He called his outpost Watering Hole #25.[5]

Along with the railroad workers, or "rails," as they were called, Watering Hole #25 soon had passengers alighting for the creature comforts they knew to expect from a frontier town: booze, gambling, and prostitution. Officially, gambling was outlawed in Nevada in 1909. In truth, games of chance hummed right along. The town fathers made a half-hearted effort to limit prostitution to block 16, down by the railroad tracks, only to see brothels appear in the back rooms of nearly every saloon in town. In such revels was the city's soul born.[6]

Clark built this hardscrabble town. And then, in 1922, he tried to destroy it, after his railroad workers joined a nation-wide strike. Ruthlessly, Clark shut down the railroad repair shop and took away three hundred jobs. Grim years ensued, until President Calvin Coolidge brought Las Vegas roaring back to life in 1928 by authorizing the massive Boulder Dam, later to be named the Hoover Dam, on the nearby Colorado River. Hundreds of laborers converged on government-built Boulder City, with keen appetites for after-work vice.

Alcohol remained illegal though obtainable, until Prohibition's end in 1933. In the watershed year of 1931, however, the sparsely populated state of Nevada, fearful the dam would fall short of counteracting the Great Depression, sanctioned almost everything else. Card games, roulette wheels, and slot machines became legal. So did prostitution and quickie marriages: no waiting period, no health certificates needed, with county clerk offices open twenty-four hours a day to rake in the marriage fees. On the same day as the gambling bill passed, so came quickie divorces. Either party, not both, now needed only to stay in the state six weeks to establish residency and get a divorce. No other state could match Nevada for such ease of marital disengagement.

With the dam's completion in 1935, fears of joblessness grew. They proved groundless. Las Vegas was on the map now. It drew travelers wanting to see Boulder Dam, the nearby national parks, and the casinos of Las Vegas, now primed with legal booze. By the late 1930s, national magazines were extolling Vegas as the great new American destination, and hinting at the naughtiness visitors might find there.

Siegel's first stake in a Vegas casino was probably the check he wrote for $18,000 to the owner of the Northern Club, one of those wagon wheel–and–sawdust joints the locals favored.

The canceled check was among those found in his security vault during the raid of his home on Delfern Drive on August 16, 1940.[7]

Buying into the Northern Club made a lot of sense for Siegel. He could learn the business as a partner, scanning the Northern Club's books. He could take a slice of the profits from its roulette wheels, slot machines, and twenty-one gaming tables. Most enticing, he could bring up the race wire from Moe Annenberg's fallen empire in southern California, pushing the casinos to pay a handsome subscription fee that would go, in part, into Ben Siegel's pocket.

The course seemed clear, with new fortunes to be made. For Siegel, the news of December 7, 1941, raised hopes for that much more. Siegel felt the same excitement with Pearl Harbor that Prohibition had stirred: the sense of a world-changing opportunity for those quick enough to capitalize on it. America's entry into World War II brought Vegas a vast new military airport. It brought the new Army Air Corps Gunnery School, where thousands of fighter pilots and bomber crewmen trained to handle machine guns mounted on B-class warplanes. It brought Basic Magnesium, where thirteen thousand workers mass-produced locally mined magnesium, the "wonder metal" used in airplane construction. Those pilots and workers wanted extracurricular pleasures, and who better than Siegel to provide them?

At one time or another, Siegel had shares in nearly every Vegas casino of the early forties, from the Pair-O-Dice and the Northern Club to the Frontier Club, the Last Frontier Hotel, the Las Vegas Club, and the El Cortez, all serving the wartime boom. Still, he hungered for more. He wanted a race wire of his own, one like Annenberg's with national reach. He wanted his own hotel-casino, too.

Siegel had hoped to seize the whole West Coast wire, but Annenberg refused to sell it to him. Instead, the ailing race wire pioneer basically gave it to one of his old pals from the

Hearst newspaper wars. It was a brief tenure. Mickey McBride renamed Annenberg's wire the Continental Press, as if gangsterdom might fail to notice its latest disposition. In almost no time at all, McBride passed it on to another old crony from the newspaper wars, James Ragen Sr. McBride never said as much, but his haste in selling was probably the result of threats from Chicago mobsters with race wire ambitions of their own. They could run a national wire as easily from Chicago as from anywhere else: all they needed was telegraph wires and betting rooms in every market.[8] Ragen, a very tough guy, declared he would be staying put in Chicago and running Continental himself. He had an ally in Meyer Lansky, who, with Annenberg, had run the wire through Florida's Gold Coast of casinos and clubs.

Siegel couldn't take Ragen on yet. At Lansky's direction, he had to work with him, along with Jack Dragna, who still ruled much of southern California, and Johnny Roselli, until recently Moe Annenberg's West Coast agent. The mobsters became a team, if a reluctant one, since each would have much preferred killing the others. Together, they represented Continental on the West Coast, working out of a downtown office run by James Ragen's son-in-law, Russell Brophy.

Siegel soon lost patience with this setup. He started his own wire, Phoenix-based Trans-American, and began taking over Continental's bookie parlors in Arizona, with L.A. in his sights. To his astonishment, he found himself blindsided by the notorious Mickey Cohen.[9]

Cohen was a hit man and all-purpose thug known back east for his "fearsome, simian manner," as Bugsy biographer Dean Jennings put it, "and the knife cuts and bullet scars that crisscrossed his stomach, along with the gold mezuzah on a light chain around his waist."[10]

Cohen had just moved to L.A. to escape a little heat from the authorities back east. He found it irksome that Continental

Press was operating without his blessing and participation. To make his sentiments clear, he paid a visit to one of Continental's offices, accompanied by a favorite henchman, Joe Sica. By great good chance, a bagman called Little Joe walked in at that moment to check on a race result. Cohen easily guessed the meaning of Little Joe's terrified look: Little Joe was en route to another race wire office with the day's haul for Siegel and Dragna. As one of the office guards reached for his gun, Cohen warned him to back off if he wanted to live out the day. The guard backed off, and Cohen pointed his gun at Little Joe. "I ain't got nuthin'," Little Joe said. "I just come here to lay a bet." Cohen took aim. "You want it in the head, quick, or slow in the belly?" Little Joe handed over a satchel of what proved to be $22,000.[11]

When news of the heist reached Siegel, he had to laugh. It was so audacious. He proposed that Cohen meet him at a YMCA where Siegel liked to work out. Another gangster might have feared for his life, but not Cohen. After a little small talk, Siegel offered him some advice. "He says to me 'you're a gutty kid, but you need some finesse and polish, or you're going to wind up being on the heavy . . . the rest of your life,'" Cohen told a biographer years later. "'You got ability that if used in the proper way would put you in a different scale.'"[12] Cohen was flattered, but still refused to give the Continental mobsters their money back. A second meeting in a lawyer's office proved no more fruitful; Siegel was beginning to lose face.

Finally, Siegel proposed that Cohen and his sidekick Joe Sica pay a visit to Continental's biggest L.A. office. Siegel and his partners might still be in business with Continental, but they had their own agenda. Ultimately they wanted either to take Continental for themselves or push Siegel's new Trans-American wire into dominating the field. Perhaps in paying this social visit, Cohen could earn back the money he'd filched.[13]

On July 21, 1942, Cohen and Sica strolled into Continental's downtown L.A. office and pulled out all the telegraph and telephone wires from the walls. Aware of the sudden silence, Russell Brophy emerged from the back office. He told the thugs to clear out. Cohen responded by striking him with a pistol butt. Together, he and Sica beat Brophy until the man lost consciousness.[14]

Siegel took Brophy's hospitalization as an opportunity to sweep through L.A. with Mickey Cohen, urging bookies to switch their allegiance to the new Trans-American wire. The two wires were basically identical: both sent out race results and information by telegraph. Continental bookies would just pay their subscription fees to Siegel and his gang, rather than to Brophy, Continental's battered man in southern California. There was an added incentive that went unspoken. Bookies who signed up with Siegel's new "association," as he called it, would not be subject to pistol-whippings, as they would if they stayed loyal to Continental. "There is no existing record that shows how many cracked skulls, or how many unsolved murders, were a direct result of Siegel's western war on Continental," wrote Jennings. "But that one incident alone—told to me with a twisted sort of pride by Mickey Cohen—is a clue to Siegel's eventual success."[15]

By one estimate, Siegel and his pals persuaded some five hundred Continental bookies in the Los Angeles area to switch teams, out of a total of some eighteen hundred. That was a lot of persuading.[16]

As a next step to expanding his empire, Siegel sent his genial number-two man, Moe Sedway, to negotiate with Continental for rights to its Las Vegas wire. Moses Moe Annenberg had been freed from prison to die at home of a brain tumor in July 1942. The next month, Sedway sealed the deal for Las Vegas rights. Siegel would pay Continental a weekly fee of $900 and keep all the race wire profits he made in Las Vegas. Perhaps not coincidentally, that was the month Ragen's son-in-law Brophy was beaten to a bloody pulp.[17]

As more casinos signed on, Siegel's deal with Continental showed real foresight. According to one report, Siegel began pocketing $25,000 a month from his Vegas race book, the equivalent of nearly $400,000 a month in today's U.S. dollars. With his management shares of various casinos, and his highly informed daily betting at the track, Siegel was said to push his overall yearly income to $500,000, or about $7 million in today's dollars.[18]

One Vegas casino owner who needed no prompting to take Siegel's race wire was the Octopus: Guy McAfee, Siegel's old L.A. nightclub rival. Run out of southern California in 1939 by a new reform-minded L.A. mayor, McAfee had decided the time had come to try his luck in Vegas. To his chagrin, the tumbleweed town had proved a challenge.[19] His Frontier Club was struggling, its nighttime business ho-hum. McAfee, it seemed, had overbuilt. Desperate to increase traffic, he suggested a sweetheart deal to Siegel. He would not only pay $300 a week to subscribe to Siegel's race wire but give him a slice of the nightly take. Anything to get customers in.

Siegel must have granted those tough terms with glee, after years of vying with the former gambling king of L.A. But both men profited. The Frontier's race wire drew a whole new daytime market of off-track horse bettors, and McAfee saw his business soar. Having tried and failed to sell the Frontier for $40,000 in 1941, he would turn down a $400,000 offer just three years later.[20] Of course, the Frontier's success did not go unnoticed. Siegel became a two-thirds owner of the place. The more a Vegas casino made on its race wire, it seemed, the bigger a slice of its overall profits Siegel was apt to take.

By February 1943, Siegel was said to run his race wire through most of the town's casinos. But that wasn't all. His territory extended to the rest of Nevada, Arizona, and southern California.

* * *

Siegel loved the money to be made in Vegas. He just hated Vegas itself: the tedious drive, the cowboy culture, and the desert around it. Los Angeles was his home. Beneath its perfect, unpolluted skies, he went to the track every day, had his barbering needs tended to, and visited the L.A. clubs and gambling dens from which he cheerfully extracted his take. Meanwhile, he and Wendy Barrie had gone so far as to get engaged. That the romance fizzled was perhaps due to Siegel's insistence on living with his family at home. George Raft's earlier warnings proved groundless: Barrie went on to a long career, her reputation unblemished by Siegel.

Despite his intent to sell the house on Delfern, Siegel still enjoyed his time there. He was in fact living a double life, often with Barrie but a family man whenever he came home. He appreciated Esther's devotion to their daughters and admired her traditional values. He knew she would never take a lover, no matter how hurtful his dalliances might be. In exchange, Siegel faithfully served as family provider, in the lavish manner his money allowed.

On one occasion, Meyer Lansky brought his wife and daughter Sandra out to stay with the Siegels. At perhaps six years old, Sandra Lansky marveled at the mansion and its expansive grounds. But she awoke the next morning to a sight that made her cry out in alarm. Her Aunt Esther seemed to have become a witch. In fact, Ben's wife was wearing a black sleeping mask to block the sunlight. "So I screamed and ran into Uncle Benny's bedroom, and what I saw there was even worse," Sandra writes in her memoir. "Not only was he, too, in a black eye mask, but he had this crazy black elastic vise around his cheeks and chin. It turned out to be some device Hollywood stars wore to bed to prevent wrinkles."[21]

Sandra's scary moment suggested a development no six-year-old would have appreciated. Ben and Esther appeared to have resigned themselves to separate bedrooms. How long their marriage had persisted in this arid state was a secret between the grown-ups, but with Wendy Barrie's relatively long-term presence in his life, Ben seemed unlikely to find any pleasure in his marital bed. As for Esther, she had married Ben at seventeen and would say, after his death, that he was the only man she had ever loved. Her consignment to a separate bedroom was probably one she rued with bafflement and chagrin.

Siegel still dressed and acted like a gangster. But he prided himself on his clean police record, so far as it stretched to the state's borders. True, he had spent the autumn of 1940 in an L.A. county jail, and faced a two-part murder trial, but both parts had ended in dismissals. That, he felt sure, was what motivated the L.A. sheriff's vice squad to stage a raid on Siegel for gambling in a room at the Sunset Towers hotel on May 25, 1944.[22]

Siegel was spending that morning with his old buddy George Raft. There with them was Allen Smiley, Siegel's Kiev-born right-hand man, in whose apartment the three men were socializing. Smiley was movie-star handsome, with prematurely gray hair and a Hollywood story to boot. Sentenced for robbery in his youth to a California reformatory, he had seized a bizarre chance: film director Cecil B. DeMille toured the reformatory in researching a movie, and Smiley managed to meet him. Upon his release, Smiley asked DeMille for a job and was given one in the wardrobe department. Soon he was pitching story ideas to stars and socializing with the likes of George Raft and Ben Siegel, who admired Smiley's pluck: in a fight at bandleader Tommy Dorsey's apartment, he was said to have sliced off part of actor John Hall's nose.[23]

The *Racing Form* and other racetrack sheets lay spread on the table. When Captain William Deal of the vice squad asked about them, Raft declared that he and his friends were doing exactly what they seemed to be doing: placing bets on horses.

Captain Deal apparently disagreed: the men were bookmaking, he declared, acting as bookies rather than betting on their own. With that, Deal took the phone from Siegel's hand and ripped its wires from the wall.

Siegel and Smiley were charged not only with bookmaking but with conspiracy, a felony that could bring significant jail time. Raft, on the other hand, was told he could leave. Furious, the actor insisted on being charged with his friends. At a preliminary hearing, Raft took the stand and heaped scorn on Captain Deal. The prosecutor finally agreed to drop the felony charges if Siegel and Allen Smiley pleaded guilty to the bookmaking count. After paying a $250 fine, the two men were freed.[24]

Raft actually benefited from the affair. His courtroom appearance with Siegel buffed his image as a real-life gangster, winning him more gangster roles. Smiley came out ahead, too. Recently he had opened a nightclub with Siegel's backing, and the press was good for business. Only Siegel lost out, his California record clean no more.

Irate, Siegel decided in earnest to sell the Delfern Drive house and move his base to Vegas, despite the desert heat. The cops and politicians in Vegas were more sympathetic, he felt, the new hotel-casinos enticing. And who was to stop him from building a casino of his own, one bigger and more dazzling than anything else on the Strip? Surely the Syndicate would back him on that.

There was another reason, just as compelling, for Siegel to sell his house and start a new life. His romance with Wendy Barrie behind him, he had met a woman so sensual and exciting that he could actually imagine divorcing Esther and marrying her. At some point in this period, he must have told Esther about Virginia Hill, because Esther moved to Manhattan with the girls, who enrolled in the Calhoun School on the Upper West Side. She had tolerated Siegel's Hollywood flings, his long cross-country absences, and more painful, his public relation-

ship with Countess Dorothy di Frasso. Esther wasn't quite
ready to ask for a divorce: the very idea appalled her, given her
conservative upbringing and the love she still felt for Siegel.
But nor did she appear willing to remain under the same roof
as her husband. To judge by the way Siegel began making the
rounds with Hill on his arm, the marriage was kaput.

Itching to acquire a hotel-casino of his own, Siegel approached Tom Hull, the owner of El Rancho Vegas, whose flat
tire four years before had led him to build the Strip's first one.
Siegel made an offer for El Rancho; Hull declined. Siegel raised
his offer; Hull declined again. "You may say for me," Hull told
the Las Vegas *Review-Journal*, "that the people of Las Vegas
have been too good to me for me to repay them in that way.
Mr. Siegel has contacted me several times with an offer to purchase, but I have told him I was not interested—and that goes
for all time."[25]

Hull's disdain only hardened Siegel's ambition to rule, or at
least dominate, Las Vegas. So eager was he to start a new life
that he put the Delfern house on the market for $85,000. A
quick bite of interest came from actress Loretta Young and her
husband, Tom Lewis, who wrote a check for the $8,500 down
payment. Soon after, they made a more detailed examination of
the place and found termites. Young and her husband asked
only that Siegel pay $350 to exterminate the bugs. "Like hell
I will," he declared. At that, they withdrew their offer, losing
their down payment but extricating themselves from a house
full of bugs. Siegel retaliated by taking them to court. A first
judge sided with Young and her husband; a higher judge did,
too. In the end, Siegel spent two years tangled in the proceed-
ings, only to sell the house at a bargain price of $75,000.[26]

Possibly unaware of the Delfern house history, and that of
its owner, a young Los Angeles woman let her curiosity lead her
to the front door. She was a wartime European refugee whose

son, a financier named Peter Gregory, tells the story to this day.[27] The woman was his mother. Curiosity led the woman to 250 Delfern, where she found herself face to face with a darkly handsome, impeccably dressed man who introduced himself as Ben, and invited her in.

The handsome owner gave Gregory's mother a tour of the place; pleasantries were exchanged. The owner then motioned her to a seat in the living room.

"I like the house very much," Gregory's mother said. "But I have to admit the price is high for me. What's the best price you could give me?"

Siegel put a hand up as if to wave off the thought. "I never do business with ladies," he said. "I'll take whatever price you offer."

Mrs. Gregory was enjoying her visit, and the intensity of the handsome owner's gaze. There was, perhaps, a trace of flirtation between them. Mrs. Gregory was a very handsome woman in her early forties, not unaware of her looks. She giggled. "Oh come on," she said. "How little would you take?"

"Whatever you want to pay is fine," Siegel said.

"Well, all right," said Mrs. Gregory. "Would you take a dollar?"

The man smiled. "Yes, of course. If you want to buy this house, I will sell it to you for a dollar."

Mrs. Gregory grinned. "You can't be serious," she said.

The owner leaned toward her. "That's where you're wrong," he said. "You can buy it for a dollar."

At that point Mrs. Gregory thought it best to leave. She promised to bring up this offer with her husband that night, and she did.

"You did *what?*" her husband said. "You offered to buy a house from Bugsy Siegel for a dollar? Do you know what he would do if we actually *did* that?" Neither Mr. nor Mrs. Gregory knew what would happen, since Mrs. Gregory never went

THE FLAMINGO

back to the house. There was something so mesmerizing and intense about Siegel, though, that Mrs. Gregory never forgot the episode. She had a feeling she really could have bought the Delfern house for a dollar and not incurred any retaliation. It was just something she saw in those brilliant blue eyes.

At some point soon after that curious encounter, Siegel moved out of the Delfern Drive house. He had done all he could, sparing no expense, to make it a perfect family home. But surely even he knew he was to blame for the failure of family life its empty rooms represented.

In the summer of 1944, in response to a letter from the U.S. Draft Board, Siegel offered a few updates on his wartime status. He had changed his address from 250 Delfern Drive to 721 North Doheny Drive, a home in Beverly Hills owned by his sister Bessie and her husband, Sollie Soloway. His annual income, he reported, was $50,000. He called himself an investment broker, and explained, "I consider various propositions concerning investments in enterprises, and if satisfactory, enter into such deals." As to the specific nature of those deals, "I do the following kind of work: I usually obtain an interest in return for my work. I'm required to make trips to appraise and investigate all matters connected with enterprises, and to negotiate terms."[28]

It was an apt description for an entrepreneur, but no less so for a freewheeling gangster about to embark on the business challenge of his life, one in which daily decisions, involving tens or even hundreds of thousands of dollars, would have to be made. Soon he would see how equipped he was to make them.

7

The Start of an Ill-Starred Romance

No RECORD EXISTS of Ben Siegel's first meeting with Virginia Hill. History does provide the next best thing: George Raft's first meeting with her, at about the time she and Ben Siegel fell into their torrid affair.

Raft liked driving his black Cadillac convertible from his home in Coldwater Canyon down to Romanoff's restaurant in Beverly Hills. There, as usual, he would be warmly greeted by "Prince" Romanoff and led to his favorite booth as all eyes followed. Decades had passed since he'd whirled lonely women around a dance floor for cash, but he still moved with a dancer's ease and grace.

This particular evening, Raft noticed a familiar figure in a nearby booth. Giuseppe Doto, better known as Joe Adonis, was a key member of the Syndicate, and one of Meyer Lansky's closest friends. With him was a beautiful young woman Raft had never seen. Intrigued, he went over to pay his respects.[1]

For a moment the two men talked of Ben Siegel and his efforts to sell the mansion on Delfern Drive. Then Joe Adonis remembered his manners. "George, I'd like you to meet a friend of mine, Virginia Hill. Virginia, this is George Raft, as if you didn't know."

Hill had iridescent gray-green eyes, a dazzling smile, and a mane of dark red hair, falling around her bare, petite shoulders. Raft was mesmerized. "You from out of town?" he asked.

"Chicago," Hill murmured. "But I'll be living here now."

"Maybe we'll be seeing you around," Raft said. He was right about that. Raft would be seeing a lot of Virginia Hill. And so would his friend Ben Siegel.

Doto had had his amorous innings with Hill—he was, perhaps, having them still—and he would say he knew just how to deal with a girl like her. She loved sex, took pride in doing it well, and saw it as sport. You didn't fall in love with a girl like that; you had fun. But somehow, Siegel was about to lose sight of that fact. He would let Virginia Hill become the love of his life, then let her take *over* his life. You couldn't separate Hill from Ben Siegel's murder, Doto would say, whoever fired the shots. Hill was charming and fun, a crazy spender, and in her way, a great beauty. But she would bring chaos into Ben Siegel's life, and chaos, in the end, was what would kill him, whether the shooter was a Syndicate hire, or a race wire rival, or someone else altogether.

It was a tragedy, really, "Joe Adonis" would say. A great tragedy for all concerned.

Later, Siegel and Hill would speak of each other as soulmates, but they were more like alter egos. Like Siegel, Hill had grown up in abject poverty. Like Siegel, she had fought her way out at an early age, self-reliant and tough. The only difference was that Hill had a sponsor in the Chicago mob, a middle-aged mole of a man named Joe Epstein, who smoothed her path.

Virginia Hill, nicknamed Onie, was one of ten children, her kid brother Chick later recounted. She was born on August 26, 1916, in the small, mostly black town of Lipscomb, Alabama. Lipscomb was dominated by the Woodward iron company, where most residents worked until they could work no more. Her father nursed a violent temper and had more interest in bartering than earning a livelihood. "He could leave home in the morning with nothing but a pocketknife," Chick later said, "and come back at night with a horse." Another account suggests "Mack" Hill's trades were crooked, and that he did nothing to support the family, womanizing and drinking and beating the children.[2]

Soon after Virginia's birth, the family moved to nearby Bessemer, a larger industrial town where her mother, Margaret, ran a boardinghouse. From an early age, Virginia took charge of her siblings, warding off their drunken father and, according to one biography, slamming him on the head with a skillet when she was as young as seven. According to that account, Hill learned to regard all men as untrustworthy, and she never let down her guard.[3]

Overwhelmed by work and her querulous brood, Margaret situated the children among relatives. Virginia ended up with a grandmother on a cotton patch and became a lifelong tomboy. Later, Hill told the Kefauver Commission on Organized Crime that she left school in the eighth grade. By one account, she eloped at fifteen with the scion of a wealthy southern family, but both sets of parents were appalled and managed to undo the marriage. This adventure reportedly yielded her a sizable settlement, starting her on a lifetime course of easy money.[4]

At the height of the Great Depression, Virginia at seventeen left home for the 1934 World's Fair in Chicago, where she found work: a waitress by one account, a midway shill by another, a prostitute by a third. Somehow she met Epstein, a trusted confederate of Al Capone. She came back to Bessemer, as Chick recalled, "in a factory-fresh LaSalle convertible, with her beautiful legs in shimmering silk, a fur neckpiece touching the new sheen of her hair, and more gems than a Reno pawnshop."[5]

Hill stayed long enough to dispense the gifts she'd bought her siblings, dazzle the good citizens of Bessemer, and get her brother Chick to pack. Then it was back to Chicago, where she and Chick began learning the race wire business, and seeing the money it brought in. "Joe gave it to her in damp bunches, like lettuce," Bugsy biographer Dean Jennings wrote. "The bookie joint grew it in clusters, and there was a new crop every day."[6] Hill's relationship with Epstein would last for years and remain enigmatic. Chick saw her treat the mob accountant with scorn. He heard her ask for more money from wherever she was, and get it by special delivery. Yet the money kept coming from Epstein even as Hill began openly dating Epstein's fellow gangsters. Perhaps Epstein was an idealized father figure, generous to a fault even as Hill threw back the rage and hurt she had felt toward her real father.

Clearly, business was part of the picture. Hill was entrusted to place bets at the tracks and be a courier with substantial sums. Chick would recall trips to nearby airports to pick up money sent by Epstein. As a bag woman, Hill met most of the mob's top figures, from Frank Costello and Meyer Lansky to Longy Zwillman and Joe Doto. At Senator Estes Kefauver's 1950–1951 hearings on organized crime, Hill would coolly acknowledge sleeping with many of her mob consorts.[7]

By 1938, Hill and her younger brother had moved again, this time to L.A. They settled in West Hollywood at the Garden of Allah residential hotel, the same year a despondent F. Scott Fitzgerald lived there. Hill began making the rounds as an actress. Like Siegel, whom she hadn't met yet, she embraced self-improvement. She loved to read Thackeray, and had a complete set of his works. She read *Vanity Fair* and identified with plucky, ambitious Becky Sharp and her rise from an orphanage to great wealth. In the copy that her brother Chick saw, she underscored a favorite passage. "This I set down as positive truth. A woman with fair opportunities, and without a positive hump, may marry whom she likes. I think I could be a good woman if I had five thousand a year."[8]

Becoming a film star was the twentieth-century equivalent of marrying well in *Vanity Fair*. With her striking good looks, and still just twenty-two years old, Hill wangled a screen test at Universal, then a seven-year contract. She was seen as a Jean Harlow type, moody and mysterious. Unfortunately, as she admitted to Chick, she had little talent, and she tore up her contract. She dined and danced at the Trocadero, the Mocambo, and the Brown Derby. Actor Errol Flynn squired her around town. They ended up in a drunken brawl at the Brown Derby, the restaurant so shaped on Wilshire Boulevard, with Hill reportedly screaming at Flynn and throwing a drink in his face.[9] The Brown Derby was one of Siegel's favorite haunts, too.

With a limitless supply of "lettuce," Hill took her brother on gambling trips to Acapulco. By one account, she was seen in the gambling joints so often, her red hair framing a flushed face, that the Mexican casino men gave her a nickname: The Flamingo.[10] But there would be other derivations for the name of Ben Siegel's extravagant castle in the sands.

Passionate and willful, Virginia went home to Bessemer long enough to marry an All-America halfback and get that marriage annulled in a week. She then married, and divorced, a Mexican rhumba dancer. Unabashed, she started over in Hollywood. She threw expensive dinners at Ciro's, inspiring one newspaper to dub her "the film city's most generous party giver." Social columnist Hedda Hopper wrote that "she had the swingingest parties in town."[11] Soon *le tout* Hollywood was mad to know who this gorgeous and mysterious young big spender was.

Hill seems to have met Siegel in New York in 1943 or 1944. She was ensconced with "Joe Adonis" Doto in one fancy hotel or another, giving $10,000 dinners at the Waldorf Astoria. Or so she recalled to the Kefauver Commission. Was it perhaps at the Madison Hotel's cocktail lounge that she met Siegel, the lawmakers ventured, there in the company of Frank Costello? The Madison was one of Costello's haunts at that time, and Costello and Siegel were close. Hill said she couldn't be sure.[12]

When Hill began turning up on Siegel's arm, there was muttering that Joe Adonis might take offense, triggering a gangland grudge war. Hill's brother Chick scoffed at the thought. Joe Adonis wasn't in love with Virginia, said Chick Hill; he wasn't going to start a war. It was Siegel whose passions had been deeply stirred.

As the married man in the picture, Siegel could hardly demand that Hill stay faithful to him. With her free spirit, and bundles of cash, she proceeded to act as freely as she had before she met him. She still saw Joe Adonis, whatever that meant, and rumors rolled in of late-night parties and other paramours. Siegel seethed with jealousy, but when he confronted her, Hill just laughed and swore right back at him.[13] Siegel had met his match at last: Hill was as fearless as he was.

One week, taking a break from Siegel's jealousy, Hill stayed a night or two incognito at George Raft's house in Coldwater Canyon. Were the two of them, his lover and best friend, consorting behind his back? The very thought drove Siegel mad, but when Hill finally surfaced, she said she had nothing to apologize for, and Raft assured his friend that Hill's stay had been purely platonic.[14]

With her endless money from Epstein, Hill was free to do as she pleased, and to sleep with whom she chose. Siegel had never met a woman so fiercely free-spirited. For the first time in his life, he was powerless. If he was like most dominating men, he probably found the experience exhilarating. Hill and Siegel were kindred spirits, both canny enough to see their chances and take them, both made of the same indestructible stuff. Surely amid Siegel's roiling emotions for Hill was sheer admiration for the way she'd clawed her way up.

With his house on Delfern Drive sold, Siegel was living with his sister Bessie and her husband, Sollie Soloway. He could hardly bring Virginia Hill there. He made do with a series of trysting places. One was the Chateau Marmont apartment hotel, as it was called then, where the couple took a penthouse as Mr. and Mrs. James Hill. Virginia would check in first and bathe her body with Chanel No. 5 in anticipation of Siegel's visit. Chick, still a teenager, would be paid to go for a leisurely walk when his sister's new boyfriend arrived. Even so, he could sense, and sometimes hear, just how passionate their encounters were. Aspiring screenwriter Edward Anhalt lived for a while in a room across from "Mr. and Mrs. James Hill" at the Chateau Marmont and heard not just lovemaking but fierce arguments that sometimes came to blows. Bea Sedway, wife of Bugsy's longtime gambling manager Moe Sedway, confirmed the two often fought, and that Hill would hurl objects at her lover. But Hill assured Bea Sedway these arguments always led to marvelous bouts of makeup sex.[15]

Despite the hotel assignations, Hill kept an L.A. home of her own. She needed space for her hundreds of pairs of shoes, her four mink coats and half dozen mink stoles, her English bone china, crystal glassware, and sterling silver service for twelve. As she moved from one large rental home to the next, she carted her treasures herself in her latest Cadillac convertible, a new model every year.[16]

Siegel added to this trove with the occasional diamond necklace or earrings, but his greatest gifts were tips at the track. Once when they were in Chicago, Hill shook her brother Chick out of a nap and put $12,000 in his hand. "Ben just called me," she said. "The race starts in fifteen minutes. *Go!*" Chick drove at high speeds to the nearest bookie joint and put the

$12,000 on the horse Siegel had named. He came back to the hotel with $30,000. At some point in the romance, Siegel also made a down payment for Hill on a house for her in Miami: about $30,000, as she recalled years later before the Kefauver Commission, though she couldn't be sure. "I think it cost $49,000, I don't know."[17]

That was romance, at least for Hill and Siegel. When they weren't buying jewels and quaffing Champagne, they loved to read aloud from a fantasy novella called *Forever*, published in 1938 by a popular writer of the time, Mildred Cram. The story's lovers were doomed to die, but passionately believed they would be reborn, to spend eternity together. Chick kept his sister's copy, and later showed Jennings a passage Virginia had underscored. "Julie: If you should go first . . . And then what if I could never find you again? Or you me?" Colin: "We'll find each other. Somewhere. Somehow. You'll be born knowing about me. Wanting me. And some day we'll come back here."[18]

The star-crossed lovers of *Forever* captivated film star Judy Garland, too. According to her biographer Gerald Clarke, she could recite its sixty pages by heart.

Not long after Pearl Harbor, Lucky Luciano was quietly recruited by the U.S. military to help protect New York's waterfront from German saboteurs. Luciano was obviously motivated by self-interest: his help might get him released from Dannemora prison. But he was, in his way, a fierce patriot, proud to help his adopted country and horrified by emerging news of the Holocaust. Lansky felt the same way: he had gone so far as to try to enlist in the U.S. Army, only to be rejected for his age (forty) and height (five-foot-four). And then there was Siegel.

If Ben Siegel played any part in the war effort, it was never made known. Aside from his rather theatrical and ineffectual brush in Italy with one of Hitler's top officials, Siegel appeared to be spending the war positioning himself to take advantage of a postwar surge in the casino business. He had his race wire deal with Continental Press, earning weekly fees from every casino that took the wire, which most of them did by now, and a slice from their nightly gaming, too. He couldn't build his own hotel-casino, not for the million or more dollars that such a venture would take. But as a test run, he could talk Meyer Lansky into backing the purchase of one of the town's existing hotel-casinos and show he could squeeze a profit from it.

Siegel never did get Tom Hull to sell him the El Rancho. By chance, however, the town's other big hotel-casino came up for sale. Just four years after its debut, the El Cortez sold on March 28, 1945, for a little more than $600,000. The buyer was Moe Sedway, Siegel's front man. The seller was unaware Sedway and Siegel were in a group of ten silent investors, headed up by Meyer Lansky.[19]

For such a lover of gambling and the lucre it brought, Meyer Lansky had only a modest interest in Vegas. He had made his own real estate investments in Florida, using front men to build or buy up casinos, clubs, and racetracks in and around Miami.[20] He had invested heavily, too, in Cuba. Vegas was a cowboy town, set in the desert, a climate Lansky abhorred as much as Siegel did. But with the Syndicate in need of new investments—it had too much cash in hand—Lansky had let Siegel talk him into the El Cortez deal. In little more than a year, Siegel on the Syndicate's behalf sold the El Cortez for $766,000, kicking back a modest but cheering profit to each of the ten partners on their respective $60,000 investments. Now they were in a more positive frame to hear Siegel's pitch for another, very different kind of casino deal. Buying and selling an existing casino was a fairly easy deal to manage. What Siegel wanted now was to build a brand-new casino from the ground up, and make it, in the process, the most elegant hotel-casino America had yet seen. And for that, he had just the place in mind.

8

Bugsy Takes Charge

WHO FIRST NOTICED the scruffy, thirty-three-acre lot with weather-beaten shacks south of Las Vegas on Highway 91 sometime in the first half of 1945? That's a story with at least three versions.

Siegel gets credit in the first version. It was he, so he said, who took Moe Sedway to the site a few miles south of the city's last humble settlements, where the desert resumed and two-lane Route 91 wove its lonely way to L.A. Siegel was in the driver's seat, Sedway in the passenger seat. "Here it is, Moe," Siegel supposedly said.[1]

Sedway saw a few ramshackle outbuildings, one with a faded sign that read "Cottages." "For God's sake, Ben," Sedway said, "what is it?"

"Thirty three acres, Moe," Bugsy chortled. "Thirty three acres for a few nickels and dimes."

In this version, taken up by actor Warren Beatty for his

1991 film *Bugsy*, Siegel rhapsodized about the potential of these acres to give rise to "the god damnedest biggest hotel and casino you ever saw."

"But for Christ's sake Ben," Sedway retorted, "miles out of town. Not a tree in sight, nothing but bugs and coyotes and heat."

Siegel admitted that the kind of place he had in mind might cost as much as $2 million to build. But Vegas was about to explode—Siegel could feel it. The highway from L.A. was better paved, the drive time shorter. For long-distance gamblers, commercial aviation now offered direct flights from New York and other far-flung venues: no more stopovers, and half the flying time. Within the casinos lay another great comfort: cool air. Until 1945, the casinos of Vegas had had to rely on "swamp coolers," modestly effective in public spaces, but of no help in guest bedrooms. That year the Carrier Corporation brought out in-room units that cooled, humidified, and dehumidified. Now all Vegas needed was an end to the war, so that homecoming soldiers could get their share of the fun.

Version 2 put Lansky in the driver's seat, with Siegel beside him and Sedway nowhere to be seen. Years later, Lansky told his trio of Israeli biographers it was he, not Siegel, who first noticed the thirty-three-acre lot for sale south of Vegas and took Siegel to it. Siegel was "too busy being a Hollywood playboy," Lansky scoffed. "What I had in mind was to build the greatest, most luxurious hotel casino in the world."[2] In Version 2, Lansky was the visionary, bringing to bear his years of building clubs, casinos, and tracks on the Florida Gold Coast. Siegel had no idea how to build a hotel, much less a hotel-casino. He would just be the front man, making Lansky's dream come true.

Then there was Version 3, in which none of the aforementioned was in the car at all. That's the version the facts support.

In Version 3, the visionary was one Billy Wilkerson, a nightclub owner and publishing magnate who took note of the For

Sale sign on his way to the Las Vegas airport, homebound to L.A. after a ruinous stretch at the gaming tables. He saw it in January 1945, long before Siegel, Sedway, and Lansky claimed to have seen it. The story of how Wilkerson got to that point, and where his fate then led him, is told by the entrepreneur's son W. R. Wilkerson III, in *The Man Who Invented Las Vegas*, which has key documents and canceled checks to make its case.[3]

The dapper Wilkerson had sailed through the 1920s with a series of New York–based movie jobs, and decided in the fall of 1929 to drive his family to Hollywood, where the opportunities seemed greater. When a friend told him to play the market at rock bottom, he had done just that, only to learn how low rock bottom could go.[4] He went west anyway, all but broke, and took charge of a trade magazine catering to the only legitimate business making money at that time: Hollywood. Soon his *Hollywood Reporter* was a powerhouse, intimidating studio heads to advertise or face having their movies panned or, worse yet ignored.

Blessed with a flair for style, Wilkerson went on to establish nightclubs and restaurants that defined L.A. in the thirties: the Trocadero, Ciro's, LaRue, Vendome, and L'Aiglon. He dressed the part, cultivating a waxed mustache and wearing white tails.[5] Siegel frequented those haunts and surely had a back-slapping friendship with the dapper club owner; when Siegel was being catered to in jail in the fall of 1940, his dinners were sent from Ciro's. Wilkerson's own meals tended to consist of canned sardines on toast and deviled-egg sandwiches.[6] Some bettors had lucky rabbits' feet; Wilkerson had his strangely Spartan cuisine, his own superstition to help him win at the gaming tables.

Unfortunately, Wilkerson was more than a run-of-the-mill gambler. He was a compulsive, hour-after-hour gambling addict, capable of winning, but more often of losing, tens of thousands of dollars at private gaming tables in southern California. He went daily, as well, to one of the horse tracks: Santa Anita, Hollywood Park, or the new Del Mar, opened in 1937. He and

Siegel probably met at the track, too. The difference between them was that Siegel's race tips were usually better.

Wilkerson often staggered away from the gaming tables trailing handwritten IOUs, some on toilet paper, that the *Hollywood Reporter* and his nightclubs had to pay, to the detriment of his employees' paychecks.[7] When Earl Warren as state attorney general cracked down on offshore gambling ships, Wilkerson took to flying to Las Vegas for its rustic—and legal—casinos. Like Siegel and Lansky, he hated the desert. But that was where the casinos were. He couldn't live without them.

Wilkerson's losses only deepened, until the dark year of 1944, when he lost even more: $1 million. The notion of owning his own casino came from one of Wilkerson's friends. It was a perfect solution for a gambling addict. The money lost would be like play money, reimbursed by the house. All Wilkerson had to do was stay out of *other* casinos.[8]

By the time he stopped beside that stretch of desert in January 1945, Wilkerson had begun dreaming up a "mammoth" hotel-casino complex. He had Monte Carlo in mind: a lavish and exclusive resort that would pull in the high rollers yet also appeal to the hoi polloi. He figured the cost to buy the land and build might be as much as $1.2 million.[9]

On that fateful day, Wilkerson walked a bit of the property, and his black mood began to lift. By his own account, Wilkerson negotiated with the property's owner, Margaret M. Folsom, a former brothel keeper in Hawaii. He agreed to give her a check for $9,500 for ten of the thirty-three acres. He waited a month to buy the rest of the land until his lawyer, Greg Bautzer, a future high-profile Hollywood litigator, returned from active duty in the U.S. Navy to finalize the deal.[10]

Apparently, Folsom came to appreciate the value of her remaining acreage to Wilkerson. Bautzer negotiated as best he could, but ended up buying the land on Wilkerson's behalf for a hefty $84,000.[11] The deed for those remaining twenty-three

acres would not change hands until September 15, 1945, however. Wilkerson needed to raise capital for the balance of that
purchase price, and for the architectural plans.

Wilkerson knew nothing about how to run a hotel-casino
complex, so he enlisted two local casino operators, Moe Sedway and Gus Greenbaum, apparently unaware, as yet, that both
were backed by Meyer Lansky and Bugsy Siegel. He suggested
that Sedway and Greenbaum run the place in exchange for a
share of the profits. The two were happy to oblige.[12]

Wilkerson felt sure he could raise the capital he needed at
the gaming tables of nearby casinos. Instead, in April, he lost
more than $200,000 in short order. To his new partners, he
wrote a candid letter steeped in despair. "I have become convinced that Las Vegas is too dangerous for me. I like gambling
too much, like to shoot craps and drive myself nuts and the only
way I can defeat it is to keep away from any place that has it."[13]

Though it tore him up, Wilkerson decided to sell the deed
to his partners, "an act of self-abnegation" as his lawyer and
friend Bautzer put it. They promised to make him a co-owner,
and give him a fair share of the spoils. Accordingly, on September 15, 1945, Sedway and Greenbaum bought the deed from
Wilkerson. Two months later, possibly after a stretch of sobri-
ety, Wilkerson declared he wanted to buy the deed back. The
war was over, and he felt a new sense of excitement about what
that would bring. Sedway and Greenbaum agreed, suggesting
that neither they nor Lansky was yet sold on the prospect of
building a mammoth hotel-casino. Better, they felt, to spend
$250,000 sprucing up the newly acquired El Cortez.[14] The
deed was returned to Wilkerson for some amount of money on
November 21.

Back in charge, Wilkerson bulldozed the shacks on the old
Folsom place in December 1945 and oversaw plans for a compound he had taken to calling the Hotel Wilkerson. It had six
buildings, including stores, a beauty parlor, and a health club.

The casino itself would be the hub of the compound: better to snare gamblers from all directions. It would have no clocks, Wilkerson decreed, and no windows. Chronic gambler that he was, Wilkerson knew the value of keeping gamblers in a fevered state, oblivious to the passage of time. Whether the casino and its neighboring structures would be connected or separate would soon be a matter of great significance.[15]

The more Wilkerson schemed, the more splendid his vision became. The Hotel Wilkerson would have a nine-hole golf course, stables for forty-five horses, squash courts, a health club, a gym, and a humongous pool. It would have private bungalows, as at the Beverly Hills Hotel, and 250 rooms, and it would be five stories higher than any other in Las Vegas. All this would cost . . . a lot. By the start of 1946, Wilkerson landed a bank loan for $600,000, and aviation entrepreneur Howard Hughes contributed another $200,000 in exchange for a year's worth of advertising in the *Hollywood Reporter* for his RKO film projects. Wilkerson figured he could earn the rest at Las Vegas' gaming tables.[16]

Again he was wrong. After another cold stretch at the tables in January 1946, Wilkerson needed another investor, this one very deep-pocketed. He found one through the boys, as he called Sedway and Greenbaum. G. Harry Rothberg was a former bootlegger who, with his brother Sam, had gone legit after Prohibition and formed the American Distilling Company. But the Rothbergs were open to doing some profitable business by fronting for Meyer Lansky.[17]

Rothberg, with no mention of Lansky, made a remarkable offer. He would give Wilkerson $1 million in exchange for a two-thirds interest in the Hotel Wilkerson. All creative decisions would be Wilkerson's. And when the hotel-casino opened, in March 1947, Wilkerson would be the front man and sole operator, charming guests and nurturing the press. Rothberg, Sedway, and Greenbaum would stay in the shadows as silent backers, with Lansky even more obscured. Wilkerson agreed, as long as all parties understood the land would stay his own. He wasn't selling the site to anyone, under any circumstances. The deal was struck in late February 1946, and Rothberg wrote Wilkerson a check for $1 million.[18]

Wilkerson's son suggests that his father was the one who changed the name of the Hotel Wilkerson to the Flamingo. "He . . . had a particular liking for exotic birds and even named some of his projects after them, like his restaurant L'Aiglon in Beverly Hills. It was no coincidence that one of his favorite nightspots was the Stork Club in New York City."[19]

More likely, the man who changed the Hotel Wilkerson to the Flamingo was the one who made a surprise visit to the construction site in March 1946, accompanied by Sedway, Greenbaum, and Rothberg. With his slicked-back hair and double-breasted, pinstriped suit, he needed no introduction, at least not to Wilkerson. Ben Siegel had just come forward as the project's latest backer.[20]

Siegel was in a jovial, almost euphoric frame of mind, and why not? He was about to sell the El Cortez, turning a profit for the Syndicate in the mere year or so since he had bought it. The money from its sale—$766,000—was probably the capital Siegel had just persuaded Lansky to invest in the Hotel Wilkerson.

That day, Siegel heaped praise upon his new and somewhat wary partner. Wilkerson was his idol, he declared. He loved Ciro's and Trocadero and L'Aiglon. These were the joints that made L.A. what it was. All he wanted was to be of help, in whatever small way he could. To help and to learn from the master. Later, a business partner of Wilkerson's, Tom Seward, put it more succinctly. "Siegel did not want to be like Billy," Seward recalled of Siegel and Wilkerson. "He literally wanted to *be* Billy."[21]

Though he might be a hindrance, Siegel did have contacts

that could be of help in rounding up scarce postwar construction materials. He made calls to Hollywood heavyweights and got them to part with stage set supplies. Other sources brought in cement, steel girders, copper tubing, and Italian marble. Apparently he had help from Nevada senator Pat McCarran, who "reprioritized" the state's building needs to accommodate construction of what was now being called the Flamingo Hotel.[22]

Virginia Hill's long, flamingo-like legs were said by some to be the inspiration for the Hotel Wilkerson's new name. With alcohol, especially tequila, Hill was said to blush dramatically, another flamingo connection. Yet another explanation had nothing to do with Hill at all. Siegel made frequent trips to Miami to do business with Lansky, and the two men liked to sit out at the Hialeah track, watching flocks of pink flamingos in the infield. "Not only was the flamingo a beautiful and exotic bird," suggests Stephen Birmingham in *The Rest of Us*, his epic narrative of immigrant eastern Europeans, "but, it was said, the Seminole Indians believed the flamingo was a symbol of good luck, and that to kill a flamingo was to invite misfortune. What better name for the ultimate gambling palace?"[23] Whatever the reason, the project's new name was a first indication that Wilkerson's backers had plans of their own, plans that might not square with his.

News of Siegel's arrival blew through Vegas like a desert sandstorm, stirring stories that might be true—or not. One was that when Siegel tried to open an account at a local bank, he was asked to take his business elsewhere. "A couple days later," recalled a local, "he walks to the bank, a couple bodyguards with him, swaggers up to the window and says, 'I want to make a deposit.' He empties a suitcase with a million dollars out on the counter—and they took the money!"[24]

Louis Wiener Jr., a local lawyer, was immersed in documents at his office when his secretary announced a visitor. He recognized Siegel when the gangster came in, with his matinee good looks and a stomach so flat you could bounce quarters on it, as Wiener later put it. "I just bought into the Flamingo Hotel and I want to hire you to represent me," Siegel declared. Wiener had once beaten him in a lawsuit, and Siegel hadn't forgotten, or so the story went. Warily, Wiener said he would have to consult his partners before he could take Siegel on as a client. "I'll tell you what," Siegel said. "I'll give you twenty-five thousand dollars a year as a retainer." Wiener was stunned: that was the equivalent of about $500,000 today. "Sure," he said weakly. "Why not?"[25]

Wiener found his new client meticulous. "He carried a pocket diary or notebook and he would ask me five, six, even ten questions a day, and I had to write him a separate answer for every question on my letterhead." The reason he did that, Wiener said, was that he didn't want any confusion later on. "I don't ever want any question being raised about you being right or wrong," said Siegel. "Nobody's going to be able to say you gave me the wrong advice when you didn't." Only later did it occur to Wiener that Siegel wasn't doing this to protect himself. He was doing it for Wiener. "I mean, he never said this but I think he was trying to protect me against criticism from his associates back east. He didn't want me to ever be put on the spot, and ever be blamed."

Siegel did have one eccentricity, his new lawyer learned. "He didn't care what you charged him to go someplace or do something, but your expenses had to be exact. If you spent two dollars and seventy-six cents for something, he didn't want you to charge him two eighty or two seventy-five; he wanted it to be two seventy-six." This was not to say Siegel was frugal, far from it. "As a matter of fact," Wiener recalled, "he used to get upset with me because I wouldn't go to better places, to better hotels, take taxicabs, do this, do that. I could have charged him five hundred dollars a day for going to San Francisco and it wouldn't have meant a thing, because that was what I thought I was worth.

But if I went to Bernstein's and I paid two dollars and seventy-six cents for something and it was really two dollars and forty-six cents he probably would have raised hell with me."[26]

John Cahlan, the pioneering Vegas journalist, was still on the beat when Siegel came in to the *Las Vegas Review-Journal* to announce that he was building the Flamingo. Cahlan began to see Siegel at Lenny Schafer's Health Club, and the two became fellow gym rats. Siegel was warm and gregarious, and of course dressed up nattily when his workout was done. "He was a perfect gentleman, a very good dresser, very immaculate," though, as Cahlan noted, "he hated any blemish on his skin, he had to get rid of it."[27] It was an odd fixation for a man who left his shooting victims in dramatically blemished states.

"I got to know him quite well," Cahlan added. "The fact of the matter is, I assisted him in getting his liquor license for the Flamingo." It was a license Siegel almost failed to get, given his reputation, and one for which the liquor license board would be given a carload of beer by Lansky at Siegel's request, prior to the board's vote in favor of granting the license. But that was the least of Siegel's problems.[28]

Within weeks, the relationship between Wilkerson and Siegel soured. Despite the agreement that Wilkerson make all creative decisions, Siegel started making his own, and undoing the legendary restauranteur's. "Siegel did not know a bidet from a Bordeaux, much less marbles from Italy," recalled Tom Seward. "Bill showed him everything." As much as Siegel needed Wilkerson, he resented him. "As time went on," wrote Wilkerson's son, "the gangster's respectful admiration disintegrated into an insane, all-consuming jealousy."[29]

To Wilkerson's amazement, Siegel started ordering the workmen around. Trucks rolled past the front gate, got their deliveries checked in by Siegel himself, then rolled out the back gates an hour or two later, to come through the front gates all over again. Siegel had no idea he was checking in his supply trucks twice, and so paying double or triple for those precious, postwar supplies.[30]

With Wilkerson more and more of a hindrance, Siegel announced a decision that made him the on-site boss. With Lansky's blessing, he created the Nevada Projects Corporation, formalized on June 20, 1946, for the explicit purpose of building a hotel-casino according to Siegel's vision, not Wilkerson's. Lest there be any doubt, Siegel named himself president, with the others mere shareholders.

How many shares the other investors got was commensurate to some degree with how much money they kicked in, but not exactly. The Rothberg brothers together were awarded 245 shares, in recognition of their $1 million investment. Siegel was the largest individual owner, with 195 shares. Wilkerson was awarded 125 shares while Lansky got 100. The initial offering raised $500,000.[31] This outcome was so pleasing that Siegel would sell shares again and again, shares that didn't exist. As for Wilkerson, he was persuaded to sell half of the property after all, in exchange for an extra clump of stock. At least the new agreement kept him in charge of construction for the casino. The hotel would be Siegel's domain. Within days, two separate teams of architects and builders were hard at work in two separate camps.

Utterly ignorant of hotel construction, Siegel began making disastrous mistakes. Wiener got a frantic call one day. His new client was apoplectic. The hotel's structure had been roughed out, with its ninety-three guest rooms, and Siegel's penthouse built atop it. Siegel had gone up to see it for the first time and nearly banged his head on a structural beam that ran across the ceiling. The architect and his crew were short enough that they could cross the room without running into the beam. So, as it happened, was Wiener. But not Siegel, or anyone else taller than five-foot-nine. "Tear that goddamn thing out of here," Siegel shouted. The crew had to take the roof off, redesign it, and remove the low beam, Wiener recalled, at a cost of $22,500.[32]

Another calamity occurred with the kitchen. A massive industrial kitchen was put in, but the ovens took too much space. "If you turn around in here you'll fry your ass," Siegel declared. As a result, the kitchen's walls had to be pushed out a critical foot or two, at a reported cost of $30,000.

The costliest mistake came with the boiler room, which proved too small for the units it had to accommodate. "I bet the concrete walls at the Flamingo must have been fourteen inches thick at least," Wiener recalled. "When they went to put the boilers in, they couldn't get them in because the rooms were too small and the hall too narrow. So they had to put the boiler room about 200 feet away, and build a structure around it." That mistake cost $115,000.[33]

Despite Siegel's agreement to stick to hotel construction, Wilkerson began noting Virginia Hill's hand in the casino's interiors. She picked out the oversized draperies that turned out to be fire hazards, and the lime-green and tomato-red tufted leather sofas and overstuffed chairs that simply looked gauche. Certainly she did nothing to encourage moderation.[34]

As a temporary residence, Siegel and Hill took the penthouse of the Last Frontier Hotel, just north on Route 91. From there they studied the Flamingo's blueprints and held meetings. Once, architect Richard Stadelman arrived to find the two in bed. Told to draw up a chair, he saw they were covered by a single sheet, and utterly nude under it, reminiscent of Siegel's barbershop style.[35]

Down the road at the construction site, a far grander penthouse suite was being built for the Flamingo's royal couple, now that the offending beam had been removed. The décor was definitely Hill's: over the top. Siegel added his own, more practical touch: an escape route starting from the coat closet.

"This led to a labyrinth of secret passageways and staircases," explained Wilkerson's son. "Although many of (the hotel's) staircases led nowhere, if you knew the layout, it was possible to descend to the garage and a waiting getaway car in less than a minute."[36]

The Nevada Projects Corporation could not have been floated a moment too soon. The money raised by its owners went right to Del Webb, Siegel's handpicked builder for the hotel to pay down the huge construction bills of $436,100 in just three months. Already, Wilkerson's back-of-the-envelope estimate of $1.2 million to build the Flamingo was looking not just unrealistic but absurd.

To no one's surprise, Siegel's marriage came to a formal end that summer. Ben and Esther had led separate lives for at least a year. Esther's only joy was her daughters—Millicent a teenager now, Barbara nearly so—though both were difficult, hurt by their father's all-too-frequent absence.

Esther knew about Virginia Hill. She had suffered any number of Siegel's affairs, but sensed early on that Hill got to her husband as no other woman had. Esther had asked Meyer Lansky to do what he could to talk sense to his old friend, and Lansky had tried, going so far as to visit Joe Epstein in Chicago. Epstein told Lansky it was hopeless. "Once that girl is under your skin, it's like a cancer. It's incurable." Lansky relayed the message to Esther, and added that he had seen Siegel and Hill together. "They're like two teenagers in love," Lansky told Siegel's wife. "There's nothing you can do about it."[37]

Lansky's advice was to threaten to sue for divorce and hope that that brought her husband around. Doc Stacher, Lansky's right-hand man, said Esther did just that—to no avail. "Siegel showed not the slightest remorse. . . . Bugsy's feelings for Virginia seemed to get stronger every day they were together."[38]

Finally, in the spring of 1946, Esther went to Reno to file

for a divorce and start the requisite six-week residency. The girls would divide their summer between an aunt in Los Angeles, Siegel's sister Bessie, and at the Last Frontier with their father, lolling by the pool and riding horses as he held stormy meetings at the new project and gnashed his teeth at rising construction costs. If Esther Siegel ever said how she felt about letting her daughters spend the summer with their father's inamorata, that sentiment was not publicly recorded.

Regretful as he was to break up his family, Siegel couldn't imagine living without Hill. All he could do was atone for his sins, giving his wife the biggest settlement he could handle. He committed to $600 a week in alimony for life, plus hundreds more for child support. Meyer Lansky, divorcing at about the same time, persuaded Anna Citron to accept a mere $400 a month for alimony, with $300 a week for child support.[39]

Siegel not only paid child support: he bought his family a good-sized apartment on Central Park West in Manhattan. Esther got full custody, though Siegel could visit the girls whenever he liked.

Months later, Siegel would sheepishly ask his ex-wife for a loan of $45,000. Esther would lend him the money, only to learn, soon after, that her ex-husband would never be able to pay her back. Nor would he write her another weekly check for $600. But all that was in the future: on August 3, 1946, she knew only that her marriage of seventeen years was over, the papers signed that day.

Sure as he was that Virginia Hill was the love of his life, Siegel was stricken with a sense of guilt he'd never felt before. Esther was the very picture of the woman his parents had wanted him to marry: decent, honest, loyal, adoring, and a loving, responsible mother. She had been faithful to him in every way. Now she had suffered the pain of her divorce without any public show of bitterness. Loyalty was Siegel's touchstone, always. He never hesitated to kill disloyal gangsters, but here was Esther, more loyal to him than anyone he'd ever known, and how did he repay her? By tearing their marriage apart.

The signatures on Ben and Esther Siegel's divorce were barely dry when another drama erupted, this one a dire business threat. The federal government was studying the Flamingo's architectural plans, and it didn't like what it saw. Siegel had settled most of his problems with a gun. Now he found himself up against an adversary that was, in every sense, bulletproof. And what that adversary wanted was to close the Flamingo down.

9

◆◆◆◆◆◆

His Every Red Cent at Risk

THE FIRST SIGN of trouble had come with a telegram dated April 23, 1946, from a new federal agency called the Civilian Production Administration. The CPA's agenda was to help veterans build homes by steering scarce construction materials to them, and not to commercial, inessential new structures—like hotel-casinos in Las Vegas.[1]

In fact, the CPA had set national guidelines that went into effect on March 26. Any project not yet started by that date would be deemed in violation of the mandate. The Flamingo's builders had ignored that edict. And so had come the telegram four weeks later, sent directly to the Flamingo, demanding an immediate halt to construction. The Flamingo consisted of several structures, the CPA declared, further violation of U.S. government rules. In this tender postwar economy, one was the limit.

Siegel's lawyer Louis Wiener, eager to prove himself worthy of his generous retainer, had flown to Reno on April 29 to plead the Flamingo's case with the CPA's regional manager. He explained that the Flamingo had broken ground on December 4 of the previous year, when the shacks were razed. He argued that the project was one large, horseshoe-shaped building, as shown by a blueprint dated January 1946. He also noted that based on the county permit issued in January, the builders had spent $444,000 to date. How were they supposed to get that money back if the project was nixed?

The CPA manager in Reno listened with a sympathetic ear and gave the Flamingo's builders written approval to forge ahead, pending a formal review that summer.[2]

The ruling pleased local authorities in Las Vegas eager to see a jobs-generating and tax-producing project go ahead. It certainly pleased U.S. Senator Pat McCarran, the recipient of weighty campaign contributions from Siegel and an unabashed supporter of mob-financed projects in Nevada.[3] It infuriated a top FBI agent named A. E. Ostholthoff, who viewed the Flamingo as a rising monument to organized crime, and Siegel as a murderous affront to justice.

Ostholthoff was in close and frequent touch with his director, J. Edgar Hoover, the two of them communicating by memo in the terse, cryptic style Hoover had crafted over the years. Ostholthoff studied the telegram of April 23. He read CPA regional head E. S. Bender's rationale for letting the Flamingo go ahead. He strongly suspected that Bender had been bribed. The builders had done no more than put sticks in the ground when the March 26 freeze order went into effect. And any fool could see there were at least three structures rising on the site. Ostholthoff was determined to shut down the Flamingo for operating under false auspices, and throw Siegel in jail while he was at it.

With Hoover's blessing, Ostholthoff ordered full-scale surveillance of Siegel and the Flamingo, starting in July 1946. His team of ten full-time agents put a "technical" surveillance bug into penthouse suite 401 of the Last Frontier Hotel on Route 91, where Siegel and Virginia Hill were residing while the Flamingo rose nearby. The agents soon learned that Siegel was using a rear office above the boiler room at the nearby Las Vegas Club to conduct his business, with four phone lines. Those lines were put under surveillance, too.

The FBI agents stood out in Vegas like comic-book characters, with their buzz cuts, black suits, narrow black ties, and "yes, sir" "no, ma'am" speech. As a result, news of the bugging of Bugsy reached its quarry almost immediately. In teletypes to headquarters, Ostholthoff bemoaned the scarcity of useful information from the technicals. The gangsters' boiler room talk was as terse and telegraphic as the FBI's internal memos, and Siegel and Hill kept to small talk in their penthouse suite. If the bug there picked up snatches of their love life, the FBI agents made no mention of it in the updates now sent almost daily to the FBI's top brass.

In a black-and-white photograph, A. E. Ostholthoff looks like a central-casting FBI agent, his dark hair neatly combed back, a patterned tie tightly knotted, his starched white shirt set off by a white handkerchief. Yet the head-and-shoulders shot shows a hint of swagger in his choice of a double-breasted dark suit with extra-wide stripes: a counterpart, almost a photographic negative, to Siegel with his own trademark suits.[4] Officially, Ostholthoff was special agent in charge of the FBI office in Cincinnati. In fact, he was one of Hoover's top men.

In his teletypes, Ostholthoff did his best to stir the director with lurid details about Siegel. "He has never engaged in honest toil," Ostholthoff wrote, "and does not legitimately have available the large sum of money so far spent in the construction of the Flamingo Hotel."[5] Ostholthoff added that it was possible that Siegel was the kingpin narcotics distributor of the West, a charge the FBI would make often in the months to come. No evidence of trafficking would ever emerge, however.

As for Siegel's consort, Virginia Hill was "a fabulous woman of mystery in L.A.," Ostholthoff wrote, "who has unlimited funds at her disposal." Hill, too, was deemed a likely trafficker.[6] "Virginia Hill is said to be in constant touch with dope dealers in the L.A. area." Again, no evidence arose. Also, Ostholthoff noted, "Virginia Hill wears daring clothes, smokes and drinks excessively, uses foul language, considerable make-up, spends money, and is promiscuous."

Ostholthoff had no doubt, he told Hoover, that Siegel had bribed various officials to push the Flamingo along. Nor did he doubt that Siegel would bribe or kill anyone else who stood in the way of his dream. But proving bribery of an elected official like McCarran would mean showing the money had bought a specific favor in return, and wasn't just a campaign contribution. "In other words," Ostholthoff wrote Hoover, "we must prove intent."[7]

As the Civilian Production Administration's formal review loomed that August, the Flamingo's construction bills soared, forcing Siegel to forage for cash. His best chance lay in making Trans-American a monopoly race wire by knocking out Continental Press. Siegel had made a fortune in Vegas with his Continental Press franchise. But James Ragen still owned the rest of Continental and seemed disinclined to sell it at any price. By the late spring of 1946, Siegel and the Chicago mob were opening Trans-American wire offices all over the country, competing with Continental. But they wanted the rest of Continental, too. This was a messy and embarrassing situation, so the Chicago mob, and apparently Siegel, agreed that James Ragen had to go.

That April, Ragen barely eluded a car full of hit men. Rather than retire summarily from the race wire business, he hired more bodyguards, to no avail. On June 24, 1946, Ragen was driving in rush hour along Chicago's State Street, alone in his car with his bodyguards in a car behind him. "A shabby old truck pulled alongside Ragen's auto," recounts historian Allan May. "As he waited for the light to change, a tarpaulin on the left side of the truck was pulled up and two shotguns blasted away, riddling Ragen's upper right arm and shoulder."[8]

Tough old bird that he was, Ragen survived the onslaught and was rushed to a hospital. He began to recover, only to have his kidneys fail. Still in the hospital, he was rushed into surgery on August 8 but died six days later. An autopsy revealed traces of mercury in his blood. In all likelihood, a doctor or nurse hired by the mob had crept into Ragen's hospital room and administered the deadly dose.[9]

Though it fell beyond their purview, the FBI agents now tapping Siegel's phones had no doubt that Siegel and his uneasy ally, Jack Dragna, knew exactly who and what had killed Ragen. In a phone chat within hours of Ragen's death, one of them told the other the good news: Ragen had been poisoned. "Both men laughed heartily at this discussion of Ragen's death," the FBI transcript noted. Dragna closed the conversation by saying he would let others know what a good job "the doctor" had done.[10]

More than money was needed to keep the Flamingo rising from Nevada's desert sands. From Washington, D.C., that August came a distinctly chilly missive from the Civilian Production Administration. The CPA, Siegel reported to Lansky in disbelief, was issuing "an order to cease building immediately or they will indict us criminally." This, despite the April go-ahead from E. S. Bender in the CPA's Reno office. "Now they tell us this order supersedes their April order!"[11]

Siegel would just have to make the best of it. He would have to work with lawyers and architects, and humbly appear before the CPA's regional offices in San Francisco. A first meeting was scheduled for mid-August.

If the commissioners could still be bribed, of course, Siegel was all for it. Knowing his phone was tapped, he tried to convey that in coded language to his somewhat slow-witted sidekick, Moe Sedway.

"Did you get that money from the places like I told you?"[12] Siegel asked Sedway in an August phone call recorded by the FBI.

"The what?"

"The money!"

"From where?"

"From the place where we made up you were to get it from."

"Yeah."

"Do you know what I'm talking about, Moey?"

"No, I don't."

"Well, did we discuss about you getting it?"

"I don't remember, just tell me."

"You have a wonderful memory. I only discussed one thing about getting some money with you for you to give some people. Don't you know where you are supposed to get it from?"

"The four thousand."

"Four thousand! Am I getting the four thousand, Moey?"

"Huh?"

"Well, what does the four thousand got to do with giving money to some people."

"Oh, you mean—I know what you mean."

"Do you get it?"

"No, I don't get it. He don't want to give no money."

"Why don't he want to give?"

"He says he don't have to give no commissioners any money. . . ."

"Alright," Siegel relented. "Don't give anybody anything."[13]

The CPA had Siegel rattled. He needed to blow off steam, and Meyer Lansky seemed resigned to listening by long distance. "I should have busted a leg before I got into this thing," Siegel told him on the phone one day. "Every time I go, I see something this jerk did, you know: contracts he signed."

One day the target of Siegel's ire was Sedway. The next day it might be Gus Greenbaum or Billy Wilkerson. Either way, the story was always the same. Siegel's partners got everything wrong, and Siegel had to fix their mistakes. "Got an ice machine for $18,000, makes 20 tons of ice a day . . . we need two. And it needs four guys to make the ice! All he is is a lot of headaches."[14]

Lansky was too discreet to note that the worst mistakes, the three-alarm headaches, were all Siegel's.

By now, Billy Wilkerson, the wax-mustached entrepreneur, wanted out as much as Siegel wanted him out. But he didn't want to just walk away, not when he owned a hefty chunk of the Nevada Projects Corporation and part of the land under which the Flamingo sat. In June, Siegel had browbeaten Wilkerson into selling him half the land for an additional 5 percent of the Nevada Projects Corporation. By August, Siegel was pushing to buy the remaining half of the land for another 5 percent in corporate stock. Again, Wilkerson acquiesced. He deeply regretted letting the land go, but he now owned 48 percent of the Nevada Projects Corporation, which was to say 48 percent of the Flamingo.[15] With a rational business partner, the future should have looked bright. But Siegel was hardly a rational partner.

Everything depended on the CPA, and on Siegel's ability to charm the commissioners in a meeting scheduled for August 13 in San Francisco.

The CPA's investigators had paced the Flamingo site more than once. It certainly seemed to them that the complex consisted of more than one building, and that the hotel in particular stood on its own, apart from the casino. But the builders showed their original blueprint of January 12, 1946, noting that it called for one large, horseshoe-shaped building. That was the project the CPA had approved in April, Siegel declared.

For a hearing likely to be rancorous, the commissioners brought in a neutral party as overseer and kept him under wraps before the meeting. Somehow, Siegel learned who he was: Stanford law professor William Owens. FBI surveillance picked up a conversation in which Siegel asked someone, in regard to Owens, "How we can get to him?" The FBI agents were concerned enough to meet privately with Owens, but the professor said no one had approached him.[16]

The meeting lasted some hours. When it was done, A. E. Ostholthoff and his fellow FBI agents were chagrined to hear Owens declare the CPA's case weak. Owens gave the government agency a choice: drop it or come back on September 5 with persuasive new evidence. The CPA chose to reconvene.

A. E. Ostholthoff suspected that the whole hearing "may have been a cover-up as they obviously did not present much of a case," he reported. He was no less irked that the Flamingo's builders now planned to erect a high fence around the hotel "in order that no one can see what is going on there." Duly blocked from sight, builder Del Webb's team poured concrete walls and floors, and added roofs that would physically connect all of the buildings. "They feel that this will completely fool the CPA," Ostholthoff wrote in disgust.[17]

Days before the September 5 meeting at which the Flamingo's fate would be decided, an FBI informant reported a fascinating meeting with Siegel that showed how vulnerable the gangster felt. Judging from how the talk turned out, the informant might well have been Professor Owens, who could honestly report that no one had approached him when the FBI asked earlier but seemed the likely contact now. In the interim, Siegel had made some calls and concluded that Owens was an "alright guy." He had learned, too, that the CPA would pay Owens just $25 a day for his expertise. "Why don't we pay him $100 and have him work for us?" Siegel said, only half joking.[18]

The FBI informant, at any rate, reported getting a call on

August 29 from someone whose voice he failed to recognize. "This is your cousin from San Francisco," the caller said. The caller asked the informant to meet him at the intersection of Eighth Street and Wilshire Boulevard in L.A. The informant realized that he was speaking with Ben Siegel, and agreed to meet with him. After hanging up, the informant tipped off the FBI, then drove as directed. When he arrived at the intersection, he noticed a car parked there, and on approaching it found that it contained Ben Siegel.

Siegel declined to talk either in his own car or the informant's. Instead, he asked the informant to go for a walk with him.

"Siegel was of the opinion that he was being persecuted by the government in connection with the construction of the hotel," the FBI reported of the conversation. "He told the informant that every red cent he owned in the world was invested in the Flamingo. If the project was not permitted to continue, he would be ruined financially."

The informant was actually quite sympathetic to Siegel, and said as much to the FBI. He stated that as far as he was concerned, Siegel's background did not enter into the picture. Whether it was "Siegel or the King of Siam," the informant continued, "the hotel [is] completely dependent on one point: the stage of construction on March 26." Siegel just needed detailed plans to show when construction began and prove, in the process, that the Flamingo was one building, not several. If Siegel could bring those plans to the CPA's follow-up meeting, the informant felt all would go well.[19]

On the morning of the CPA review—September 5, 1946— Siegel convened a war room in his suite at San Francisco's St. Francis hotel. There he met with his lawyers and architects in advance of the 1:00 P.M. CPA meeting. The FBI was listening in; its agents had bugged his suite, along with an adjacent one occupied by Virginia Hill.

The main topic of war room debate was who should take

the stand and make the case that construction had started before March 26. One candidate was declared too nice, another not suitably informed. The consensus pick seemed to be an architect from Del Webb's office, though he seemed reluctant. "Here's one thing I don't want you to ask me and that is how the two buildings connect," he declared, "because I don't know!"[20]

Siegel and his war cabinet trooped over to the CPA offices for a meeting that went on all afternoon without a verdict. That night in Siegel's suite back at the St. Francis, a marathon card game commenced. Siegel groused that he had lost $200,000 in the stock market in the previous three days. But that only whetted his appetite to win it back at poker. The game went on until 4:15 A.M., the FBI duly reported.

The CPA was to meet again on September 6, but the meeting was postponed to September 12, in order to get the opinion of a "non-interested" architect whose name would be held until the start of the final day of deliberations. "They are going to indict us now so what's the difference," Siegel grumbled.[21]

The September 12 meeting started badly. The CPA's D.C. office relayed that in its judgment, the Flamingo was clearly three separate buildings. Siegel's team said no: the buildings were in fact connected by underground tunnels with foundations conjoining them. What about the outside windows and doors at either end of the casino and the Flamingo's hotel? Didn't they indicate separate buildings?[22]

To the surprise of many in the room, particularly FBI agent A. E. Ostholthoff, the architect brought in as a neutral party found Siegel's argument persuasive. He had no problem with the buildings being conjoined by their foundations. Builder Del Webb's team admitted construction on the hotel had not begun until April. But so what? All that mattered was that some other part of the project had gotten under way beforehand.[23]

After seven hours' deliberation, the CPA's San Francisco chairman announced his decision. The Flamingo was a single building, and construction had begun before the CPA's freeze order. Its builders could go forward after all.

Siegel had done more than stymie the CPA. He had won a battle against A. E. Ostholthoff, the FBI agent set on bringing him down. In effect, he had fought off the agent's boss too: J. Edgar Hoover. Not many targets of the FBI could make that claim.

Construction on the Flamingo had never stopped. Now, with the CPA appeased, it went into high gear, the bills piling ever higher. Sometime in late September, Del Webb, the builder, informed Siegel that he was owed nearly $500,000—again. Webb vowed to shut down construction and throw the Flamingo into bankruptcy if he wasn't paid soon.[24] Webb was the one who had a jarring chat with Siegel one night about how many men Siegel had killed. That was when Webb had turned pale, and Siegel had begun to laugh. "There's no chance that you'll get killed," he told the builder. "We only kill each other."[25]

Siegel knew the money they had sunk into the Flamingo was already approaching $4 million. Still, he felt the end was in sight. He needed a loan of $1.5 million, he figured. With that, he could get Webb to finish the hotel, and the Flamingo would open at last. But he knew that no bank would lend him even a fraction of the money he needed. He would have to get it from his East Coast associates.

In early October 1946, Siegel flew to New York. He stayed with his family at 88 Central Park West, as FBI surveillance confirmed, but spent most of his time selling his dream of the Flamingo to Syndicate leaders. He hung out at the Copacabana with Frank Costello, the Italian boss who, like Siegel and Lansky, had started on bootleg runs years ago for Arnold "The Brain" Rothstein. According to Costello's lawyer, George Wolf, the gangster heard Siegel's pleas and sympathized. Not long after Siegel's return to Vegas, the lawyer recounted, Costello sent an underling with $1 million in two suitcases of cash to the Flamingo.[26] Another version had Costello and others ponying up $3 million to Siegel.[27] Whatever the exact amount, Costello soon learned that Siegel needed even more. "What worried Frank was that many members of the mob had put in money on his say so," the mob lawyer recounted. "Now that crazy Bugsy in Vegas was swallowing up millions and the damn hotel would never be finished and even if it was, it would be so deep in the red it would go bankrupt."[28]

In a phone call with Meyer Lansky, Siegel shared his financial woes, perhaps hoping that Lansky might put in more money to get the Flamingo done. Instead, his old friend urged him to sell it at a loss and wash his hands of the whole thing. Siegel talked openly of doing that. If he gave Del Webb $250,000 in cash and the balance of $250,000 in corporate notes, maybe Webb would wipe the slate for bills due. Some unnamed third party might then take a hefty interest in the Flamingo. One story had Siegel flying west to Webb's office and dumping a case of cash on his desk: $400,000.[29]

If Siegel had hoped Del Webb would absolve the bills due for a case full of cash, he was mistaken. Some money must have changed hands, however, because Del Webb kept his men on the job, enough of them that the casino might still get finished by Siegel's self-imposed deadline of March 1947. Reportedly, Siegel also offered to sell the Trans-American race wire to get the Flamingo finished. "The problem was," suggests mafia historian Thomas Reppetto, "the Chicago mob thought they already owned it."[30]

That fall, A. E. Ostholthoff and his agents learned of a flight that Siegel and Hill took to Mexico. They felt sure the two were coordinating a big drug deal to pay Del Webb's mounting bills. But again, no evidence of drug trafficking surfaced.

A girlfriend of Virginia Hill had her own version of why Siegel and Hill made that trip to Mexico: to get married. "Siegel had bought a ruby and diamond ring," Hill's friend recalled, "and he slipped it on her finger. When the Spanish ceremony was over, they left there as man and wife." It was a $500 ring—$6,500 in today's dollars. For a woman who spent $10,000 on a dinner party, the ring was a trinket, but perhaps a sentimental one. Hill was thrilled, recounted her girlfriend in Bugsy biographer Dean Jennings's account, and declared, "I'll never take it off."[31]

By now the money pit was so deep that Siegel felt he might as well spend lavishly on the Flamingo's finishing touches. One flourish was an illuminated tower at the entrance that would be visible for miles around. Another was a moat, furnished with . . . pink flamingos.

"There were between six and eight of these birds," Ben's daughter Millicent later recalled, "and as the days went by, they were dropping like flies." The climate was just too hot for them. "My dad stood out there and said 'Those goddamned flamingoes are dying on me!' They never lasted very long. I think he replaced them once or twice and that was it."[32]

As Del Webb's bills kept mounting, Siegel spent as he pleased. Surprisingly, his personal expenses included worthy causes, particularly Jewish ones. The story of Meyer Lansky and his vigilantes breaking up Bund rallies before the war was one inspiration. In fact, most Jewish gangsters increased their giving to Jewish causes as the Holocaust's scale became known. Lansky gave generously to his synagogue, Temple Sinai in Hollywood, Florida, as well as to Brandeis University, as mafia historian Robert A. Rockaway notes. He gave more to the cause of creating a state of Israel.[33] So did Siegel, in a memorable scene recounted by Rockaway.

To help create and sustain a Jewish state, a seasoned military officer named Reuven Dafni came to L.A., raising funds from prominent Jews in the movie industry. One day he got a call from Siegel's pal and right-hand man, Allen Smiley. "Tell me what you're doing," Smiley said. "The boss is interested."

Dafni gave his pitch, and Smiley rang off. Shortly after, Dafni was directed to the back room of LaRue, a new Billy Wilkerson restaurant on Sunset Boulevard, recounts Rockaway. After a few pleasantries, Smiley left the room and two toughs walked in to check Dafni for weapons. Once they had left, Siegel entered. Dafni made his pitch for arms and money. "When he finished," Rockaway recounted, "Siegel asked, 'you mean to tell me the Jews are fighting?'

" 'Yes,' replied Dafni.

"Siegel, who was sitting across the table, leaned forward until the two men's foreheads were almost touching. 'You mean fighting, as in killing?' Siegel asked.

" 'Yes,' said Dafni.

"Siegel looked at him for a moment and said 'I'm with you.'

" 'From then on,' recalled Dafni, 'every week I got a phone call to go to the restaurant. And every week I received a suitcase filled with $5 and $10 bills. The payments continued until I left LA.' " Dafni guessed that Siegel contributed $50,000 in all to the cause.[34]

Giving to Israel was clearly gratifying to Siegel. In a way, though, it underscored just how desperate his financial straits were: $50,000 was a drop in the bucket in the grand scheme of his expenses, so why not help the Jews?

But was Siegel trying to help the Jews—or redeem himself? "Judaism has an innate sense that people regret evil, and crime, which is why we have Yom Kippur," suggests Peter Rubenstein, emeritus rabbi at Central Synagogue in Manhattan. "Of course, simply attending services means very little, nor does giving to good causes. If you're still killing people, giving to charity is not going to redress the balance. If you stop your crimes, then one could argue that maybe you could do good." But murder, he notes, is in a special category. "Only the victims can forgive the murderer, and they're not around. Which is to say the murderer really can't be forgiven." "God sentences Cain not to death," Rubenstein adds, "but to ceaseless wandering, friendless and alone." Ultimately, Siegel's only salvation was that his wandering wouldn't last for long.[35]

Still in a mood of atonement the night of November 28, 1946, as he flew from Las Vegas to L.A., Siegel asked a stewardess for a few sheets of writing paper and a pencil. Esther had written him to complain about Millicent's adolescent issues, and to point out that Ben was doing nothing to help. Siegel responded, in a schoolboy scrawl, at some length. His advice, coming from anyone else, would have sounded mundane. From a vicious killer, it was downright bizarre.

"Esta, I well realize the problem you have with the girls and you know that I always have and I always will do all I can to help you with them," Siegel began.

> Our love for them and our responsibility to them is something we will always share. So do not be so overwrought and feel that you are carrying the burden alone. Unfortunately, business interests have me so tied up that I cannot be with you to solve all the problems that come up in the rearing of two adolescents.
>
> First, you must remember that children do not automatically give parents respect—as you speak of your neglect to your father. Parents have to earn it. Now I know you have always acted in the very best interest of the children, and that you love them dearly. But sometimes we do not love too wisely and I suppose we are to blame for Millicent's misdeeds, too. As you yourself said she is a fine healthy smart child who I believe is going through a stage of antagonism towards us now, because we have constantly thwarted her. Perhaps a little more love and understanding on our part would be more helpful now than constant criticism and pun-

ishments. I dislike the idea of her dy[e]ing her hair as much as you do, but I think if you tell her that if she'll wait until she is seventeen, and if she still wants her hair lighter we will see to it that it will be done properly in a good beauty salon.

The same thing goes for the smoking. You know I never like you to smoke and yet you have for many years. So you see you must be more tolerant with her. I don't like the idea of her smoking at all, but I would rather we knew about it than have her cheat behind our backs. That is what you must impress upon her. Tell her she may have an occasional cigarette with you in the house to see if she really enjoys it. When she gets older she can then indulge in moderation if she so desires. I would point out to her that it is not at all ladylike or nice to smoke on the street, and that her home is far the better place.

Frankly, I hope she won't continue to smoke, and I dislike the habit in women, and when I see her I will tell her just that. As to her lying, you know that you, I and everyone else is guilty now and then of that habit. None of us likes to admit our faults, yet I feel that you, as the mother who is with her all the time, must be patient and more understanding and try to encourage her to confide in you about her boyfriends and all her social activities. As to her staying out so late, I do not approve of that either, except an occasion when something big is on. Firmly but pleasantly make her realize that you want the name and telephone number of her companion for the evening. This is in case she is unduly late for some reason, so that you can reassure yourself that she is all right. Tell her that you are doing this not to check up on her but because you love her and worry about her. You and she should also agree on a reasonable hour when you expect her home and if she doesn't live up to her part of the bargain then she can't go out on her next date.

And on it went. Some seventy years later, the letter hangs framed on a wall of Siegels 1941, a Bugsy-themed restaurant in the still-standing El Cortez casino, a testament to Ben Siegel's curious commitment to parenting. Just days later, he would show his dark side, all but threatening Billy Wilkerson with physical assault if his frazzled partner didn't do as he wished.

Wilkerson had watched Siegel make one mistake after another as his own expertise was ignored. A few days after finishing his fatherly letter to Esther, Siegel demanded that Wilkerson help keep the Flamingo afloat by taking out a loan for $600,000, a loan on which Wilkerson would be the sole signatory, pledging his stock as collateral. Or else.

"Billy was in a difficult spot," explained Wilkerson's lawyer Greg Bautzer in a posthumous biography.[36] "If Wilkerson signed, he would be sucked into a whirlpool of corruption and insanity. If he did not sign, he might kill [Siegel's] project and lose his investment." Wilkerson signed, only to learn that Siegel was now planning his grand opening of the Flamingo for December 26, three months ahead of schedule. Not only was it the night after Christmas, but the hotel wouldn't be finished! This was a blunder to eclipse all the others, Wilkerson felt. Grimly, he asked for a meeting with Siegel, to which both men brought their lawyers.

Siegel had come to a conclusion about Wilkerson, the partner with whom he had been so enamored just six months before. He wanted Wilkerson out completely. To that end, he wanted to buy Wilkerson's 48 percent of the Nevada Projects Corporation, which was to say the Flamingo. But there was a problem. In order to raise more money, Siegel had sold excess shares of stock in the Nevada Projects Corporation, stock that didn't exist. Apparently he hoped the Flamingo's success would float all boats. Shares in the Nevada Projects Corporation would rise so high that the new stockholders would be made whole by the original ones, who would quietly sacrifice a bit of their legitimate stock as needed. Wilkerson was shocked to learn of this scam, the more so to learn that he was expected to make it work by sacrificing a big chunk of his 48 percent interest in the venture. "You're gonna have to part with your portion of the interest," Siegel declared. "You're not gonna be paid anything for it, and you'd better have all the interest in hand."

"Just a minute," Bautzer said. "Are you telling this man, who has a legal and valid right to that interest, that he's gonna have to part with it? Cause he's not going to have 'to do' anything."

"He's gonna have to do this," Siegel explained. "I've sold one hundred fifty percent of this deal, and I don't have one hundred fifty percent—only 100 percent—and everybody's gonna have to cut, including Wilkerson."

"Well, you'd better find another way out," said Bautzer, "cause he ain't gonna cut."

As Bautzer's biographer James Gladstone relates, Siegel's famous temper began to erupt. "I can only tell you if I don't deliver the interest to the people in the east, I'm gonna be killed." He turned to Wilkerson. "And before I go, you're gonna go first. And don't take that lightly. I'll kill you if I don't get that interest."

But Bautzer had a temper to match Siegel's. "Sit down and shut up," he shouted. He proceeded to tell Siegel exactly what would happen next. As soon as he got back to his hotel room, Bautzer would write up an affidavit recording exactly what Siegel had said, and send that affidavit to the district attorney, the FBI, and the police in two states. If anything happened to Bautzer or Wilkerson, Siegel would be arrested right away.

With that, Bautzer took Wilkerson by the arm and led him out of Siegel's office, without once looking back. As they reached their rooms, Wilkerson made a sheepish admission to his lawyer: he had just wet his pants.

Bautzer made out the affidavits just as he had said he would, sent them out by wire, and brought Wilkerson home to L.A. without further incident. He advised Wilkerson to stay out of

Vegas for a while. Wilkerson sailed immediately from New York to Paris via the *Île de France* and checked in to the George V Hotel. His partnership with Siegel was clearly at an end. All that remained was for the two men, through their lawyers, to agree on what it would take for Siegel to buy Wilkerson's ownership shares—assuming that he had any money left by the time they sat down to work out that deal.

Wilkerson, whose vision more than anyone else's had brought the Flamingo to this point, made the wise choice to stay in Paris for the gala opening on December 26. In fact, he stayed away through the next tumultuous months, letting his lawyers do the deal that would buy Wilkerson out of his 48 percent. He never set foot in the Flamingo again. He did do radio interviews for the opening night. He just neglected to say he was doing them from Paris, rather than from the floor of the Flamingo.

For Siegel, Wilkerson's departure was a relief. The Flamingo was his now, his dream about to come true. All he needed was an opening night so star-studded and glamorous, and so dizzyingly profitable, that the Flamingo would be, from its first night, the most famous and successful hotel-casino in the world.

10

The Flamingo's First Flight

BY THE WEEK before Christmas, the Flamingo looked ready. The casino's big double doors swung open, the swimming pool shimmered, and at night, the tall, illuminated waterfall cast the desert in vibrant hues. Only a walk-through revealed how much needed to be done. Work on the hotel, Siegel's personal priority and responsibility, was lagging, many of its ninety-three guest rooms awaiting beds and furniture, their bathrooms so incomplete that some had merely a hole in the floor where the toilet or bidet should be. The casino had its gaming tables and roulette wheels in place, but piles of two-by-fours lay in dim corners. As of December, some $4 million had been spent on construction.[1] But that didn't include the other loans and funds needed to finish the hotel. All told, Siegel was in the hole for . . . $5 million? $6 million? Who could count the losses anymore?

At the start of that propitious month, Siegel and Hill moved from the Last Frontier Hotel into the Flamingo's fourth-floor penthouse, the airy suite that Hill had designed just for them. The offending low beam was gone. Hill was thrilled to settle in with Siegel to what felt like their home as man and wife. To celebrate, she splurged on a top-tier radio phonograph from the Penny-Owsley Music Company in L.A. for a whopping $1,129.80 and had it sent gift-wrapped.[2] Quite possibly, the radio phonograph served an ulterior motive, giving its owners privacy in bed without being overheard by the FBI's "technical surveillance" team.

To the hastily departed Billy Wilkerson, now hiding out in Paris, Siegel's decision to open the Flamingo on December 26, 1946, was a catastrophe in the making. Entertainers and their audiences alike would want to be home the night after Christmas. So would gamblers. Even gangsters would want to be with their families, singing Christmas carols and quaffing eggnog. What was Siegel thinking? As his blowup with Wilkerson suggested, he may have had no choice. His East Coast confederates were ready to hear the jingle of big money coming in, holidays be damned.

Siegel had planned to charter two or three planes for the stars whose presence would shine up the place. But by mid-December, a disturbing pattern was emerging. The stars were declining, one by one, to come, and more than holiday timing was to blame. "I don't like to tell you this, Ben," George Raft finally admitted, "but old man Hearst has passed the word around the studio that he's against the whole idea, and everybody's been told to stay away." The studio was Metro-Goldwyn-Mayer, which produced press magnate William Randolph Hearst's nationally broadcast newsreels. That gave Hearst sway over MGM and its stars, including Joan Crawford, Greer Garson, Spencer Tracy, and Ronald Colman. All were Raft's friends, but the charming gangster-actor had no sway over Hearst.[3] Raft at one point tried to weasel out of going himself, but Siegel's silence on the other end of the line was too menacing for him to ignore.[4]

At one point that month, Siegel was ready to cancel the opening altogether, or so Virginia Hill's kid brother Chick later recalled. He was furious and heartbroken, also a bit contrite. Maybe Wilkerson was right about the post-Christmas opening. Maybe they should have kept to the original date of March 1, 1947, and let the East Coast Syndicate stew. But Hill had just been sent a flaming orange-red $3,500 gown designed by couturier Howard Greer and created for the occasion, and insisted on wearing it.[5]

In the end, there would be three opening nights, not just one, Siegel decided: December 26, 27, and 28. The first, noted in full-page ads, would be for the locals: good public relations, and a way to paper the house if too many of the stars failed to show. Siegel had at least lined up comedian Jimmy Durante as his headliner, along with singer, comedian, and radio star Rose Marie, backed by the Xavier Cugat band.

The morning of December 26, Siegel made frantic rounds, picking up cigarette butts left by the construction workers and fussing over the stacks of cocktail napkins. He went outside to inspect the multihued waterfall, only to find it dark. A pregnant cat had gotten into the waterfall's sump pump and had six kittens there. A groundskeeper proposed turning off the system and flushing out the mother and her brood so the waterfall could be up and working that evening. "You bother those kittens and you just lost a job," Siegel snarled. For a gambler, touching a cat was bad luck. The cats would find their way out on their own, Siegel decreed; the waterfall would stay off on opening night.[6]

Some stars promised to come despite Hearst's ultimatum, as long as Siegel was willing to fly them up by charter plane. Lucille Ball signed on, as did William Holden, Ava Gardner, Veronica Lake, and a twenty-three-year-old Peter Lawford. But then, as if the Flamingo were in thrall to a higher power, storms swept the West Coast. In desperation, Siegel chartered an all-

Pullman Union Pacific train. But nary a celebrity clambered aboard.[7]

Some stars did manage to make the trip. George Raft drove up. So did British actor George Sanders; Sid Grauman, who pioneered putting stars' hands onto wet cement in front of his Chinese Theatre; entertainer and master of ceremonies Georgie Jessel; and Georgia-born actor Charles Coburn. They found an outdoor spectacle of palm trees spotlit in red and blue, a veritable forest of greenery, and scores of local cars, a traffic jam in the desert waiting to reach the front doors.[8]

The casino they entered was glamorous, but very unfinished. The bar in tufted green-and-tomato leather looked over the top, even for a casino in the desert. So, too, the statues, thick draperies, and deep plush carpeting. Everywhere were massive bouquets of flowers. Jimmy Durante twitted Siegel that "da place looks like a cemetery wid dice tables and slot machines."[9] Yet according to Wilkerson, who was hearing the blow-by-blow long distance from Paris, the lobby was draped with dropcloths, and the air-conditioning conked out with annoying frequency.[10]

Distraught at the lack of stars, Siegel made his appearance early that evening in a sports shirt with no tie or jacket. "You crummy peasant!" Hill reportedly said. "Go back and get into a dinner jacket." Siegel vanished without a word, and came back suitably attired.[11]

As the casino filled, Siegel's scowl gave way to a grin. "Siegel was the most accommodating guy, most likable fellow, had the best personality you ever seen," observed legendary Texas gambler Benny Binion, who was there that night. "If he was a bad guy, he damn sure didn't show it from the outside."[12]

Erskine Caldwell, Georgia-born author of *Tobacco Road* and *God's Little Acre*, was no less impressed. "With his handsome physique and his expensively tailored dark-blue suit worn with a white-on-white monogrammed shirt and black silk necktie,"

Caldwell wrote, "it was a magical combination that stated Bugsy's presence in unmistakable terms."

At the bar, Caldwell added, loud talk dropped to a whisper as Siegel ordered drinks. "Bugsy blew a puff of cigar smoke at one of the (scantily) costumed cocktail girls," Caldwell recalled. "She stopped as if mesmerized and stood there panting with a heaving of her breasts until he motioned for her to go away."[13]

"The dining room is packed all evening," reported the *Las Vegas Review-Journal*. "Cugat and his orchestra are presiding on the podium, and when he starts his rhythms there are more people on the dance floor than you can shake a sacroiliac at. . . . Durante is sharper than a GI bayonet during the evening and while he is on the stage he rips apart a $1600 piano and scatters Cugat's music all over the dance floor."[14]

The crowd swelled, and the headlining acts captivated the room. But by midnight, something was seriously wrong at the gaming tables. The house was losing cash by the buckets. Rival casinos had sent their best card counters. Siegel's own croupiers and stickmen were said to be working with Greek shills, splitting the ill-gotten gains. So suggested Mickey Cohen's biographer. "These handsome croupiers, imported from Havana, stole huge sums of money from the house." Guy McAfee, Siegel's nemesis for more than a decade, walked out with thousands of dollars; so did his girlfriend, starlet June Brewster. One world-famous gambler, Nick the Greek Dandolos, left with $500,000 after three nights, reported columnist Dorothy Kilgallen.[15]

Out-of-towners, whether they lost or won at the tables, left early that night and the two opening nights that followed. What choice did they have? They needed rooms for the night, and they weren't going to find them at the unfinished Flamingo. Instead, they took rooms at other casinos, and spent the rest of their gambling cash there. The El Rancho and Last Frontier, just north on Route 91, did especially well, welcoming overnighters for $5 a room and gently separating them from their money before they fell into bed.

One of the Flamingo's few losers that night was George Raft who, after making the three-hundred-mile car trip for his old friend, saw $65,000 melt away in a game of chemin de fer. He came back for the second opening night, December 27, and drew up a chair, set on winning it all back. To his shock and hurt, Siegel refused to let him play. "I stuck my neck out and drove up here from L.A. because you begged me to," Raft said. "I dropped sixty-five G's last night, and I'm entitled to another shot." Siegel glared at the other players. "If anybody deals a hand to Raft," he reportedly said, "this game's closed for the night." Perhaps by then, Siegel had his own men working the game, and didn't want to see his old friend lose again. Or maybe he didn't want to see Raft's luck change and burn a deeper hole in the Flamingo's losses from that first night. With Siegel, it was hard to tell.[16]

Buoyed by gushing coverage from columnists and paid flacks, the Flamingo did better—much better—on its third and final opening night of December 28. The West Coast storms had passed, and a number of Hollywood figures flew up after all. Vaudevillian Jessel played master of ceremonies, and the other first-night entertainers were back. Some of their numbers, and Jessel's patter, were broadcast on national radio.[17]

A dashing Siegel presided over his kingdom with a queenly Hill on his arm. An FBI memo reported that she arrived on each of the three opening nights with an entirely different hair color and style: platinum blond on the first night, jet black on the second, and finally a return to her naturally red hair on the third. So relayed the earnest FBI agents. Walter Winchell reported that the Flamingo in those first three nights drew twenty-eight thousand people.[18]

The Flamingo was certainly a spectacle. But as a business, it was a bust. The house kept losing, as much as $300,000 in its first two weeks.[19] Corrupt croupiers or not, Siegel had just tried to do too much himself. "Siegel had been unbearably autocratic about every activity in the hotel," suggested his hard-boiled biographer Dean Jennings. "He was so emotionally involved in his beautiful but soulless castle in the desert that he had lost perspective. . . . He tried to supervise the kitchen crew, hire the big name entertainers, appoint the pit bosses, choose the décor for the hotel rooms, and personally approve every employee. He simply could not stay in the background, nor was he able to clear his reputation as a gangster with a vile temper. He came there as Bugsy Siegel. He remained Bugsy Siegel."[20]

As Siegel was staging his opening nights, an ominous group was meeting thousands of miles away in Havana, Cuba. Lucky Luciano had called this meeting of family leaders, in the Hotel Nacional, soon to be owned by the Syndicate, to address key business matters. Siegel wasn't invited, a slight that no one in the underworld took as a coincidence. The meeting, after all, was to a large extent about him.

A lot had happened to Luciano since his sentencing in 1936 to thirty years in prison for running a prostitution ring. When the USS *Lafayette*—formerly the French ocean liner *Normandie*—just refurbished and sitting at anchor, caught fire and sank, U.S. Navy authorities suspected German sabotage and solicited Luciano's help: no one was better able to suss out spies malingering on the docks, or, for that matter, to control the dockworkers, who were militating to go on strike. Luciano had proven helpful in those regards. He had played another secret role in helping the allies take Sicily with an amphibious campaign in 1943. Luciano had put them in touch with the Sicilian mafia, who wanted Mussolini gone as much as the Allies did. The mafia supplied maps of the harbors and coastline, as well as maps through minefields laid by the Fascists. The locals also led the way to Mussolini's Italian naval command, hidden in a villa nearby.[21]

Luciano agreed to help U.S. forces with no guarantee that he would regain his freedom. Yet his help was so significant that with the war's conclusion Thomas E. Dewey, now governor of New York, personally pardoned Luciano in January of 1946. The pardon wasn't absolute: Luciano's freedom would involve deportation to his native Sicily. Still, it was a lot better than thirty or forty more years in Dannemora prison. A month later, Luciano was transported to Ellis Island and put aboard the *Laura Keene* for his one-way passage.

The night before his departure, Luciano was reportedly toasted aboard the boat by his old compadres, including Siegel. "We were all there," recalled Lansky associate Doc Stacher. "It was like old times. . . . Maybe the only shadow on the celebration was the coolness between Bugsy and Joe Adonis. Bugsy had taken over Joe's former girlfriend . . . as his number one mistress. Bugsy was really in love with Virginia, the first time in his life he had fallen so hard. And Virginia was crazy about him, though she'd had a lot of lovers before, including several of our guys."[22]

When the ship churned out from the New York waterfront the next day, bound for Genoa, Luciano was aboard, accompanied, according to Stacher, by a special detail of U.S. government agents.[23]

Officially, Luciano remained the Syndicate's leader even after his deportation. But the *capo di tutti i capi* was too canny to think he could maintain control from across an ocean without making an appearance now and again. The Havana Conference, as it came to be called, was the perfect venue. The crime families could meet easily and legally there; they could stay in the Hotel Nacional, overlooking the sea. Havana was also a port Luciano could reach by boat and plane without crossing into U.S. territorial waters. And so Luciano could use the occasion to reaffirm his power in the Syndicate.

That Christmas week, a formidable group of mobsters gathered in Havana. Among them were Santo Trafficante Jr., Frank

Costello, Albert Anastasia, Vito Genovese, and Meyer Lansky. No one ever revealed exactly what transpired in those rooms, but the gist came, decades later, from Lansky's right-hand man Stacher, the garrulous gangster who spoke with Lansky's blessing to his Israeli biographers.[24]

The most important order of business at the Havana Conference was to shore up Luciano's status, permanent resident as he was now of Sicily, and that was certainly achieved. By accepting the traditional envelopes of cash from all in the room, Luciano confirmed his power as titular head of the major families. Anything more explicit was unnecessary: Luciano was fully backed by Lansky, and everyone knew what that meant.[25]

Narcotics were also discussed at the meeting, specifically whether and how to develop the heroin market. The different families, it was decreed, could handle drugs in their own ways without undercutting each other, a short-lived fiat.

Then came the most painful subject of the conference: Ben Siegel and the Flamingo. Many in the room had invested in the Flamingo at Lansky's bidding. They had heard rumors about runaway costs. Now, to their shock and dismay, Lansky confirmed that the Flamingo's budget had gone from $1 million to $6 million. Lansky reassured them that the profits would soon be rolling in, but the leaders were dubious, and not at all happy to know they were in business with Virginia Hill. More than one participant believed Hill was guilty of more than reckless spending. She had been skimming the enterprise, some said, and making trips to Zürich, where she had stashed half a million dollars or more in a Swiss bank account. Mickey Cohen's biographer, Tere Tereba, suggested that Hill had also taken a long-term lease on a Zürich apartment.[26] Some thought Siegel was in on the skim. What else could account for the $5 million in construction overruns? By now, the Syndicate surely knew that Siegel had sold shares of Nevada Projects Corporation stock two or three times over, so that as one historian notes, "people who thought they owned ten percent found out they only owned a half of one percent."[27]

"This sort of behavior meant only one thing in the underworld," Stacher later explained. "Bugsy was going to be hit. Everyone knew that, too, but [Meyer] did all he could to save his friend. He begged the men to be patient. . . . It was the first time I ever heard Meyer become so emotional. He pleaded with everybody there to remember the great services that Bugsy had performed for all of them. They looked at him stony-faced, without saying a word."[28]

Frank Sinatra had come to the Nacional to sing on Christmas Eve, the highlight of the holiday gathering, and the gangsters gathered in pride to hear him. Halfway through the evening, Stacher later recalled, Luciano took Lansky aside. "Meyer, I know your feelings for Bugsy," Luciano allegedly told him. "I know you love him as much as you love your own brother, even your sons. But Meyer, this is business and Bugsy has broken our rules. He's taking our money and stashing it away in Switzerland. He is betraying us. He is cheating us. He knows it and you know it.

"If you don't have the heart to do it, Meyer, I will have to order the execution myself."[29]

Back in Sicily, according to one newspaper report, Luciano made his sentiments just as clear to Siegel. "Lucky made three long-distance calls to Bugsy in Las Vegas. He told him in no uncertain language." Unless Siegel began to generate windfall profits, he would not survive the next year. According to the article, Siegel replied that he knew what he was doing, and the Syndicate would be grateful soon enough.[30]

On the Flamingo's stage, the Xavier Cugat band played a holdover two-week run in early January, along with headline singer Lena Horne. Beneath the glamour lay desperation and a growing sense of doom. Siegel went from one game to the next, looking for shady croupiers and card-counting bettors. He found a few, and tossed them out, but the magnitude of his gaming losses remained a mystery.[31]

Added pressure came from the town's other casinos. They had let the Flamingo have its opening nights. Now they weighed in with marquee entertainment names of their own, forcing Siegel to pay as much as $25,000 a week to compete.[32] Lena Horne brought down the house, as did Abbott and Costello, and a smattering of Hollywood stars came to hear them—Wallace Beery, Van Heflin, Gary Cooper, and more—but at a cost. For Horne, extracting top pay was about more than money. Upon her arrival in Vegas, she was relegated to the black section of town, which had no running water or sewage system. "Bugsy relented and allowed her to stay near the casino in a cabana, though every morning the maids burned her bed linens."[33] Horne took her revenge in cold cash.

The other great, unrelenting cost was construction. The hotel's ninety-three guest rooms remained unfinished. One estimate put their furnishing at $3,500 a room, roughly $325,000 in all. And still, as yet, only a small fraction of the Flamingo's guests could stay the night.

Again and again, Virginia Hill urged Siegel to bring in a hotel manager from New York. But he couldn't bring himself to delegate. Better to sell it, he told her, but his East Coast partners wanted to see him turn a profit first, and a sizable one at that.

Between the lovers, tensions grew. One day, Hill was in the penthouse suite, reading a copy of *Time* magazine in which Siegel was pictured. Why, Siegel asked, was she reading that rag?

"I'll read what I damn well like," Hill replied.

Siegel knocked the magazine from her hand and gave her a shove. "She was on her feet like a cat, clutching her left shoe like an ice pick, and the long sharp spiked heel cut a deep gash in Siegel's neck," Dean Jennings reported. "She hit him again and again, until blood ran down over his eyes." Before Siegel could wipe his face clean, Hill was in a taxi to the airport, taking the first flight to L.A. "She knew him well enough to stay away until his anger cooled," Jennings wrote, "and a full week passed before he saw her again."[34]

Day by day, the crowds at the Flamingo dwindled. Siegel felt the victim of a campaign from the other casinos, sure the competition was painting him as a violent murderer, one who might pull out a gun at the slightest provocation. Much of the muttering, in fact, was done by the FBI, as A. E. Ostholthoff and his special agents interviewed local informants and passed rumors from one to the next. Yet for all of Siegel's reckless spending and terrible management, the FBI found no hard evidence of any crime committed.

Ostholthoff had his suspicions. He felt sure Siegel had bribed CPA commissioners to keep the Flamingo from being shut down, and possibly bribed Senator McCarran as well. But where was the proof? The straight-arrow agent referred liberally in his memos to Siegel's and Hill's rampant drug trafficking with Mexican wholesalers. He said Siegel was the biggest drug dealer on the West Coast. Yet the agents had no proof of that, either. There was not one credible witness, not one border interception, not one buyer who could say that Ben Siegel was his dealer.

On January 16, 1947, Ostholthoff was forced to acknowledge a bitter truth. "I reluctantly concur in the attached recommendation that the Bureau at this time discontinue all active investigation of 'Bugsy' Siegel, including the maintenance of technical and physical surveillance."

Ostholthoff told J. Edgar Hoover that since the previous July, the Bureau had expended some one thousand agent days of investigation effort in coverage of Siegel and his activities without developing "a scintilla of evidence" of any activities in violation of federal statutes within the Bureau's jurisdiction.[35]

Siegel still faced a thicket of issues, but the FBI, to his pleasant surprise, was no longer one of them.

* * *

By the end of January, Siegel made a painful decision. He would temporarily close the Flamingo and fix what remained undone, starting with the hotel's guest bedrooms.

Hill, plagued by allergies in the desert, took the Flamingo's closing as a chance to spend time in L.A. She rented a Moorish-style mansion in Beverly Hills at 810 North Linden Drive from her friend Juan Romero, an art dealer who also owned Falcon Lair, the late matinee idol Rudolph Valentino's home, where Hill and Siegel had enjoyed a few trysts.

Siegel and Hill were still tightly bound, enough that Hill gave Siegel a solid-gold key to the front door of the house on Linden. But she was sick of the casino and Siegel's deepening financial straits.

So desperate were Siegel's finances, and so widely known, that one of his few true friends, Countess di Frasso, made an extraordinary effort to help. The romance between them was long over, but the countess remained devoted to him, bristling at anyone who called him Bugsy. Now she went so far as to offer to pawn some of her jewelry for him. It would bring $50,000, she said.

"You're a real sweetie, Dottie," Siegel told her, "but I don't need it now."

"Don't try to fool me, Ben," she said. "Everybody knows you've been losing your shirt."

"We're coming out of it now," Siegel insisted, "we're doing okay."[36]

If the story was true, it was a graceful moment on Siegel's part. He knew how little impact $50,000 would have on his finances; why squander his old friend's jewels? He felt no such tug of conscience with George Raft, however. Once again, the price of friendship for Raft proved dear. Siegel asked for a loan of $100,000 from the actor's annuity fund, with no collateral. Reluctantly, Raft complied. He had to know he would never see that money again. As Siegel's debts mounted during the shutdown, he went back to Raft and asked that the actor buy $65,000 in Flamingo stock. Again, Raft obliged his friend. Raft must have been unaware that Siegel had sold at least 150 percent of the stock: the certificate he gave Raft wasn't worth the paper it was printed on.[37]

By one account, both Meyer Lansky and Frank Costello helped get the Flamingo's guest rooms finished in time for the March 1 reopening.[38] Certainly they had incentive enough to see the place succeed. Perhaps, too, both were still rooting for Siegel: if he could just turn the place around, the Syndicate might relent.

The Flamingo's closing stung Siegel's creditors, Del Webb chief among them. Siegel was able to keep him working by wangling a $350,000 loan from an Arizona bank.[39] Most if not all of that money went to Del Webb to finish the hotel. No one expected it to get the Flamingo into the black.

The doors opened once more, as announced, on March 1. Once again, Siegel was there to greet arriving guests, including those checking in for the night. Some rooms still lacked rugs and draperies, and some beds needed making. Not more than an hour before, Siegel had asked his hotel manager whether all the bed sheets had been turned down. The manager lied and said yes, then slid away to lead a swat team of staffers from room to room, turning every sheet down.[40]

The Andrews Sisters sang that night to a full house, and the roulette wheels spun and spun. Still the losses grew. By mid-March, Siegel was forced to sign a "notice of completion" allowing creditors to file liens on the property. One of Del Webb's liens alone came in at $1,057,000.21. Webb said that to date, he had been paid only $2.5 million of the $3.6 million he was owed. As a goodwill gesture, Siegel wrote Webb two checks totaling $150,000. Both bounced.[41]

Webb was one of Siegel's tormentors, Billy Wilkerson another. Having decided in December to buy out Wilkerson's shares and cut all ties with him, Siegel now had to sit with Wilkerson's lawyer and agree on what Wilkerson's 48 percent of the Flamingo was worth. Greg Bautzer, Wilkerson's lawyer, wasn't in on these negotiations: he felt, after the confrontation in December, that both he and Wilkerson should stay as far away from Siegel as possible. Instead, Wilkerson's partner, Tom Seward, did the negotiating by phone from L.A.

As an opener, Seward demanded $2 million on Wilkerson's behalf. That would be Wilkerson's price for selling nearly half the Flamingo to Siegel and being free of any liabilities. Siegel, through his lawyer, countered at $300,000. Seward, on Wilkerson's behalf, dropped his demand to $1 million. Siegel came back at $600,000. Half of Wilkerson's payoff would be remitted in May, the balance in August. Wilkerson was torn. Siegel was buying him out for a pittance, but a pittance was better than nothing. More important, Wilkerson wanted his life back. Reluctantly, he called Seward to say they had a deal.[42]

In early March 1947, Seward braved the trip from L.A. to get documents signed and countersigned, ending Billy Wilkerson's business dealings with Siegel. He found himself sitting in a booth along with Siegel and Meyer Lansky. At one point, recounts Wilkerson's son in *The Man Who Invented Las Vegas*, "Siegel made a symbolic revolver out of his hand and pointed the barrel at Seward's head. Seward recalled feeling the pressure of the gangster's fingers against his skull.

"'If your partner were here right now I'd blow his fucking brains out,' Siegel said."[43]

Seward was terrified, and high-tailed it out of the Flamingo without getting any of the documents signed. Not until March 19 did Siegel and G. Harry Rothberg sign an official document releasing Wilkerson from any liability on the project. In late April, he got the first half of his $600,000, according to his son.[44] He would receive the balance in August. Or so the parties agreed.

* * *

As the Flamingo's losses continued to rise, Siegel ranted against the injustice of having to pay his ex-partner any money at all. His front man Moe Sedway got the bum's rush as well. Sedway had arguably done more to build Siegel's fortune than anyone else, getting the Vegas race wire exclusive from Continental Press back in 1942, and comanaging the El Cortez. Now he was working to expand Siegel's Trans-American turf, but he was having trouble delivering.[45] That in itself made Siegel angry, but what really lit his fuse was Sedway's involvement in local philanthropy.

Ever since his arrival in Vegas, Sedway had downplayed his close association with Siegel. That was his job, to be the front man, but Sedway had taken the role a bit too much to heart. Like Siegel, he longed for legitimacy. He had involved himself with the United Jewish Appeal, and donated enough money to become its Las Vegas chairman. He had taken a seat on the board of the Clark County Library. Now he was being asked to run for the Nevada State Assembly and had agreed to do so.[46] Siegel was furious. "We don't run for office!" he railed at Sedway. "We *own* the politicians."[47]

That argument ended, or so it was said, with Siegel literally kicking Sedway out of the Flamingo and telling him never to come in again. By one account, Siegel had concluded that Sedway was a stool pigeon for the FBI. He went on about the obsequious Sedway with Hill's brother Chick. "Before I die," he told Chick one night, "there's two guys I'm gonna kill. Sedway and Wilkerson, the two biggest bastards that ever lived."[48]

Siegel may have derived enormous satisfaction from drop-kicking Sedway out of the Flamingo, but the story reportedly found its way to the Syndicate, where it was received with dismay. Sedway was a longtime colleague they could trust. More to the point, he was an old and close friend of Siegel's. If Siegel was capable of treating Sedway like this, it was another sign that Siegel was growing unhinged, and jeopardizing the Syndicate's dough.

With the Flamingo's reopening, Hill was back in the hotel's penthouse suite, unhappily so. She took large doses of Benadryl for her allergies, only to feel groggy and sick. Later, she would say that she now came to Vegas only when friends flew up to visit. Always quick to seethe with jealousy, she noticed that Siegel seemed drawn to the pretty young girl at the cigarette concession stand. At Siegel's next flirty exchange with her, Hill leapt into action, grabbing the girl by the hair and scratching her face, until Siegel pulled her away. Later, before the Kefauver Commission, Hill admitted, "I hit a girl in the Flamingo and [Ben] told me I wasn't a lady. We got into a big fight. I had been drinking, and I left." The girl, diagnosed at the hospital with deep facial scratches and a dislocated vertebra, filed a lawsuit. According to one report, Siegel told Hill she could come back to him only if she apologized.[49]

Beneath Hill's rage, it seemed, lay insecurity and a self-destructive streak. A day or so after the attack on the cigarette girl, Hill took an overdose of sleeping pills. Siegel found her comatose in their penthouse suite. His quick response probably saved her life: together, he and Chick carried her down the secret passage and into Chick's new Cadillac. They raced to the hospital at ninety miles an hour, drawing police in their wake. A stomach pump at the hospital brought Hill back from the brink. This suicide attempt was apparently her first; it would not be her last.

There were many examples that spring of Siegel's temper or, perhaps more accurate, his mental deterioration. One concerned the entertainment director for the El Rancho Vegas, one Abe Schiller. As a courtesy, the town's casinos let anyone use their pools. Schiller, so went the story, took his wife and children to check out the Flamingo's pool. This was in early March; the Flamingo had just reopened, and some two hundred guests were ranged around the pool.

At the sight of Schiller, Siegel began seething. Apparently the flack had been warning visitors away from the Flamingo and its hoodlum clientele. Siegel reportedly pulled out his .38 and pistol-whipped him. Then he made Schiller crawl around the pool on his hands and knees as his horrified family looked on.[50]

Siegel's mood swings had grown extreme. Yet he was still capable of generous acts. One night that spring, he hosted a fundraiser for Eddie Cantor's cancer drive. Along with underwriting the evening and urging guests to dig deep, he wrote a check of his own. "He came across with a sum that surprised me," Cantor later related to columnist Florabel Muir. "He didn't do it for publicity, either, because no one knew how much he gave us."[51]

Later that spring, Siegel hosted another cancer fundraiser, this one for the new Damon Runyon fund. The Broadway journalist and short story writer had died of cancer the previous year, and his friend Walter Winchell had inaugurated the fund for cancer research. Again Siegel donated the Flamingo for the evening, and again he made an anonymous gift. This time he couldn't resist pulling a prank on his lawyer as he did.[52]

"He told me to bid on a fur for my wife," related Louis Wiener, Siegel's lawyer, of the auction that climaxed the evening. "He said 'you can probably get it for five hundred dollars.'" Siegel melted into the crowd, and when the time came, Wiener bid $500 for what was, in fact, a silver fox fur, most prized of the various fox kinds. To his mild annoyance, another bettor raised him to $550. Back and forth the bidding went, with Wiener sweating as it reached $950. Set on winning the fur—he could hardly do otherwise, given that retainer of $25,000 a year that he and his firm continued to earn from the

Flamingo—he heard himself croak a bid of $1,000. Mercifully, his unseen rival dropped out. A bit shaken, Wiener walked over to the "cage" for a cash advance. Siegel came up behind him and innocently asked, "What happened?"

"Well, someone bid me up to a thousand dollars and I didn't bring that much money with me," Wiener said, not entirely able to hide his irritation. Siegel started to laugh, and Wiener got the joke at last. Still, he thought he'd bought the coat—the cage advanced him the thousand dollars he asked for, and Wiener walked over to the auction table to plunk down his cash for the fur. Instead, his money was pushed back across the table to him, along with the silver fox fur. Siegel had paid for it himself.

Wiener wasn't the only unwitting front for Siegel's generosity that night. Brigham Townsend, a publicist who had helped organize the evening gratis as part of representing Siegel, sat with his volatile client through the auction.[53] "Whenever an item was going for far less than it should, Benny would have me push up the bidding." Siegel would slip him the bills that clinched the winning bid, and crooner Gene Austin, the evening's auctioneer, would look on in amazement. All told, the evening would raise $8,000—a lot of money in 1947. Most of that money came from Siegel.

The two men were seated on barstools as the guests began to leave. Every one of them came over to thank Ben Siegel—not Bugsy—for hosting the night. "When the last guest had departed," Townsend recalled, "Benny turned to me, wiped a tear from his eye, and said 'Gee kid, they shook my hand.'" Townsend, who wrote a regular column for the *Las Vegas Review-Journal*, made no mention in print of Siegel's largesse.

These shows of philanthropy were more than pro forma. On April 17, 1947, Ben's father died at sixty-seven and was buried in Mt. Zion cemetery in Queens, his gravestone scrunched between others, a poor man to the last. For years, Ben had provided for his parents. He could take consolation that his father Max had lived far longer, under his care, than if he had kept working in a pants factory. But those first years had been so hard. Money had helped, and Ben had taken pride in all he could do to support the family. His parents had never embraced him for that. Ben was the Siegels' persona non grata. Maurice had done well, moved up, become a doctor. There was no need to say more than that.

Admirable as Ben's philanthropy was, motivated as it might be by grief at his father's passing, it also spoke to a sort of mania. Siegel could no more afford to make charitable gifts at this point than to run for president.

Amid the grim portents was one surprisingly positive bit of news: sometime in May, the Flamingo turned a profit. Siegel was euphoric. Maybe the whole crazy extravaganza was turning around at last.

11

Time Runs Out

LITTLE ABOUT Siegel's last days suggested the end was near. In early June 1947, he seemed optimistic, at ease, good-natured, even philosophical, if that could be said of a gangster.

One source of Siegel's improved mood was obvious. The Flamingo's day-to-day operation was in the black at last, with $250,000 in profit in May.[1] Siegel finally had croupiers he could trust, good counters in the cage, and a growing clientele, now that the hotel's bedrooms were done and bettors could stay the night. Luck played a part, too. Siegel believed deeply in luck, as any true gambler does. Luck had come to the Flamingo not a moment too soon, he thought, but not too late, either. Of course, the Flamingo was still millions in debt on construction costs.

After several tempestuous months, Siegel was feeling philosophical about Virginia Hill as well. He felt resigned to the odds that their romance, whether a marriage or not, was over.

They loved each other, and always would, like the characters in their favorite book. But the two were so volatile, their fights so fierce, that both were relieved whenever Hill left Las Vegas for L.A. Hill's brutal takedown of the cigarette girl had felt like a turning point.

Hill's house on North Linden Drive in L.A. had given her some of the freedom she craved, but Vegas had worn her down. She was tired of being queen of the Flamingo. She hated the desert. She could hardly venture out into the searing heat without triggering her allergies. She felt suffocated, literally and figuratively, by Siegel. If she kept going to Vegas at Siegel's command, she felt sure she would overdose again.[2] What she needed after that, she told her friend and landlord Juan Romero, was a real getaway.

Romero asked whether Hill had been to Paris. She had not. As the two drank Champagne, Romero painted a vivid picture of the city. Hill knew one Frenchman already, he reminded her, and pointed to the bottle they were emptying. Just weeks before, Romero had introduced Hill to Nicolas Feuillatte, a young heir to the Mumm's Champagne fortune. Feuillatte could be her guide. Hill laughed at the very idea: Was Nicolas even twenty-one? Possibly, Romero said, possibly not. But Hill wasn't that much older than Feuillatte, Romero teased. How old was she, again?

Hill was twenty-nine. A lot had been packed into those years, though Feuillatte didn't have to know that. To him, she would be a great adventure: beguilingly chic, beautifully dressed, and an all-star in bed.

Hill flew up to Vegas to tell Siegel she was planning a summer in Paris—on her own. His first reaction was a flat no. Siegel had been through a lot with Hill, between the overdose and the frequent fights, and he didn't need any more aggravation. Hill was ready for that. "You don't own me, Ben Siegel," she said, according to her brother Chick's recollection.[3]

Later, Virginia Hill would tell investigators that she and Siegel had broken up that day. "He was a constant strain on my nerves," she said. "We couldn't be together five minutes without arguing. When he barked at me, I packed my bags and left the hotel."[4]

Siegel decided he would take his daughters to Vancouver for a summer vacation. Meanwhile, he declared, Hill could travel around France as much as she liked. At summer's end, they would see how they felt about getting back together. At least this was the story that Virginia's brother Chick told investigators. Both, he said, were "too nervous" to stay together. Doc Stacher, Meyer Lansky's right-hand man, dismissed that theory. His view was that Siegel just needed to keep the Flamingo in the black another three months, after which the lovers would reunite, more ardent than ever.[5]

Whatever their true feelings, Hill let Siegel stay in the capacious Linden Drive house when she left L.A. for Paris on June 10. He had the gold key Hill had given him, and he could take his time packing his clothes: the lease on the Linden Drive house expired on June 23. Hill also allowed her brother Chick and his new girlfriend Jerri Mason to stay there in her absence, on the stern proviso that they not do something foolish, like get married. Hill even bought Chick a new Cadillac to keep him happy while she was away.[6] Siegel would use the house as a brief base of operations, pitching more investors for the Flamingo.

First stop for Hill was Chicago, where she had dinner with the long-suffering Joe Epstein, her adoring mob accountant, and stayed the night in his apartment. That evening, she and Siegel exchanged their last words. "I phoned goodbye to him from Chicago and I said I was going to Europe," Hill later said to a reporter. "That was the last I heard from him."[7] The next morning, Epstein flew with her to New York, and the pair took a suite at the Hampshire House on Central Park South. One order of business was getting a passport for Hill. On the application form, she noted that she would be setting up an import business for French wines from the Feuillatte family. That was probably a stretch, given that she had just written to Nicolas to ask him to guide her around Paris, but it would serve.

The young Feuillatte was delighted. So were his parents, who had no idea that the woman hiring their son as a guide was a notorious gun moll. On June 16, Hill flew from New York to Paris. By one report, she was carrying $76,000 worth of furs as excess baggage. Perhaps she liked having her choice of furs for the Parisian summer. Or were the furs making a one-way trip to Europe?

Four days later, gangsters and detectives alike would be left wondering if Virginia Hill had had an ulterior motive for flying to Paris when she did.

Siegel was still in Vegas as Hill flew off from New York. He had a special guest to welcome at the Flamingo. Rumor had it that Meyer Lansky stayed away from the gaming tables and barely left his room. Still, word of his presence traveled, as it always did. Most likely, he was there to preside over a forced conclave of major race wire operators. Siegel had just announced that he was doubling their subscription fees to the Trans-American race wire and giving them no choice to go elsewhere. Siegel needed more money for the Flamingo, it was as simple as that. The operators were furious.

Possibly in that group of disgruntled mobsters sat the one who would become Siegel's murderer.[8] A good prospect was Russell Brophy, son-in-law of the late James Ragen and victim of that ferocious beating in 1942 by Mickey Cohen and Joe Sica. At the meeting, Brophy reportedly demanded a much bigger chunk of Siegel's turf: Arizona, southern California, and Nevada. Decades later, Doc Stacher reported on how that turned out. "He was informed that he not only couldn't have

Siegel's territory but would lose five other western states that he already owned for being so greedy."[9]

According to Stacher, Lansky did his best to defend Siegel to the end, giving him business advice and reporting the casino's upturn to the boys back east. Later, another version of Lansky's Vegas trip surfaced. Perhaps Lansky had flown out to bid Siegel goodbye, knowing a gunman was about to act.[10] Yet Siegel seemed jovial when Lansky departed. As for Lansky, he would deny, for what it was worth, playing any role in Siegel's murder. "Ben Siegel was my friend until his final day," he told his Israeli biographers. "I never quarreled with him."[11]

A warning of sorts came one June night at the Linden Drive house in L.A. Siegel was still in Las Vegas. Virginia Hill's younger brother Chick and his girlfriend Jerri Mason were at the house on their own, in a second-floor bedroom. They heard a scuffling and scraping, followed by a sharper impact. Chick came down to find the kitchen door wide open, its latch jimmied, and heard receding steps. Or so he said.[12]

In Paris, Billy Wilkerson picked up his phone at the George V to receive a much more explicit warning. He had planned on coming back to Las Vegas at last, to get the second half of his $600,000 buyout money. Now he heard a raspy voice saying, "wait till it's over." The phone clicked.[13] Wilkerson chose to take the advice, though it would cost him the rest of his buyout money.

By one account, Siegel received several threatening calls, too. Enough of them came on June 19 at the Flamingo that he told the switchboard not to connect anyone he didn't know well. Still, Siegel seemed at ease. He called Chick Hill to say he would be flying down that night of June 19. He had business in L.A. the next day and would be staying at the Linden Drive house. Chick and Jerri shouldn't wait up, he advised: he wouldn't get to the house until 3 or 4 A.M.[14]

Before flying down, Siegel reportedly called one of his most trusted bodyguards, "Fat Irish" Green, to his office. There, according to legend, he popped open a locked case filled with cash.[15] Green was accustomed to seeing wads of cash; he had run the wire service book at El Rancho for six months. But this was really big. Later estimates of the cash varied from $60,000 to $600,000.

Siegel asked Green to keep the case while he did a little business in L.A. The very idea made Green nervous. Money like this had a way of getting its owner killed. "Don't worry, no one else in Vegas knows about it," Siegel assured him.

Days later, after Siegel was dead and buried, Fat Irish reportedly handed over the still-locked case to Meyer Lansky. By one report, even Lansky was astounded when he forced the case open. He had known nothing about a secret case of money, or of anyone holding it for him. And yet there it was: tens or even hundreds of thousands of dollars in small, unmarked bills.[16] Deeply touched, he declared that Fat Irish Green could live the rest of his life rent-free as a guest of the El Cortez hotel. And so he did.

Neither of the authoritative Meyer Lansky biographies includes the Fat Irish Green story, but Dean Jennings's early Bugsy biography does. "For the past nineteen years," Jennings wrote in 1967, "Green has been living at the El Cortez in Las Vegas. He has never had a bill for room and board, and he gets small cash handouts now and then to pay for drinks and the other needs of life."[17] The story of Fat Irish and his suitcase of cash, living happily ever after, may be embellished. It may not be true. But it *is* a good story.

Either way, Siegel flew down to L.A. on the night of June 19 with his friend Swifty Morgan, a racetrack tout notorious for always needing money, sometimes selling hot jewels in nightclubs to pay off his gambling debts. They reached L.A. at about 2:30 A.M. and took a taxi to Linden Drive. Chick Hill was there

to greet them, but Siegel went right to one of the upstairs bedrooms, after putting Morgan in another. The next morning, Virginia Hill's Chinese cook served them breakfast. Later, Chick
would remember the calls coming in, a few at first, then more,
with more insistence.[18]

First Siegel called his ex-wife to check on the girls. Esther
was putting Millicent, sixteen, and Barbara, fourteen, on the
Super Chief sleeper train from New York's Penn Central Sta-
tion to Los Angeles, with the promise of summer fun with their
father. The girls had never traveled so far alone before. They
were thrilled to have their own sleeping coach.

There were business calls to be made, so Siegel repaired to
one of the Linden Drive bedrooms and closed the door. When
he reappeared, his mood had darkened. Allen Smiley had come
by in the meantime. He was the partner who had been arrested
with Siegel for bookmaking in the Sunset Towers, back in 1944;
he was the Russian Jew who had arranged for Siegel to meet
with Israeli activist Reuven Dafni. Siegel had a full day of meetings, almost certainly in order to scrounge for more operating
funds for the Flamingo. "Let's go," he said tersely to Smiley.

The two drove to Mickey Cohen's house in Brentwood.
Siegel got out of the car and told Smiley to take a walk, while
he went in to confer with Cohen. Years later, Cohen would say
that Siegel in the meeting said he might need a shooter, asking
Cohen who was in town.[19]

From there, Siegel and Smiley drove over to George Raft's
place in Coldwater Canyon. Raft later said that Siegel looked
pale, "with jerky speech and movements." Raft told him to take
a few days off. "I'm tired, Georgie," Siegel admitted.[20] But he
was buoyed by the prospect of seeing his daughters and taking
them to Lake Louise in Canada.

On the last day of his life, Siegel indulged himself with a
stop at Harry Drucker's hair salon. Siegel had his usual that

day: haircut, shave, manicure, neck and shoulder massage, and his shoes shined to a high gloss.[21]

A visit to his L.A. lawyer's office rounded out Siegel's afternoon. At one point the lawyer passed over an unreimbursed receipt—for thirty-five bucks. Siegel's temper flared, and the lawyer felt a stab of fear. Muttering, Siegel pulled out his wallet, counted three hundred-dollar bills, and stuffed them into the lawyer's hand. "Now you're not busted," he said.[22]

Back at the Linden Drive house, Siegel had an odd exchange with Chick Hill. Up in the bedroom that Hill and Mason had been sharing was a gun on a bureau. Siegel asked Chick to put the gun in the room's wall safe. Chick spun the dials, opened the door, and put the gun beside a heaping mound of jewelry. "You know that's all Virginia's stuff," Chick said. Much of it had been given to her by Siegel. Shouldn't he insure it, Chick asked? Or put it in a bank safety box?

"That's your sister's worry, kid," Siegel retorted. "I got enough on my mind." Anyway, he added, Chick shouldn't worry. "You're in Beverly Hills," Siegel said with a laugh. "Cops come along this block every half hour."[23]

Perhaps the full treatment from Drucker's had put Siegel into a better mood. He had no bodyguards that day, and when Allen Smiley came back over, Siegel seemed cheerful again. He didn't even close the draperies of the living room's plate-glass windows—the windows that looked directly on to Linden Drive.

The four headed out for dinner in Smiley's new powder-blue, slope-backed Cadillac coupe: Siegel, Chick Hill, and Jerri Mason, with Smiley at the wheel. Their destination was Jack's, a new restaurant overlooking the sea in the Ocean Park neighborhood of Santa Monica. Chick Hill recalled that they stayed about ninety minutes. The older men joked with Chick and Jerri about their romance getting serious, and Siegel picked up the tab. As they waited for a valet to bring them their car, a restaurant worker handed Siegel a copy of the next morning's *Los*

Angeles Times. On the front page was stamped "Good Night Sleep Well, with the compliments of Jack's."[24]

Back at the house, Siegel slid out the passenger side of the big car and strode up to the front door, reaching in his pocket for the gold key Hill had given him. As he switched on the living room lights, a strong smell of flowers stopped him in his tracks. When Siegel called their attention to it, Chick recalled a saying of his mother's, down in Bessemer, Alabama. "When someone smells flowers and there aren't any in the house, it means they're going to die."[25] In fact, the scent was from the late-blooming jasmine outside a window. A window that was open, through which nine shots were about to be fired.[26]

At about 10:45 P.M., Siegel and Smiley sat in the living room, each with an open section of the *Los Angeles Times* on his lap. Siegel was on the chintz davenport in front of the plate-glass windows, the draperies still open. Smiley was on an adjacent sofa. Chick and Jerri had gone upstairs.

Outside, an unseen figure set his .30-.30 carbine on the rose trellis dividing the Linden Drive mansion from its neighbor. By one report, the rifle was fourteen feet from its target; by another, it was fifteen. Either way, the shooter could hardly miss from such close range, and didn't. A first bullet tore directly into Siegel's head and out the other side, propelling his right eye fifteen feet across the room into the opposite wall. A second bullet found its mark, too, pushing through Siegel's brain and neck. Two more bullets passed through his chest, another through another part of his body. In all, he was hit by five bullets, killing him instantly. One of the other bullets grazed the sleeve of Allen Smiley's coat.[27]

To Smiley, the first bullets sounded like fireworks. "For a second, I thought it might be a gag," Smiley told investigators. "But I looked up at Siegel's face and saw blood all over it so I instinctively fell on the floor for my own protection."[28] Smiley started screaming, "Shut the lights, shut the lights!" By the time someone did, the firing had stopped. In the darkness, Jerri called the police and screamed into the receiver that someone was firing a gun into the house. Chick was more rational. He went into the upstairs wall safe, pocketed the gun, and dumped his sister's jewelry into the partially filled laundry chute.[29]

The police were at the house within minutes. Once they had determined the shooter was gone, a police photographer took gruesome pictures of Siegel's blood-covered body, sprawled on the sofa. These are some of the grisliest photographs ever taken in the annals of organized crime.

The first journalist to arrive at the scene was Florabel Muir, the syndicated columnist. Hours before, Siegel had called her to thank her for a favorable review of a Flamingo floor show. Now she coolly lifted the blood-spattered newspaper on Siegel's lap to see what he had been reading. She measured the distance between Siegel's corpse and the eye that had hit the opposite wall. Then, she recalled, she picked up the sliver of flesh from which his long eyelashes extended.[30]

Up in Vegas that evening, shortly before Siegel's shooting, a strange scene had unfolded at the Flamingo's floor show. Eight large, broad-shouldered men had sat together in silence as singer and guitarist Tito Guizar, the Mexican Roy Rogers, performed. Toward the end of the show, another man went around the table, whispering in their ears. With that, the men left the room and took up posts around the casino, apparently guarding the premises.

Within minutes of the L.A. murder, Moe Sedway and Gus Greenbaum appeared in the lobby of the Flamingo. Sedway hadn't dared show his face at the casino after his summary banishment, but here he was now, with his old partner Greenbaum and another casino executive, Morris Rosen, who worked for Meyer Lansky. They announced to the crowd that Ben Siegel had died, and that there had been a change of management. They were the Flamingo's owners now.[31] With that, their roles grew to legend. Mario Puzo in his 1969 novel *The Godfather* named his Vegas casino owner Moe Greene, an amalgam of Moe Sedway and Gus Greenbaum. Both in the novel and the epic 1972 movie that followed, Moe Greene was clearly based on Siegel as well. Like Siegel, Greene was a hot-headed casino owner who refused to sell out to the Syndicate. Like Siegel, Greene was killed by a bullet through the eye—in Greene's case while getting a massage.

Within an hour of his death, Siegel's body was driven to the Los Angeles County morgue and put on a sliding slab in crypt 6. His personal effects, duly recorded, were a platinum wristwatch, a gold ring with an amber stone, a Mexican gold coin made into a money clip, a set of diamond-and-platinum cuff links, an alligator billfold containing about $400, a gold cigar punch, and six keys, two of them gold plated. The next day, the *Los Angeles Herald-Express* published a front-page picture of Siegel's right foot, with a toe label that read "homicide."[32]

The murder suspects were legion. As the last person who saw Siegel alive, Allen Smiley briefly topped the detectives' list. He could have set up the kill and positioned Siegel right in front of the plate-glass windows. Except that Smiley had been Siegel's loyal friend and fixer for nearly a decade, and there was, in any event, no evidence of his complicity.

The investigators also questioned Chick Hill and Jerri Mason. Both said they had been in their upstairs bedroom when the shots were fired. Jerri had called the police as soon as the shooting ended. It was a short interrogation.

The likeliest suspects, directly or indirectly, were Siegel's lifelong associates: the Syndicate leaders who, according to Doc Stacher, had approved Siegel's execution at the Havana Conference the previous December. Stacher had no doubt that Lucky Luciano had followed through on his warning. Luciano had made clear that Siegel would have to die. If the job was too personal for Lansky, Luciano would get it done for him. In fact, Stacher said later, Lansky had hired Mickey Cohen to guard Siegel, and warned Cohen of the consequences if Siegel was killed. As a result, Stacher theorized, "Bugsy's death must have involved Lucky Luciano because Meyer had told Mickey Cohen to stay close to Bugsy, and yet he hadn't been there with Bugsy at the end. That could only have meant that Luciano pulled Mickey off the case."[33]

Still, there were pieces that just didn't fit. Why, if the order had been handed down the previous December, couldn't the Syndicate have gotten the job done within days or weeks? And why, if the fix was in, did Meyer Lansky keep visiting his oldest and dearest friend at the Flamingo? Why did he help under-write the cost of finishing the hotel, and talk Frank Costello, among others, into investing with him? Why visit Siegel at the Flamingo just days before his death?[34] Most bafflingly, why kill Siegel when the Flamingo was generating money at last? Didn't it make more sense to put personal feelings aside, and partake of the profits?

These queries bolstered the odds of a race wire shooter, possibly Russell Brophy. The race wire grumblers had just lost serious future income, and killing Siegel might undo the damage, or at least satisfy the need for revenge.[35]

Beverly Hills Police Chief Clinton Anderson had another suspect in mind: Moe Sedway. Over the years, Sedway had done all he could to buff Siegel's image, steer the race wire his way, and fend off his rivals. Yet Siegel had banished him. Sedway seethed with resentment, and his appearance at the Flamingo the night of Siegel's shooting, alongside Gus Greenbaum, seemed to suggest he had played a role.

Sedway could hardly be accused of the Beverly Hills shooting himself when he was three hundred miles away in Vegas. But he certainly could have ordered the hit, or found the right man to do it. Chief Anderson had a hunch that Sedway might hustle back down to L.A. to clean up any of the dead man's unfinished business. The chief was right. When his men brought Sedway in, he was trembling and struggling for breath. He asked if he could postpone the interview until the next day. The police chief had no evidence on which to hold him and so, reluctantly, he agreed. The next morning, the chief learned that Sedway had been rushed to a hospital in Hollywood. When Anderson's men came by, they found their suspect in a private room marked "No admittance, Oxygen." They entered anyway. Again, Sedway pleaded for time. That night, the casino manager took a late-night train to Vegas, putting himself outside the Beverly Hills police department's jurisdiction. "I never had a chance to talk to him," Anderson said later, "but I was convinced, and still am, that he had a hand in the Siegel killing. He knew who did it."[36]

Gus Greenbaum, another of the three men who took over the Flamingo that fateful night, was just as likely to have known who killed Siegel. He never said a word about it, and no evidence of his complicity ever emerged. A decade or so later, after managing the Flamingo to great profitability, he would let gambling and drugs slide him into skimming. The punishment for skimming was always especially violent, as Siegel's story had underscored. Greenbaum and his wife were found dead in their Arizona home, their throats cut so brutally that their heads were nearly severed.[37]

There was another, equally plausible suspect in Siegel's murder. What if the love of Siegel's life had had something to do with his death—if not caused it, then allowed it to happen?

Virginia Hill had never traveled to Europe before. Yet she crossed the Atlantic on June 16 for an extended stay. How unlikely was it that Joe Epstein might have warned her Siegel was about to die, and advised a long vacation in a faraway place?

Perhaps, if she did get wind of the shooting to come, Hill

could have tipped off Siegel and fled with him to some South Sea island. But that was a course Siegel would never have taken. As Doc Stacher said of Siegel, "he knew there was no point in running away. He was never a coward. He would stay in the United States and face whatever was coming to him."[38]

Hill, for her part, said she first heard the news of Siegel's death at a party outside Paris—perhaps the early evening of June 21, likely on the Feuillattes' houseboat near Fontainebleau, where Hill was sharing a bedroom with Nicolas's mother. "We got to talking about calisthenics," Hill recounted, "and I told another American girl, 'I know a fellow who loves calisthenics and does them very well—Ben Siegel.' She looked at me strangely and replied. 'Why, he's dead. Didn't you know?'"[39]

Shortly after, a Paris-based reporter tracked Hill down to the Claridge, her hotel near the Champs Élysées. During a brief interview, Hill cried more than once. She said her last quarrel with Siegel was over whether he should wear a sport shirt to a dinner he was attending. "I told him he could not go to dinner with all those people in a dirty white sports shirt. I can't believe who shot him, or why." As she talked, Hill kept nervously crossing her legs, and the reporter noticed several bruises on them. They came, Hill said, from horseback riding in the Fontainebleau forest.[40]

Chick Hill said that his big sister called him from the Claridge, hoarse with grief. As they talked on the phone, cars filled with gawkers inched along past the Beverly Hills house. According to Chick's later account of that night, Hill asked Chick who had done it; Chick said he had no idea.[41]

"What about my stuff in the safe?"

Chick said he had it all.

"Take my things and ship them to Florida," Hill commanded, meaning the house in Miami that Siegel had helped her buy. "I'll meet you there."

There was a lot more to pack than jewelry. Over the next

day or two, Chick and Jerri packed silverware, dishes, linens, Hill's wardrobe, and more. At Hill's instruction, they called Joe Epstein in Chicago for cash: a packet with several thousand dollars arrived. They then set out in Chick's new car for Hill's house in Miami. Chick Hill was never questioned again about the murder. Two decades later, Bugsy biographer Dean Jennings would get him to sit for hours of interviews, studded with fascinating details about his time with Siegel and Hill. Chick's openness seemed to underscore his innocence in the affair. Or did it?

Millicent and Barbara were still on their cross-country train trip the morning of June 22. "I know we stopped in Chicago, but we didn't see the newspaper," Millicent said decades later. "We were kids."[42] The Super Chief sleeper chugged westward, until something very odd happened. The train came to a full stop at a depot one hundred miles from Los Angeles, and a big black Packard rolled up.

As Millicent later described, Allen Smiley was in the car. So was Dr. Maurice Siegel, Ben's younger brother. And so, to their amazement, was their mother. Esther had flown out from New York as soon as she heard the news. From the L.A. railroad terminal, she had been driven north to this meeting point, where her daughters could disembark without being mobbed by the flashbulb-popping press awaiting them in L.A.[43]

Millicent recalled that the car ride proceeded in grim silence to Maurice's house. "That's where they told us," she said. She felt grateful, at least, that she and Barbara had not found out from the headlines while the train was en route, forcing them to absorb the news without their mother. "I don't know what the two us would have done," she said. "It was a shock."[44]

At some point that day or the next, Esther was obligated to visit the office of an L.A. district attorney and submit to a polite but probing interrogation. She came dressed in black, with black-netted demigloves. Nervously, she smoked one cork-tipped cigarette after another. She had married Siegel eighteen years before, she told the investigators. They had been schoolmates, she explained, and stayed close through their teenage years until Siegel asked her, at seventeen, to marry him. "Benny was in the garage business then," Esther offered.

Esther had never thought she'd seek a divorce, she declared. "I divorced him only because I was tired of being alone. His business interests kept him away all of the time. He was a wonderful husband, a good father to our two children and a good provider." Asked about various gangsters with whom Siegel had done business, she denied knowing any of them. Nor, she added, had she ever heard of Virginia Hill. "I never knew or heard about Virginia Hill until I saw her name in the papers after the murder," Esther declared.[45]

In a breach of Jewish tradition, Siegel's body remained at the county morgue for three days. Finally on June 25, Maurice had his dead brother's body brought to the Groman Mortuary at 830 West Washington Boulevard in L.A. Siegel was embalmed, a further breach of tradition, and by one newspaper account "clothed in a blue suit, white shirt, blue tie, with a white handkerchief tucked in his breast pocket."[46] Only the mortuary staff saw this choice of clothing, since Siegel's mutilated body was then placed in a hermetically sealed $5,000 silver-plated casket.

The next day at 8:50 A.M., a limousine rolled up to the mortuary, where a gaggle of reporters and news photographers was waiting. Out came Esther, Millicent, and Barbara, along with Maurice, Allen Smiley, and one other of Ben's siblings, his sister Bessie Soloway. Inside the chapel lay the casket flanked by white candelabra, with two amber spotlights fixed upon it. According to one published report, there were no flowers, no eulogy, only a hurried Twenty-Third Psalm and a short Hebrew prayer intoned by Rabbi Max Kert to four hundred empty seats.

"It was all over in five minutes, at 8:55 AM," the *Examiner* reported. "Smiley and the four women slipped through a casket room, went through a little-used door and down a rubbish-littered alley to a gate which was unlocked for them. They hurried to a waiting car a block away and were gone, neatly escaping the press. Dr. Siegel, hatless, walked quietly out the mortuary's front door, unrecognized by photographers."[47]

Without further ceremony, Siegel was interred at the local Beth Olam cemetery, the Jewish section of one hundred–acre Hollywood Forever Cemetery. The poor Jewish boy who had dreamed of becoming a star was now assured of the company of stars in perpetuity. Already, the cemetery included Rudolph Valentino and Douglas Fairbanks; soon these would be joined by Judy Garland, Marion Davies, Fay Wray, Peter Lorre, John Huston, and so many more.[48]

Back in New York, a plaque in Ben's name was added to the memory wall at the Bialystoker synagogue at 7-11 Bialystoker Place, the old neighborhood from which Ben had so fiercely set himself free. Right above his plaque was the one for his father Max, put up just two months before. To the end, the relationship between father and son had been based on the pact that Max and Jennie never allude to the source of Ben's largesse. The elephant remained in the room, but it allowed Ben to be the provider that his father had struggled and failed to be, and for his parents to live comfortable lives after working themselves to the bone. Almost certainly, Ben had paid for his father's memorial plaque at the Bialystoker synagogue. Just as likely, Ben's brother Maurice, the respected doctor, paid for Ben's two months later.

Shortly after the funeral, Maurice petitioned to become administrator of his brother's Nevada and California estates. Together, he found the estates worth all of $113,969, most of it in stock in the Flamingo, which was to say the Nevada Projects

Corporation. Ben's stock was worth a fraction of its face value, given his reckless choice to inflate the stock by selling the same shares again and again. Whether it had any worth at all would depend on how the Flamingo was run now.

Esther had hoped the estate story might be very different. Hadn't her ex-husband vowed to pay her $600 a week in alimony for the rest of her life, and to support their daughters? Perhaps she should not have been surprised: here was only the latest and last example of Ben's improvidence. As a practical matter, Esther sued the estate for $800,000, the money promised her for her life expectancy of forty more years from the time her ex-husband died. But that money, she came to realize, simply didn't exist. Most of what remained went to creditors, the largest of which was the IRS: Siegel hadn't paid his taxes for the last three years, and owed $22,000 plus interest.[49]

In the month of Siegel's death, the Flamingo again turned a profit, albeit a modest one. Its investors were relieved, but in no mood to wait for the Flamingo to earn back its $6 million cost at the gaming tables. They wanted to be made whole, or at least mostly so. Two outside groups submitted proposals for running the place in alliance with the Syndicate. The winning group was led by Sandy Adler, owner of El Rancho. The Adler group reportedly paid $3.9 million for 49 percent of the Flamingo in early July, though Nevada tax records showed that Adler and his partners paid only $3 million.[50] Billy Wilkerson was said to be one of the selling parties, but his son, Billy Wilkerson III, doubts that his father got anything out of the deal. "When Siegel was shot," Wilkerson says, "the new owners flatly refused to honor any deals Siegel had done with anyone."[51]

Wilkerson might be left high and dry, but Lansky and his fellow Syndicate backers could take comfort in the $3 or $4 million they'd netted from their newest partner. It was a sizable sum, enough to relieve their anxiety, and a clear indication that

Ben Siegel's folly had promise after all. Soon enough, the Flamingo would start pulling in $4 million a year, assuring the rise
of modern Las Vegas.

Was Virginia Hill next on the Syndicate's murder list that
summer, given the rumors of Swiss bank accounts? To reporters who sought her out, she scoffed when asked if her life might
be at risk. "I spoke to my lawyer in Los Angeles by transatlan-
tic phone and he said I have nothing to worry about," Hill declared in Paris. "I guess I'll go ahead with my plans and stay
two or three months in Europe."[52]

Nevertheless, Hill checked out of the Hôtel Claridge in
Paris on July 2, leaving no forwarding address. She drove to
Monaco and spent time at the casino. The morning after a long
night at the tables, she was found unconscious in her room,
barely in time for doctors to save her life. For the second time,
just months after her first serious overdose in Vegas, she had
again nearly died from barbiturates. There was a third overdose at the Ritz in Paris, and then a fourth when Hill got to
Miami to learn that her brother had married Jerri Mason.[53]

Hill had always nursed a violent temper: it was part of what
had made her Ben Siegel's alter ego. She flared like a brushfire;
she plunged, for days after, into a deep despond. But the overdoses were new. At the least, they suggested growing anxiety
in the last weeks of Ben Siegel's life, and deep depression after
his death. But was this not also, perhaps, a woman struggling
under a burden of enormous guilt? A woman, perhaps, who
knew when the love of her life would be killed, and who would
do the deed?

Anyone who writes about Bugsy Siegel ends up nursing his
own murder scenario. My own is based on simple logic. The
Syndicate felt sure that Hill had begun skimming serious money
into Swiss bank accounts. Whether or not she *had* begun skimming, the Syndicate *thought* she had. Why, then, would Frank

Costello or Lucky Luciano not send shooters to Hill's hotel in Europe, force her to cough up the money, and kill her once they did?

That the Syndicate bosses didn't do that suggests a deal got made, weeks or months before Ben's death. To keep the money she'd squirreled away, and to keep from being killed, Hill had to perform some duty that would allow her to keep those Swiss bank accounts. My guess is that Hill assigned Chick, her little brother, to orchestrate the killing by hiring a fellow U.S. infantryman with rifle expertise. He himself had just been discharged from the military, where he had trained with a rifle. Hill then left for Paris to be an ocean away when the deed got done.

Chick was in the Linden Drive house the night of Siegel's murder. He might easily have coordinated with a shooter to await the return of the group from dinner. For that, Chick had at least two motives. One was to keep his big sister from being physically assaulted any more by Ben: the two had fought more bitterly, and physically, of late.[54] Another was to allow Hill to keep the money in the Swiss bank account, both for her benefit and his own. If Hill and her brother didn't murder Ben Siegel, someone else would: his sentence was written. The only difference was that if someone else did the deed, Hill would still be on the hook for the money she'd skimmed. Ben's death was in a sense his last gift to her. He just didn't know it. The cost to Hill was that she had to live with the knowledge that she'd made her brother kill the love of her life. Certainly that would explain the four overdoses, and the ones that followed, and her tragic, spectacular decline.

One subscriber to that theory, or rather some variation of it, is mafia historian Nick Pileggi: he feels that Chick Hill was the shooter. Chick could easily have been motivated by the fights that Siegel and Hill were having, Pileggi theorizes, enough for Chick to kill his sister's tormentor.[55] The detail of the rifle was telling in another way. "I never recall anyone else ever shooting with a rifle," Pileggi says, meaning hired hit men. "And if it was a wiseguy," he says, meaning an experienced mobster, "they're not going to shoot through the window. [Siegel] would have disappeared, you would have put him in the desert."

For what it's worth, Meyer Lansky suspected Chick Hill as well, or so he stated through a spokesman to the *Los Angeles Examiner.* He said he believed the "hot-headed southerner," as he described Chick Hill, might have killed Siegel "because of Siegel mistreating [Virginia] Hill."[56] By then, the authorities had all but given up hoping to solve the murder. "We have the gambling angle, the love angle, the racing news syndicate angle, the narcotics angle—you can take your choice," one investigator said. "Everyone tells us how much they loved him, but it's a cinch somebody didn't."[57]

In the time that was left to her, Virginia Hill would try to kill Jerri Mason by pistol-whipping her. She would marry an Austrian ski instructor in Sun Valley, Idaho, give birth to a son, and make a memorably profane appearance before the Kefauver Commission hearings on organized crime in 1951. The money stream from Joe Epstein would finally dry up, leading to a government auction of all her possessions. She would end up in Klosters, Switzerland, skiing and drinking with a group that included legendary actress Greta Garbo and best-selling novelist Irwin Shaw. In March 1966, she drove to an Austrian mountain village called Koppl, walked into the woods with a vial of twenty-eight pills, and gulped them down with clear brook water. She succeeded at last, with this sixth or seventh overdose, in killing herself.[58]

The other women in Ben Siegel's family circle fared only marginally better after Ben Siegel's death. The Syndicate promised his widow Esther that it would protect her and her daughters, and help the daughters marry well. This pledge was made by Morris Rosen, the top Lansky man who with Gus Greenbaum and Moe Sedway had taken control of the Flamingo the night of Ben's death. Morris was an odd one to make that pledge, since he almost certainly had something to do with Ben Siegel's murder. But business was business, and Rosen was, according to his granddaughter Wendy, a key Syndicate businessman, as powerful as Lansky. "If Meyer needed money, he got it from my grandfather Morris," Wendy recalls. "He was the financial backer for Murder Inc. My grandfather was a very wealthy man." Also smart: almost nothing was ever written about him. "His hands were never dirty."

Barbara, the younger of Ben's daughters, chose not to take Morris Rosen up on his offer. As soon as she could, she ran away from home bound for the midwest. She got as far as Detroit, where she married a man who became successful in real estate. For the rest of her life, she had almost nothing to do with her sister and mother, and never mentioned her father to her midwestern friends.

Millicent, the older daughter, let her life be steered by the Syndicate. Barely eighteen, she married Morris Rosen's son Jack. She had known him since birth: he had pushed her pram. The match was essentially arranged. It astonished Sandra Lansky, daughter of Meyer Lansky and childhood friend of Millicent. "How could Millicent marry into the family that so bloodily replaced her father, unless she hated her father, way beyond hatred?" So mused Sandra Lansky in her memoir.[59] Wendy Rosen felt she knew exactly why her mother married Jack Rosen. "Having Millicent marry Jack was the best way to provide for her, and protect her."[60]

Meyer Lansky, too, had committed to help Ben Siegel's widow and daughters. He paid for Millicent's wedding to Jack Rosen at the Waldorf Astoria. An eight-by-ten black-and-white photograph shows Millicent in a white wedding gown with a white lace veil, on her march into matrimony. Behind her walks a ghostlike Meyer Lansky. From his pained expression, one can easily imagine that he had something to do with the death of his childhood friend and is trying to atone by marching that friend's daughter up the aisle.

The last of the women in Ben Siegel's family circle was, of course, Esther, his long-suffering wife, who spent her last years alone in Manhattan. "She lived on East End Avenue, a tiny little apartment," recalls Wendy Rosen, her granddaughter, who grew up nearby. "I would go there on Saturday, and she would make me tuna fish sandwiches in this tiny kitchen—I see it now. She had these portraits of my mother [Millicent] and my aunt Barbara in her living room." The portraits were painted, ornately framed, and huge. "I can't even describe how big they were." Very likely, they had been displayed in the mansion on Delfern Drive. They were much too big for Esther's tiny living room.

The apartment smelled of perfume, Wendy recalls, and it had a bedroom door that Esther kept closed. Wendy was too polite to push it open. One time, though, Esther forgot to close the door, and while she was making tuna sandwiches in the kitchen, Wendy got a good look in. "It wasn't just a bedroom," Wendy recalls. "It was like a shrine, filled with pictures of Ben. Framed pictures on the bureau and bedside tables, larger ones hanging on the walls." That was when Wendy realized how much her grandmother still loved her husband. "She worshiped him."

When Esther died in 1982, she left almost no money or assets, aside from the memorabilia Wendy had glimpsed, despite the Syndicate's pledge of lifetime care and protection. She did have one request. She wanted to be interred at the Hollywood Forever cemetery, as close to Ben as possible. There she lies, in a crypt along the same corridor as Ben's, though at a distance of perhaps one hundred feet, in death as in life not close enough, but as close as she could get.

Epilogue

Over the next decade, the Syndicate would finance, or help finance, many of the Strip's big casinos, from the Thunderbird, where Harry Belafonte helped break the city's color barrier, to the Desert Inn, the Sands, the Sahara, the Riviera, the Dunes, the Stardust, the Tropicana, the Royal Nevada, and Caesars Palace, where Frank Sinatra, Dean Martin, Sammy Davis Jr., and the rest of the Rat Pack held court. Others would be built by gangsters from Chicago, Cleveland, Philadelphia, Detroit, Kansas City, or Milwaukee, often borrowing, for building capital, from the Teamsters Union's retirement fund. Most of the builders in this new age of Vegas were Jewish; nearly all had shady pasts. Virtually none wore flashy suits and swaggered like Bugsy. They were *businessmen.* Moe Dalitz, for one, opened the Desert Inn in the late 1940s, but stayed a silent backer, never acknowledging his ties to organized crime. He liked to be known as a civic leader. When the local press dubbed him

Mr. Las Vegas, he was pleased. Ben Siegel would have been horrified.

As ever more dazzling hotel-casinos arose, the Flamingo changed hands and slid into a state of desuetude. One chunk after another was replaced, though not with Siegel's sense of style. Now it stands as a large but low-class casino, known for cheap food and rooms, surrounded by grander resorts. Aside from its name, the Flamingo's only commemoration of Ben Siegel is a trio of amateurish plaques, set rather high overhead as if to discourage passersby from reading them through.

And yet Ben Siegel's imprint on Vegas grows with each next brand-new super resort. The Bellagio, the Wynn, the Venetian, the Mandalay, the MGM Grand—all in a sense pay homage to the man whose manic ambition got the Flamingo finished and showed what could be done. Would someone else have led the way? Would Vegas be the Vegas we know? Possibly a valley of cookie-cutter houses would have filled either side of the Strip before enough hotel-casinos got built to inspire the rest, and keep the houses at bay.

A few miles from today's droopy Flamingo, in downtown Las Vegas, stands one more tribute to Ben Siegel and his colleagues in crime: the Mob Museum, opened in 2012 in the building used by U.S. Senator Estes Kefauver for his 1950 hearings on organized crime. The museum marks a sea change for Las Vegas: recognition, after decades of squeamishness from city officials, that mobsters helped shape its culture and history.

Along with accounts of Bugsy's life and career, the museum includes two personal items: a tortoiseshell-framed pair of aviator sunglasses, donated by George Raft, and a long white silk scarf, monogrammed with large, art deco–style initials. Together, the glasses and scarf suggest a dashing figure, one who lived a glamorous, even recherché life, if also a deadly and unforgivable one, a boy from the immigrant slums of the Lower East Side who fought to have the life he wanted, whatever anyone else might say, and who had that life, just as he'd hoped, until the moment at about 10:45 P.M. on June 20, 1947, when in a split second, too fast for any pain or conscious thought, it stopped.

NOTES

Prologue

1. Jacob Riis, *How the Other Half Lives*, quoted in Laurence Bergreen, *As Thousands Cheer: The Life of Irving Berlin* (Boston: Da Capo, 1996), 7.
2. Quoted in Fried, *Rise and Fall*, 37.
3. Author interview with Nick Pileggi.
4. Fried, *Rise and Fall*, 232.
5. Malcolm Gladwell, "The Crooked Ladder," *New Yorker*, August 3, 2014.
6. Birmingham, *The Rest of Us*, 278.
7. Fried, *Rise and Fall*, 250.
8. Cohen, *Tough Jews*, 150.

Chapter 1. The Lure of the Streets

1. Ship's manifest, the SS *Etruria* on its voyage from Liverpool to New York City, June 23–July 1, 1900. Max Siegel is on the

immigrant passenger list. Microfilm Serial: T715, 1897, 1957; Microfilm Roll: Roll 0136; Line: 3; p. 91.

2. Gragg, *Benjamin "Bugsy" Siegel*, 2.

3. 1910 US Federal Census report for Max and Jennie Siegel.

4. Hill-Hauser family tree, Ben Siegel, https://www.ancestry .com/family-tree/person/tree/161160880/person/402104221638 /facts.

5. Gershon David Hundert and YIVO Institute for Jewish Research, *The YIVO Encyclopedia of Jews in Eastern Europe* (New Haven: Yale University Press, 2008), 560–567.

6. Birmingham, *The Rest of Us*, 46.

7. The Lower East Side Tenement Museum, 103 Orchard Street, New York, tours of immigrant life in the early twentieth century.

8. Statement of Benjamin Siegel, Taken by Chief Deputy District Attorney Eugene D. Williams, August 16, 1940, Investigation in LA, CA, 1934–59, 2, Box 1, Folder 3, Murder Inc Series, Kings County DA Files, Municipal Archives of the City of New York.

9. 1910 US Federal Census report for Max Siegel household; 1940 US Federal Census.

10. 1940 US Federal Census; 1930 US Federal Census; 1910 US Federal Census.

11. Laurence Bergreen, *As Thousands Cheer: The Life of Irving Berlin* (Boston: Da Capo, 1996), 7, 6.

12. Joselit, *Our Gang*, 18; David Weinstein, *The Eddie Cantor Story* (Waltham, MA: Brandeis University Press, 2017), 10; author interview with Wendy Rosen.

13. 1930 US Federal Census.

14. Epstein, *At the Edge of a Dream*, 83.

15. The PS 110 *Observer*, centennial issue, May 30, 2015, PS110 PTA.org.

16. Joselit, *Our Gang*, 33.

17. Ibid., 6.

18. Lincoln Steffens, *The Autobiography of Lincoln Steffens* (1931; Berkeley, CA: Heyday, 2005).

19. Carpozi, *Bugsy*, 13.

20. Joselit, *Our Gang*, 19; Fried, *Rise and Fall*, 39.

21. Jennings, *Kill Each Other*, 23.

22. Lacey, *Little Man*, 34–36; Eisenberg, Dan, and Landau, *Meyer Lansky*, 55.

23. Cohen, *Tough Jews*, 42.

24. Eisenberg, Dan, and Landau, *Meyer Lansky*, 56–57.

25. Robert Rockaway, "Hoodlum Hero: The Jewish Gangster as Defender of His People, 1919–1949," *American Jewish History* 82 (1994): 215–235.

26. Author interview with Wendy Rosen.

27. Lacey, *Little Man*, 36.

28. Author interview with Robert Rockaway.

29. Author interview with Nick Pileggi.

30. Lacey, *Little Man*, 49.

31. Heinze quoted in Gragg, *Benjamin "Bugsy" Siegel*, 16; Luciano quoted in Cohen, *Tough Jews*, 57; Lansky quoted in Rockaway, *Good to His Mother*, 10.

32. Reppetto, *American Mafia*, 134.

33. Costello quoted in AZ quotes.com, https://www.azquotes.com/author/30200-Frank_Costello.

34. Fried, *Rise and Fall*, 122.

35. Eisenberg, Dan, and Landau, *Meyer Lansky*, 72.

36. Friedrich, *City of Nets*, 370.

37. Wolf, *Frank Costello*, 48–50.

38. Denton and Morris, *Money and Power*, 50.

39. Wolf, *Frank Costello*, 54–55.

40. Jennings, *Kill Each Other*, 27.

41. 1940 US Federal Census report for Max Siegel.

42. Florabel Muir, *Headline Happy* (New York: Holt, 1950), 157.

43. Fried, *Rise and Fall*, 110.

44. "Las Vegas: An Unconventional History," American Experience, WGBH-TV, https://www.pbs.org/wgbh/americanexperience/features/lasvegas-early/.

Chapter 2. Marriage and Murder

1. Eisenberg, Dan, and Landau, *Meyer Lansky*, 286–287; *Los Angeles Evening Herald and Express*, November 19, 1940. Siegel's police record reviewed, with the rape charge said to have been filed January 3, 1926, in Brooklyn, dismissed January 12, 1926.

2. Carpozi, *Bugsy*, 17.

3. Lacey, *Little Man*, 60.

4. "'X, Z' Suspects Accused of Part in Gang Slaying," *Los Angeles Examiner*, August 20, 1940; "Slaying in Los Angeles," *Los Angeles Times*, August 21, 1940.

5. Rockaway, *Good to His Mother*, 22.

6. Author interview with Wendy Rosen.

7. Lacey, *Little Man*, 69.

8. Lansky and Stadiem, *Daughter of the King*, 23, 26.

9. Rosen interview.

10. Wedding licenses for Ben Siegel and Estelle Krakauer: Register no. 1195 New York State Department of Health, New York County, City of New York, January 16, 1929; marriage certificate January 27, 1929, 332 Rogers Avenue, New York, County and State of New York. Marriage License for Meyer Lansky of New York City in county and state of New York, and Annie Citron of Brooklyn, New York, April 25, 1929, Register no. 6697, New York State Department of Health.

11. Fried, *Rise and Fall*, 116.

12. Ibid., 144.

13. Cohen, *Tough Jews*, 153.

14. Eisenberg, Dan, and Landau, *Meyer Lansky*, 70.

15. Lacey, *Little Man*, 56–68.

16. Jennings, *Kill Each Other*, 23–24.

17. Eisenberg, Dan, and Landau, *Meyer Lansky*, 129, 130.

18. Lacey, *Little Man*, 91.

19. Fried, *Rise and Fall*, 122–126.

20. Eisenberg, Dan, and Landau, *Meyer Lansky*, 120–124; Lacey, *Little Man*, 63–65.

21. Gragg, *Benjamin "Bugsy" Siegel*, 10–14.

22. Rockaway, *Good To His Mother,* 23; Eisenberg, Dan, and Landau, *Meyer Lansky,* 127–135; Reppetto, *American Mafia,* 137.

23. Eisenberg, Dan, and Landau, *Meyer Lansky,* 136–141; Lacey, *Little Man,* 62–64.

24. The possibly apocryphal quotation can be found at www .azquotes.com/author/30189-Lucky_Luciano.

25. New York Police Photograph 133-13: People v. Buchalter et al.: Police Investigation, 1936–41, Box 4, Folder 34, Murder Inc Series, Kings County DA files.

26. Carpozi, *Bugsy,* 23–24; Eisenberg, Dan, and Landau, *Meyer Lansky,* 166.

27. Carpozi, *Bugsy,* 24–29.

28. Eisenberg, Dan, and Landau, *Meyer Lansky,* 175, 176.

29. 1940 US Federal Census report, in which residence information circa 1935 was included.

30. O'Connor, *A Sort of Utopia,* 98–99.

31. Lacey, *Little Man,* 89.

Chapter 3. Sportsman in Paradise

A note on the FBI's Bugsy Siegel files

Over time, the FBI has made public files on certain figures of general interest. These are provided through an online portal titled "The Vault." As it happens, a voluminous file exists on Ben Siegel at the Vault, readily available by means of a few key clicks. The most direct URL is https://www.fbi.gov/@@search?Searchable Text=Bugsy+Siegel&pageSize=20&page=1&sort_on=&sort_order =descending&after=&searchSite=vault.fbi.gov. Most of the relevant FBI documents and fragments deal with the FBI's months-long surveillance of Bugsy in Las Vegas in 1946–1947.

That said, the Bugsy trove is a mess. Files are presented in mixed-up numerical order. Documents within those folders are disordered and redundant. Many passages are, of course, redacted, which only increases the challenge of dealing with them.

So jumbled are these documents that I saw no point in trying to beat them into a usable order, to which end notes could actually be attached. Instead, I went through the files myself, pruning out the frequent redundancies and creating my own rough chronological master file. After days of organizing them in files that seemed somewhat comprehensible to me, I began sifting through them using relevant keywords. This proved immensely helpful for me in my efforts to squeeze useful information from the files.

As a result, I am making my reorganized FBI files available to anyone who would like to use them. Critics may want to test whether I've been accurate in using these FBI files in my research. Other writers about Bugsy Siegel and Jewish gangsters may find that a readily accessible FBI master file on Bugsy is helpful to them. Whatever the motive, I am happy to assist by emailing my FBI master list to anyone who requests it. The material is public to begin with, and thus belongs to all of us, and the organized version, it seems to me, ought to be just as available. Just write me to request the file at michaelshnayerson@gmail.com.

Once you have the master file, go back to the book and look for end notes with "keywords" relevant to your subject of interest. Then open the master file and search for that word. Presto—passages with that subject pop up, without the onerous obligation of sifting through all the disorganized documents, again and again.

1. Gragg, *Benjamin "Bugsy" Siegel*, 22.
2. Astaire, *Steps in Time*, 125, 126.
3. Jennings, *Kill Each Other*, 20.
4. Ibid., 36.
5. Tereba, *Mickey Cohen*, 47–49.
6. Jennings, *Kill Each Other*, 38.
7. 1940 US Federal Census report for Benjamin Hymen Siegel, in response to questions about where he lived in 1935. Also, Siegel's draft card circa 1941, in which he lists his home as 250 North Delfern Drive, L.A., his date of birth as February 28, 1906, and his telephone number as BRadshaw 23815. See Benjamin Siegel, birth date February 28, 1906, at Ancestry.com, https://www.ancestry.com/family-tree/person/tree/161160880/person/40210 4221638/facts.
8. 1940 US Federal Census.

9. FBI Bugsy Siegel files.

10. Wilkerson, *Hollywood Godfather*, 209.

11. Author interview with Wendy Rosen.

12. Gragg, *Benjamin "Bugsy" Siegel*, 23.

13. Rockaway, *Good to His Mother*, 17.

14. Fried, *Rise and Fall*, 187–192.

15. Ibid., 190–192.

16. Cohen, *Tough Jews*, 165–168.

17. Carpozi, *Bugsy*, 38.

18. Author interview with Nick Pileggi.

19. "The Daughter of Las Vegas: An Interview with Bugsy Siegel's Daughter, Millicent," interview with Millicent Siegel by Diana Edelman, d travels 'round, July 25, 2012, dtravelsround.com /2012/07/25/daughter-las-vegas-interview-millicent-siegel/.

20. Munn, *Jimmy Stewart*, 77.

21. Carpozi, *Bugsy*, 58; Munn, *Jimmy Stewart*, 77–80.

22. Jennings, *Kill Each Other*, 48.

23. "1930s Holmby Hills Estate Built for Mobster Bugsy Siegel Torn Down after Selling for $17.5M," Pricey Pads.com, August 9, 2019, https://www.priceypads.com/1930s-holmby-hills-estate -built-for-mobster-bugsy-siegel-redeveloped-after-selling-for-17 -5m-photos-video/.

24. Gragg, *Benjamin "Bugsy" Siegel*, 27.

25. Jennings, *Kill Each Other*, 47.

26. Ibid., 39–40.

27. Friedrich, *City of Nets*, 372.

28. Florabel Muir, *Headline Happy* (New York: Holt, 1950), 163; Parsons, *The Gay Illiterate*, 142.

29. "Dorothy Di Frasso Wiki, Biography, Net Worth, Age, Family, Facts and More," wikifamouspeople, https://www.wikifamous people.com/dorothy-di-frasso-wiki-biography-net-worth-age -family-facts-and-more/.

30. Gragg, *Benjamin "Bugsy" Siegel*, 31; Parsons, *The Gay Illiterate*, 143; Lewis Yablonsky, *George Raft* (Lincoln, NE: I.Universe. com.Inc, 2001) 181–197.

31. Fried, *Rise and Fall*, 170, 171.

32. Jennings, *Kill Each Other*, 106.

33. Gragg, *Benjamin "Bugsy" Siegel*, 30.

34. Jennings, *Kill Each Other*, 123–124.

35. Friedrich, *City of Nets*, 372.

36. Rockaway, *Good to His Mother*, 163, 164.

37. Turkus and Feder, *Murder, Inc.*, 270.

38. Jennings, *Kill Each Other*, 48.

39. Gragg, *Benjamin "Bugsy" Siegel*, 42; also see "George Bruneman," MafiaWiki, https://mafia.wikia.org/wiki/George_Brunemann.

40. UPI report, October 28, 1981.

Chapter 4. The Masterminds of Murder Inc.

1. Fried, *Rise and Fall*, 194–195.

2. Ibid., 196.

3. Robert A. Rockaway, "Why Gangsters Who Broke Every Law Still Went to Services on Yom Kippur," *Tablet*, October 2, 2014.

4. Rockaway, *Good to His Mother*, 135.

5. Fried, *Rise and Fall*, 205.

6. Carpozi, *Bugsy*, 24.

7. Cohen, *Tough Jews*, 97.

8. "Bugsy's Angel Midwestern Millionaire," *Los Angeles Examiner*, November 23, 1940; Gragg, *Benjamin "Bugsy" Siegel*, 34, 35; Jennings, *Kill Each Other*, 36–37.

9. "Bugsy's Angel Millionaire."

10. FBI Bugsy Siegel files.

11. "Bugsy, Lepke, 3 Others Indicted," *Los Angeles Examiner*, August 21, 1940; FBI Siegel files, chrono 3, word search: Chi chi; Lacey, *Little Man*, 110.

12. Allan May, "The History of the Race Wire Service," *Crime*, October 14, 2009; Jennings, *Kill Each Other*, 80.

13. Gragg, *Benjamin "Bugsy" Siegel*, 32; Jennings, *Kill Each Other*, 67; James Kaplan, *Frank: The Voice* (New York; Anchor, 2011), 256–258.

14. Florabel Muir, *Headline Happy* (Holt: New York, 1950), 199–200.

15. Munn, *Jimmy Stewart*, 77, 78.

16. Ibid., 79.

17. Jennings, *Kill Each Other*, 106.

18. Ibid., 43, 44.

19. Gragg, *Benjamin "Bugsy" Siegel*, 25, 26.

20. Friedrich, *City of Nets*, 373.

21. Jennings, *Kill Each Other*, 43, 44, 46.

22. Ibid., 52–60.

23. "Trip Finances under Scrutiny," *Los Angeles Times*, January 13, 1939; "Bello Challenge to Love Duel on 'Hell Ship' Bared," *Los Angeles Examiner*, January 13, 1939.

24. Jennings, *Kill Each Other*, 57.

25. "Treasure Hunt Recounted by Countess Di Frasso," *Los Angeles Examiner*, January 14, 1939.

26. "The Daughter of Las Vegas: An Interview with Bugsy Siegel's Daughter, Millicent," interview with Millicent Siegel by Diana Edelman, d travels 'round, July 25, 2012, dtravelsround.com /2012/07/25/daughter-las-vegas-interview-millicent-siegel/.

27. Interview with Millicent Siegel, *Las Vegas Sun*, November 3, 2010.

28. William Bradford Huie, "My Christmas with Bugsy Siegel," *American Mercury*, January 1951, pp. 7–22. See also Muir, *Headline Happy*.

29. Gragg, *Benjamin "Bugsy" Siegel*, 44.

30. Jennings, *Kill Each Other*, 62.

31. Fried, *Rise and Fall*, 212.

32. Jennings, *Kill Each Other*, 76.

33. Gragg, *Benjamin "Bugsy" Siegel*, 38, 39; Jennings, *Kill Each Other*, 75–78.

34. Eisenberg, Dan, and Landau, *Meyer Lansky*, 185, 186.

35. Cohen, *Tough Jews*, 189; Robert Rockaway, "Hoodlum Hero: The Jewish Gangster as Defender of His People, 1919–1949," *American Jewish History* 82 (1994): 215–235.

Chapter 5. Going After Big Greenie

1. "Bugsy, Lepke, 3 Others Indicted," *Los Angeles Examiner*, August 21, 1940.

2. Eisenberg, Dan, and Landau, *Meyer Lansky*, 168.

3. Ibid., 166.

4. Fried, *Rise and Fall*, 214; Cohen, *Tough Jews*, 203.

5. Jennings, *Kill Each Other*, 82–85.

6. Gragg, *Benjamin "Bugsy" Siegel*, 48–51.

7. Cohen, *Tough Jews*, 103.

8. "Slaying in Los Angeles," *Los Angeles Times*, August 21, 1940.

9. "Bugsy, Lepke, 3 Others Indicted."

10. Rockaway, *Good to His Mother*, 159.

11. Turkus and Feder, *Murder, Inc.*

12. "Murder Inc.! 3 Accused Here in Gang Killings," *Los Angeles Evening Herald and Examiner*, August 16, 1940; Gragg, *Benjamin "Bugsy" Siegel*, 52.

13. "Seize Bugs Siegel as Slaying Suspect," *Los Angeles Examiner*, August 17, 1940.

14. Jennings, *Kill Each Other*, 99–103.

15. Statement of Benjamin Siegel, Taken at Kipling Hotel, Room 521, 4077 West Third Street, LA, CA, by Chief Deputy District Attorney Eugene D. Williams, at 1 pm, August 16, 1940.

16. Death notice for Morris Louis Annenberg, *Alabama Journal*, July 21, 1942.

17. "Seize Bugs Siegel."

18. "Fear Man Sought in Gang Killing Slain," *Los Angeles Evening Herald and Express*, August 22, 1940.

19. "Bugsy Feared Gang Assassination," *Los Angeles Examiner*, August 22, 1940.

20. "'Just a Retired Business Man,' 'Bugsy' Tells Judge," *Los Angeles Examiner*, August 18, 1940.

21. "Ask Court to Set Bail for Bugs Siegel in Murder Inc. Case," *Los Angeles Evening Herald and Express*, September 30, 1940.

22. "Fear New L.A. Gang Slaying," *Los Angeles Evening Herald Express*, August 22, 1940.

23. "Ask Court to Set Bail."

24. "Bugsy Siegel Jail Parties Probed," *Los Angeles Examiner*, November 19, 1940.

25. Jennings, *Kill Each Other*, 118.

26. Gragg, *Benjamin "Bugsy" Siegel*, 57; Jennings, *Kill Each Other*, 119–120.

27. "Dr. Blank Suspended 30 Days in Siegel Inquiry," *Los Angeles Examiner*, November 23, 1940; "Blank Served Formal Notice of Ouster; Will Fight Charges," *Los Angeles Examiner*, December 10, 1940.

28. Jennings, *Kill Each Other*, 121–122.

29. "Siegel Free, Sorry," *Los Angeles Examiner*, December 12, 1940.

30. "Siegel Free, Sorry."

31. "Final Pleas in Siegel Hearing," *Los Angeles Evening Herald and Express*, May 27, 1941.

32. "Hunt Bugsy in Greenie Killing," *Los Angeles Evening Herald and Express*, September 23, 1941; "Bugsy Still Missing as Case Up," *Los Angeles Evening Herald and Express*, September 24, 1941.

33. Cohen, *Tough Jews*, 223, 224, 228.

34. Jennings, *Kill Each Other*, 127, 128.

35. Eisenberg, Dan, and Landau, *Meyer Lansky*, 170; Cohen, *Tough Jews*, 232–233.

36. "Carbo Trial Goes On, Siegel Freed 2nd time in Murder Case," *Los Angeles Evening Herald and Express*, February 6, 1942; "Bugsy Siegel Freed in Gangland Murder Case," *Los Angeles Times*, February 6, 1942.

Chapter 6. The Flamingo

1. John Cahlan oral history interview, Collection #: OH-00151, October 4, 1978, audio recording transcript, 2 tapes, Special Collections and Archives, University Libraries, University of Nevada, Las Vegas.

2. Ibid.

3. Gragg, *Benjamin "Bugsy" Siegel*, 70–74.

4. Thelma Coblentz oral history interview, Collection #: OH-00400, February 17, 1980, audio recording transcript. Project: Early Las Vegas–Rosky project, Special Collections and Archives, University of Nevada, Las Vegas.

5. Gragg, *Benjamin "Bugsy" Siegel*, 70–74.

6. Denton and Morris, *Money and Power*, 92–99.

7. Gragg, *Benjamin "Bugsy" Siegel*, 74.

8. Ibid., 74, 75.

9. Jennings, *Kill Each Other*, 69–70.

10. Ibid., 69–73.

11. Ibid., 69, 70.

12. Tereba, *Mickey Cohen*, 53.

13. Reppetto, *American Mafia*, 235.

14. Jennings, *Kill Each Other*, 80–82.

15. Ibid., 80.

16. Gragg, *Benjamin "Bugsy" Siegel*, 82.

17. Ibid., 77.

18. Ibid., 79; Friedrich, *City of Nets*, 373.

19. Denton and Morris, *Money and Power*, 98.

20. Gragg, *Benjamin "Bugsy" Siegel*, 78.

21. Lansky and Stadiem, *Daughter of the King*, 9, 10.

22. Jennings, *Kill Each Other*, 44, 45; Gragg, *Benjamin "Bugsy" Siegel*, 84.

23. Gragg, *Benjamin "Bugsy" Siegel*, 84–85.

24. Ibid., 85.

25. "El Cortez Sold," *Las Vegas Review-Journal*, March 28, 1945.

26. Jennings, *Kill Each Other*, 146–147.

27. Author interview with Peter Gregory.

28. Letter from Siegel to US Draft Board, July 29, 1944, in FBI vault.

Chapter 7. The Start of an Ill-Starred Romance

1. Jennings, *Kill Each Other*, 41, 42.

2. Ibid., 86; Edmonds, *Bugsy's Baby*, 6, 7.

3. Edmonds, *Bugsy's Baby*, 8, 9.

4. Carpozi, *Bugsy*, 119, 120, 121.

5. Ed Reid, *The Mistress and the Mafia: The Virginia Hill Story* (New York: Bantam, 1972), 24; Jennings, *Kill Each Other*, 89.

6. Jennings, *Kill Each Other*, 90.

7. Ibid., 93; Kefauver Commission on Organized Crime hearings, part 7, 1145–1170.

8. Jennings, *Kill Each Other*, 108.

9. Florabel Muir, *Headline Happy* (New York: Holt, 1950), 185; Edmonds, *Bugsy's Baby*, 55.

10. Jennings, *Kill Each Other*, 112.

11. "They Make the News," *Berkeley Daily Gazette*, November 12, 1941; Harrison Carroll, "Behind the Scenes in Hollywood," *Times and Daily News Leader*, November 15, 1941; Gragg, *Benjamin "Bugsy" Siegel*, 87; Jennings, *Kill Each Other*, 131.

12. Virginia Hill testimony, Kefauver Commission, March 16, 1951; Edmonds, *Bugsy's Baby*, 181–191.

13. Jennings, *Kill Each Other*, 146.

14. Ibid., 146.

15. Ibid., 130.

16. Ibid., 132.

17. Ibid., 135; Virginia Hill testimony, Kefauver Commission.

18. Jennings, *Kill Each Other*, 154.

19. "El Cortez Sold," *Las Vegas Review-Journal*, March 28, 1945.

20. Eisenberg, Dan, and Landau, *Meyer Lansky*, 157, 158.

Chapter 8. Bugsy Takes Charge

1. Jennings, *Kill Each Other*, 148.

2. Eisenberg, Dan, and Landau, *Meyer Lansky*, 225, 226.

3. "Siegel Killing Clues Hunted in Las Vegas," *Los Angeles Times*, June 22, 1947; Wilkerson, *Man Who Invented Las Vegas*, 4–10.

4. Wilkerson, *Hollywood Godfather*, 50–60.

5. Lacey, *Little Man*, 152.

6. Wilkerson, *Man Who Invented Las Vegas*, 18.

7. Ibid., 19.

8. Ibid., 25, 26; Gragg, *Benjamin "Bugsy" Siegel*, 90.

9. Gragg, *Benjamin "Bugsy" Siegel*, 92.

10. Gladstone, *The Man Who Seduced Hollywood*, 84.

11. Wilkerson, *Man Who Invented Las Vegas*, 39; Gragg, *Benjamin "Bugsy" Siegel*, 89.

12. Gragg, *Benjamin "Bugsy" Siegel*, 92; Wilkerson, *Man Who Invented Las Vegas*, 52.

13. Wilkerson, *Man Who Invented Las Vegas*, 55.

14. Gladstone, *The Man Who Seduced Hollywood*, 85, 56, 57; *Las Vegas Review-Journal*, March 28, 1945.

15. Wilkerson, *Man Who Invented Las Vegas*, 46, 47.

16. Gragg, *Benjamin "Bugsy" Siegel*, 92.

17. Wilkerson, *Man Who Invented Las Vegas*, 60.

18. Ibid., 61, 62.

19. Ibid., 49.

20. Gragg, *Benjamin "Bugsy" Siegel*, 94, 95.

21. Wilkerson, *Man Who Invented Las Vegas*, 76; Carpozi, *Bugsy*, 143.

22. Wilkerson, *Man Who Invented Las Vegas*, 75.

23. Birmingham, *The Rest of Us*, 301.

24. Jack Bullock oral history interview, Collection #: OH-00287. Local oral history project—Rosky, Special Collections and Archives, University Libraries, University of Nevada, Las Vegas.

25. Louis Wiener Jr. oral history interview, Collection #: OH-01974, January 24, 1990; February 4, 1990; February 23, 1990, transcript, Oral History Research Center, Special Collections and Archives, University Libraries, University of Nevada, Las Vegas.

26. Ibid.

27. John Cahlan oral history interview, Collection #: OH-00151, October 4, 1978, audio recording transcript, 2 tapes, Special Collections and Archives, University Libraries, University of Nevada, Las Vegas.

28. FBI Bugsy Siegel files, surveillance, search word: carload.

29. Wilkerson, *Man Who Invented Las Vegas*, 76, 77.

30. Jennings, *Kill Each Other*, 152.

31. Ibid., 51.

32. Wiener interview.

33. Wilkerson, *Man Who Invented Las Vegas*, 83.

34. Ibid., 84, 83.

35. Ibid., 71.

36. Ibid., 83.

37. Eisenberg, Dan, and Landau, *Meyer Lansky*, 237, 238.

38. Ibid.

39. Lacey, *Little Man*, 138.

Chapter 9. His Every Red Cent at Risk

1. Gragg, *Benjamin "Bugsy" Siegel*, 98, 99.

2. FBI Bugsy Siegel files, chrono 1, word search: division at Reno.

3. Ibid., word search: Senator McCarran.

4. A. E. Ostholthoff portrait is at https://outlet.historic images.com/products/ned72774. Alternatively, Google A. E. Ostholthoff images.

5. FBI Siegel files, chrono 1, word search: honest toil.

6. Ibid., word search: fabulous.

7. Ibid., word search: intent.

8. Allan May, "The History of the Race Wire Service, Parts I, II, and III," *Crime Magazine*, 2009.

9. FBI Siegel files, chrono 1, word search: intent; Gragg, *Benjamin "Bugsy" Siegel*, 82–83.

10. FBI Siegel files, chrono 2, word search: overdose.

11. Ibid., chrono Bugs and Meyer, word search: supersedes.

12. Ibid., chrono 2, word search: get that money.

13. Ibid., word search: Did you get that money.

14. Ibid., chrono Bugs and Meyer, word search: headaches.

15. Wilkerson, *Man Who Invented Las Vegas*, 85.

16. Gragg, *Benjamin "Bugsy" Siegel*, 99.

17. FBI Siegel files, chrono 2, word search: cover-up; ibid., word search: concrete floors.

18. Ibid., word search: how much the commissioner; ibid., word search: $100.

19. Gragg, *Benjamin "Bugsy" Siegel*, 99–100.

20. FBI Siegel files, chrono 2, word search: because I don't know.

21. Ibid., word search: indict us.

22. Ibid., word search: outside windows.

23. Ibid., word search: not started until April.

24. Ibid., chrono 3, word search: would stop building; also see Gragg, *Benjamin "Bugsy" Siegel*, 104.

25. Jennings, *Kill Each Other*, 17.

26. Wolf, *Frank Costello*, 172.

27. Reppetto, *American Mafia*, 237.

28. Wolf, *Frank Costello*, 173.

29. FBI Siegel files, chrono 3, word search: met with Costello; Pearl, *Las Vegas Is My Beat*, 20.

30. Reppetto, *American Mafia*, 237.

31. Jennings, *Kill Each Other*, 154.

32. "The Daughter of Las Vegas: An Interview with Bugsy Siegel's Daughter, Millicent," interview with Millicent Siegel by Diana Edelman, d travels 'round, July 25, 2012, dtravelsround.com/2012/07/25/daughter-las-vegas-interview-millicent-siegel/; author interview with Wendy Rosen.

33. Robert Rockaway, "Hoodlum Hero: The Jewish Gangster as Defender of his People, 1919–1949," *American Jewish History* 82 (1994): 215–235.

34. Ibid.

35. Author interview with Peter Rubenstein, rabbi emeritus of Central Synagogue, New York.

36. Gladstone, *The Man Who Seduced Hollywood*, 88–91.

Chapter 10. The Flamingo's First Flight

1. Gragg, *Benjamin "Bugsy" Siegel*, 105.

2. Jennings, *Kill Each Other*, 158.

3. Ibid., 159.

4. Gragg, *Benjamin "Bugsy" Siegel*, 116.

5. Ibid., 159.

6. Friedrich, *City of Nets*, 377.

7. "New Downpour Drenches L.A.; Another Due," *Los Angeles Examiner*, December 27, 1946.

8. Friedrich, *City of Nets*, 377.

9. Ibid., 117.

10. Wilkerson, *Man Who Invented Las Vegas*, 101.

11. Jennings, *Kill Each Other*, 161.

12. Lacey, *Little Man*, 153.

13. Erskine Caldwell, *With All My Might: An Autobiography* (Atlanta: Peachtree, 1987), 240, 241.

14. "Flamingo Resort Hotel Jammed at Opening," *Las Vegas Review-Journal*, December 27, 1947.

15. Tereba, *Mickey Cohen*, 79; Gragg, *Benjamin "Bugsy" Siegel*, 119, 125.

16. Jennings, *Kill Each Other*, 163.

17. Gragg, *Benjamin "Bugsy" Siegel*, 118.

18. FBI Bugsy Siegel files, chrono 3, word search: platinum blonde; Gragg, *Benjamin "Bugsy" Siegel*, 119.

19. Denton and Morris, *Money and Power*, 56.

20. Jennings, *Kill Each Other*, 180.

21. Lacey, *Little Man*, 124, 125.

22. Ibid., 223, 224.

23. Eisenberg, Dan, and Landau, *Meyer Lansky*, 222–225; see also Lacey, *Little Man*, 127, 128.

24. Eisenberg, Dan, and Landau, *Meyer Lansky*, 231–233, 235.

25. Ibid., 235.

26. Tereba, *Mickey Cohen*, 78.

27. Reppetto, *American Mafia*, 247.

28. Ibid., 236, 237.

29. Ibid., 238.

30. "Lucky Luciano Told Siegel That He'd Be Put on Spot," *Los Angeles Examiner*, June 23, 1947.

31. Friedrich, *City of Nets*, 378.

32. Gragg, *Benjamin "Bugsy" Siegel*, 123.

33. Denton and Morris, *Money and Power*, 56.

34. Jennings, *Kill Each Other*, 172–173.

35. FBI Siegel files, chrono 3, word search: scintilla.

36. Jennings, *Kill Each Other*, 175.

37. Ibid., 171, 176.

38. Lacey, *Little Man*, 156.
39. Gragg, *Benjamin "Bugsy" Siegel*, 121.
40. Jennings, *Kill Each Other*, 172.
41. Gragg, *Benjamin "Bugsy" Siegel*, 130.
42. Wilkerson, *Man Who Invented Las Vegas*, 105, 106.
43. Ibid., 107.
44. Wilkerson, *Hollywood Godfather*, 239.
45. FBI Siegel files, chrono 3, word search: race wire.
46. Fischer, *When the Mob Ran Vegas*, 17.
47. Jennings, *Kill Each Other*, 169.
48. Ibid., 169.
49. Virginia Hill testimony, Kefauver Commission on Organized Crime, March 1951; Jennings, *Kill Each Other*, 177; "Siegel Killing Clues Hunted in Las Vegas," *Los Angeles Times*, June 22, 1947.
50. Jennings, *Kill Each Other*, 181.
51. Gragg, *Benjamin "Bugsy" Siegel*, 130.
52. Louis Wiener Jr. oral history interview, Collection #: OH-01974, January 24, 1990; February 4, 1990; February 23, 1990, transcript, Oral History Research Center, Special Collections and Archives, University Libraries, University of Nevada, Las Vegas.
53. Brigham Townsend, public relations director: *News from Brigham Townsend*, June 4, 1947, Special Collections and Archives, University Libraries, University of Nevada, Las Vegas.

Chapter 11. Time Runs Out

1. Eisenberg, Dan, and Landau, *Meyer Lansky*, 240.
2. Jennings, *Kill Each Other*, 188.
3. Ibid., 188.
4. "Virginia Hill, in Paris, Tells of Siegel Quarrel," *Los Angeles Times*, June 23, 1947.
5. "Heiress' Broken Romance with a Slain Siegel Disclosed; Brother of Girl Tells of New Car and Sister's Plans," *Los Angeles Times*, June 28, 1947; Eisenberg, Dan, and Landau, *Meyer Lansky*, 240.

6. Jennings, *Kill Each Other*, 189.

7. "Virginia Hill Tells of Siegel Quarrel."

8. Jennings, *Kill Each Other*, 192.

9. "Who Killed Siegel? What Was Motive?" *Las Vegas Evening Review-Journal*, June 20, 1947.

10. Friedrich, *City of Nets*, 380.

11. Eisenberg, Dan, and Landau, *Meyer Lansky*, 158.

12. Jennings, *Kill Each Other*, 193.

13. Wilkerson, *Man Who Invented Las Vegas*, 110.

14. Jennings, *Kill Each Other*, 193, 194.

15. Ibid., 194.

16. Fischer, *When the Mob Ran Vegas*, 43–47.

17. Jennings, *Kill Each Other*, 195–204.

18. Ibid., 206.

19. Ibid., 195.

20. Ibid., 196.

21. Ibid.

22. Ibid., 197.

23. Ibid., 198.

24. Ibid., 200.

25. Ibid., 201.

26. Florabel Muir, *Headline Happy* (New York: Holt, 1950), 197.

27. "Police Probe Siegel Rub-Out," *Boulder City Journal*, June 21, 1947.

28. "Underworld Keeps Its Secrets about Siegel," *Los Angeles Times*, June 26, 1947.

29. Jennings, *Kill Each Other*, 204.

30. Muir, *Headline Happy*, 197–198; Friedrich, *City of Nets*, 381.

31. Friedrich, *City of Nets*, 381.

32. "Slayer of Ragen Hunted in Siegel Death Mystery," *Los Angeles Evening Herald Express*, June 23, 1947.

33. Eisenberg, Dan, and Landau, *Meyer Lansky*, 241.

34. Friedrich, *City of Nets*, 379.

35. "Siegel Murder Ascribed to Gambling Racket Grab," *Los Angeles Times*, June 23, 1947.

36. Anderson, *Beverly Hills Is My Beat*, 129.

37. Harry Belafonte with Michael Shnayerson, *My Way: A Memoir of Art, Race, and Defiance* (New York: Vintage, 2012), 184–185.

38. Eisenberg, Dan, and Landau, *Meyer Lansky*, 240.

39. "Who Killed Siegel?"

40. "Virginia Hill Tells of Siegel Quarrel."

41. Jennings, *Kill Each Other*, 213.

42. "The Daughter of Las Vegas: An Interview with Bugsy Siegel's Daughter, Millicent," interview with Millicent Siegel by Diana Edelman, d travels 'round, July 25, 2012, dtravelsround.com/2012/07/25/daughter-las-vegas-interview-millicent-siegel/; author interview with Wendy Rosen.

43. Lansky and Stadiem, *Daughter of the King*, 72.

44. "Millicent Siegel Talks about Her Father Bugsy's Name, Reputation, and Legacy," *Las Vegas Sun News*, November 3, 2010.

45. "Probe Siegel's Link with Girl," *Los Angeles Examiner*, June 28, 1947, including "Quiz Widow"; also, "Heiress' Broken Romance with a Slain Siegel Disclosed."

46. "Bugsy's Funeral Hasty, Despite $5,000 Coffin," *Los Angeles Examiner*, June 27, 1947.

47. "Brief Rites Held for Ben Siegel," *Los Angeles Times*, June 26, 1947.

48. Ibid.; "Love Tangle Suspected as Siegel Murder Cause; Funeral Plans Speeded," *Los Angeles Times*, June 27, 1947.

49. "Gangster's Estate Small," *New York Times*, January 21, 1954.

50. "Sanford D. Adler Buys Flamingo Resort Hotel," *Las Vegas Evening Review-Journal*, July 12, 1947.

51. Author interview with Billy Wilkerson III.

52. "Probe Siegel's Link with Girl."

53. Jennings, *Kill Each Other*, 215, 218.

54. Ibid., 177.

55. Author interview with Nick Pileggi.

56. "Bugsy's Funeral Hasty."

57. "Officials Admit Siegel's Slaying May Go Unsolved," *Los Angeles Times*, June 29, 1947.

58. Jennings, *Kill Each Other*, 249.

59. Lansky and Stadiem, *Daughter of the King*, 73, 74.

60. Author interview with Wendy Rosen.

Anderson, Clinton H. *Beverly Hills Is My Beat.* New York: Popular Library, 1962.

Astaire, Fred. *Steps in Time: An Autobiography.* New York: Harper and Brothers, 1959.

Birmingham, Stephen. *The Rest of Us: The Rise of America's Eastern European Jews.* Syracuse, NY: Syracuse University Press, 1999.

Carpozi, George, Jr. *Bugsy: The High-Rolling, Bullet-Riddled Story of Benjamin "Bugsy" Siegel, of Murder Inc.* New York: Pinnacle, 1973.

Cohen, Rich. *Tough Jews: Fathers, Sons, and Gangster Dreams.* New York: Vintage, 1999.

Denton, Sally, and Roger Morris. *The Money and the Power: The Making of Las Vegas and Its Hold on America.* New York: Vintage, 2002.

Edmonds, Andy. *Bugsy's Baby: The Secret Life of Mob Queen Virginia Hill.* New York: Birch Lane, 1993.

Eisenberg, Dennis, Uri Dan, and Eli Landau. *Meyer Lansky: Mogul of the Mob.* New York: Paddington, 1979.

Epstein, Lawrence J. *At the Edge of a Dream: The Story of Jewish Immigrants on New York's Lower East Side, 1880–1920.* New York: Wiley, 2007.

Fischer, Steve. *When the Mob Ran Vegas: Stories of Money, Mayhem, and Murder.* Omaha, NE: Berkline, 2007.

Fried, Albert. *The Rise and Fall of the Jewish Gangster in America.* New York: Columbia University Press, 1993.

Friedrich, Otto. *City of Nets: A Portrait of Hollywood in the 1940s.* New York: Harper Perennial, 2014.

Gabler, Neal. *An Empire of Their Own: How the Jews Invented Hollywood.* New York: Anchor, 1989.

Gladstone, James B. *The Man Who Seduced Hollywood: The Lives and Loves of Greg Bautzer, Tinseltown's Most Powerful Lawyer.* Chicago: Chicago Review Press, 2014.

Gragg, Larry D. *Benjamin "Bugsy" Siegel: The Gangster, The Flamingo, and the Making of Modern Las Vegas.* Santa Barbara, CA: Praeger.

Jennings, Dean. *We Only Kill Each Other: The Life and Bad Times of Bugsy Siegel.* Englewood Cliffs, NJ: Prentice-Hall, 1968.

Joselit, Jenna Weissman. *Our Gang: Jewish Crime and the New York Jewish Community, 1900–1940.* Bloomington: Indiana University Press, 1983.

Lacey, Robert. *Little Man: Meyer Lansky and the Gangster Life.* Boston: Little, Brown, 1991.

Lansky, Sandra, and William Stadiem. *Daughter of the King: Growing Up in Gangland.* New York: Weinstein, 2014.

Lynum, Curtis O. *The FBI and I.* Victoria, BC: Trafford, 2004.

Munn, Michael. *Jimmy Stewart: The Truth behind the Legend.* New York, Skyhorse, 2014.

O'Connor, Carol A. *A Sort of Utopia: Scarsdale, 1891–1981.* Albany: State University of New York Press, 1983.

Parish, James Robert. *The George Raft File.* New York: Drake, 1973.

Parsons, Louella. *The Gay Illiterate.* Garden City, NY: Doubleday, Doran, 1944.

Raab, Selwyn. *Five Families: The Rise, Decline, and Resurgence of America's Most Powerful Mafia Families.* New York: St. Martin's, 2006.

Reppetto, Thomas. *American Mafia: A History of Its Rise to Power,* New York: Henry Holt, 2004.

Rockaway, Robert A. *But He Was Good to His Mother: The Lives and Crimes of Jewish Gangsters.* Jerusalem: Gefen, 2000.

Tereba, Tere. *Mickey Cohen: The Life and Crimes of L.A.'s Notorious Mobster.* Toronto: ECW, 2012.

Turkus, Burton B., and Sid Feder. *Murder, Inc.: The Story of the Syndicate.* New York: Da Capo, 1992.

Wilkerson, W. R., III. *The Man Who Invented Las Vegas.* Las Vegas: Ciro's, 2000.

———. *Hollywood Godfather: The Life and Crimes of Billy Wilkerson.* Chicago: Chicago Review Press, 2018.

Wolf, George, with Joseph DiMona. *Frank Costello: Prime Minister of the Underworld.* New York: William Morrow, 1974.

ACKNOWLEDGMENTS

Thanks so much to Ileene Smith, editor-in-chief of the Jewish Lives Series, who took a chance on me with Bugsy Siegel, and thanks to Leon Black, without whose generosity the series would not exist. Thanks to the team at Yale University Press, including Heather Gold, Dan Heaton, and Margaret Otzel. Thanks to Nick Pileggi, great guru of organized crime, who kindly spoke with me at length about Bugsy and his world; thanks also to Professor Robert Rockaway, for insights of his own about Bugsy and Meyer Lansky; and thanks to Wendy Rosen, daughter of Bugsy's daughter Millicent, who shared Siegel family lore with me. Ken Cobb, crack researcher in the Department of Records, New York Municipal Archives, guided me to key documents; J. D. Aarden did the same with me at the Center for Jewish History.

Thanks above all to my wife Gayfryd, who did so much to polish and improve this book along the way.

INDEX

Abbott and Costello, 153
Adler, Sandy, 180
Adonis, Joe (Giuseppe Doto): Lansky and, 22; at Luciano's deportation party, 150; Masseria murder and, 26; Murder Inc. and, 51; in Rothstein organization, 13; in the Syndicate, 28; Virginia Hill and, 100–101, 103, 104–5
Agua Caliente horse track, 36–37, 53
air conditioning, 110, 146
Ambassador Hotel (Los Angeles), 33
American Distilling Company, 114
American Jewish History, 10
American Mercury, 60
Anastasia, Albert "The Mad Hatter," 13, 25, 26, 51, 151
Anderson, Clinton, 174–75
Andrews Sisters, 156
Anhalt, Edward, 106
Annenberg, Moses Moe, 54, 75, 89–90, 92

Armstrong, Louis, 33
Army Air Corps Gunnery School, 89
Astaire, Fred, 33
Atlantic City, 22–23
Atomite (explosive), 66
Austin, Gene, 161

Back of Ratner's, 17
Balaban and Katz Theater Corporation (B&K), 44
Ball, Lucille, 145
Bals, Frank, 83
Bara, Theda, 34
Barrett, John, 14, 24
Barrie, Wendy, 78–79, 94, 95
Basic Magnesium plant (Las Vegas), 89
Basswood Lake, 52–53
Bautzer, Greg, 112, 113, 140–41, 157
Beatty, Warren, 37, 109–10
Beery, Wallace, 153
Belafonte, Harry, 186
Bellagio Resort (Las Vegas), 187

30–31, 36; Siegel's death and,
177–78; at Siegel's funeral, 178–79;
Siegel's last contact with, 169;
the Syndicate's commitment to,
183–84
Siegel, Esther (sister), 3
Siegel, Ethel (sister), 3, 36
Siegel, Jennie Riechenthal (mother),
1–3, 60, 78, 179
Siegel, Lil (sister-in-law), 37
Siegel, Maurice/Morris (brother), 3, 7,
37, 79, 162, 177, 178–79
Siegel, Max (father), 1–3, 7, 17, 60, 61,
64, 78, 161–62, 179
Siegel, Millicent (daughter): birth of,
25; death and burial of, 10; on
Flamingo Hotel, 136; Harlow as
"godmother" to, 40; Huie and,
61; informed of Siegel's death,
177; life after Siegel's death,
184–85; in Los Angeles, 59, 61,
64; parents' divorce and, 121–22;
portrait in Esther's apartment,
185; at Siegel's funeral, 178–79;
Siegel's parental advice regard-
ing, 138–40
Siegels 1941 (Las Vegas restaurant),
139–40
Silvers, Phil, 54–55
Simpson, Adeline E., 6
Sinatra, Frank, 54, 55, 152, 186
Smiley, Allen, 95–96, 137, 169, 170–71,
173, 177, 178
Soloway, Bessie Siegel (sister), 3, 99,
106, 122, 178
Soloway, Sollie, 99, 106
Speed (film), 78
Stacher, Doc: Greenberg murder and,
69–70; at Havana conference of
the Syndicate, 151, 152, 173–74; on
Lansky's attempts to protect
Siegel, 166–67; at Luciano's de-
portation party, 150; rape charge
against Siegel and, 19; Reles's
death and, 83; on Siegel-Hill
relationship, 121; on Siegel's
death, 165, 176

Stadelman, Richard, 120
stage extras union, 44–45
Stardust casino (Las Vegas), 186
Steffens, Lincoln, 7–8
Stewart, Gloria, 40, 55–56
Stewart, Jimmy, 40, 55–56, 78
Stolla, Rose, 4
Sunset Strip, 35
Sunset Towers Hotel (Los Angeles),
95, 169
Syndicate: Bruneman murder and, 47;
commitment to Esther Siegel,
183–84; creation of, 11, 27–28;
Dragna and, 35; El Cortez pur-
chase and, 108; financing of
Vegas casinos, 186; Flamingo
and, 156, 180; Greenberg murder
and, 69, 70–71, 72–73, 82; Havana
Conference of, 149–52, 173;
Lansky and Siegel awarded all
gambling rights outside New
York City, 31; Murder Inc. and,
49, 50, 51, 65; race wire and, 34;
Schultz murder and, 38–39; Sedway's ejection from Flamingo
and, 158–59; Siegel's loyalty to,
15; Siegel's profitability for, 37;
stage extras union and, 44–45; as
suspects in Siegel's death, 173–74;
Virginia Hill and, 181–82. *See also
specific individuals*

Tannenbaum, Albert "Allie Tick
Tock," 71–73, 76–77, 79–83
Taylor, Dorothy. *See* Di Frasso,
Dorothy
Taylor, Elizabeth, 59
Teamsters Union, 186
Teitelbaum, Harry, 39
Temple Sinai (Hollywood, Florida), 136
Tereba, Tere, 151
Terranova, Ciro, 26
Thackeray, William Makepeace: *Vanity
Fair*, 103–4
Thunderbird casino, 186
Tibbett, Lawrence, 37, 40
Tijuana dog track, 53

Alfred Dreyfus, by Maurice Samuels
Elijah, by Daniel Matt
Anne Frank, by Ruth Franklin
Betty Friedan, by Rachel Shteir
George Gershwin, by Gary Giddins
Allen Ginsberg, by Ed Hirsch
Ruth Bader Ginsburg, by Dorothy Samuels
Herod, by Martin Goodman
Abraham Joshua Heschel, by Julian Zelizer
Jesus, by Jack Miles
Josephus, by Daniel Boyarin
Louis Kahn, by Gini Alhadeff
Maimonides, by Alberto Manguel
Louis B. Mayer and Irving Thalberg, by Kenneth Turan
Golda Meir, by Deborah E. Lipstadt
Arthur Miller, by John Lahr
Robert Oppenheimer, by David Rieff
Ayn Rand, by Alexandra Popoff
Man Ray, by Arthur Lubow
Sidney Reilly, by Benny Morris
Hyman Rickover, by Marc Wortman
Philip Roth, by Steven J. Zipperstein
Edmond de Rothschild, by James McAuley
Ruth, by Ilana Pardes
Jonas Salk, by David Margolick
Rebbe Schneerson, by Ezra Glinter
Baruch Spinoza, by Ian Buruma
Henrietta Szold, by Francine Klagsbrun
Elie Wiesel, by Joseph Berger
Billy Wilder, by Noah Isenberg
Ludwig Wittgenstein, by Anthony Gottlieb